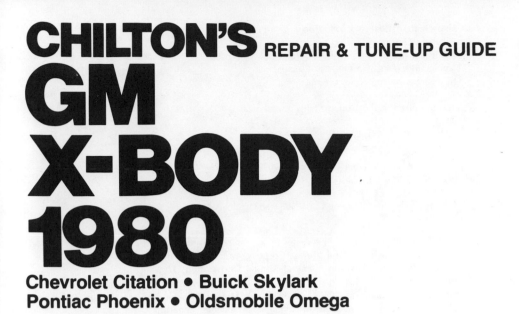

CHILTON'S REPAIR & TUNE-UP GUIDE
GM
X-BODY
1980

Chevrolet Citation • Buick Skylark
Pontiac Phoenix • Oldsmobile Omega

Managing Editor KERRY A. FREEMAN, S.A.E.
Senior Editor RICHARD J. RIVELE
Editor THEODORE COSTANTINO

President WILLIAM A. BARBOUR
Executive Vice President RICHARD H. GROVES
Vice President and General Manager JOHN P. KUSHNERICK

CHILTON BOOK COMPANY
Radnor, Pennsylvania
19089

Manufactured in the United States of America

1234567890   9876543210

Chilton's Repair & Tune-Up Guide: GM X-Body 1980
ISBN 0-8019-6909-3 pbk.

Library of Congress Catalog Card No. 79-8316

The Chilton Book Company expresses its appreciation to the Chevrolet Motor Division, General Motors Corporation, Detroit, Michigan
48202; Oldsmobile Division, General Motors Corporation, Lansing,
Michigan 48921; Pontiac Motor Division, General Motors Corporation, Pontiac, Michigan 48053, and the Buick Motor Division, General Motors Corporation, Flint, Michigan 48550 for their generous as-
sistance.
The author would particularly like to thank Fritz Bennetts at Oldsmobile and Ralph Kramer at Chevrolet for their help.

Information has been selected from Chevrolet, Oldsmobile, Pontiac,
and Buick shop manuals, owner's manuals, data books, brochures,
service bulletins, and technical manuals.

SAFETY NOTICE

Proper service and repair procedures are vital to the safe, reliable
operation of all motor vehicles, as well as the personal safety of those
performing repairs. This book outlines procedures for servicing and
repairing vehicles using safe, effective methods. The procedures contain many NOTES, CAUTIONS and WARNINGS which should be
followed along with standard safety procedures to eliminate the possibility of personal injury or improper service which could damage the
vehicle or compromise its safety.

It is important to note that repair procedures and techniques, tools
and parts for servicing motor vehicles, as well as the skill and experience of the individual performing the work vary widely. It is not possible to anticipate all of the conceivable ways or conditions under
which vehicles may be serviced, or to provide cautions as to all of the
possible hazards that may result. Standard and accepted safety precautions and equipment should be used when handling toxic or flammable fluids, and safety goggles or other protection should be used
during cutting, grinding, chiseling, prying, or any other process that
can cause material removal or projectiles.

Some procedures require the use of tools specially designed for a
specific purpose. Before substituting another tool or procedure, you
must be completely satisfied that neither your personal safety, nor the
performance of the vehicle will be endangered.

Contents

Quick Reference Specifications

For quick and easy reference, complete this page with the most commonly used specifications for your vehicle. The specifications can be found in Chapters 1 through 3 or on the tune-up decal under the hood of the vehicle.

PROCEDURES PAGE 33

TUNE-UP *SPECS. PAGE 34*

Firing Order *{PAGE 65*

Spark Plugs:

Type *R44TS*

Gap (in.) *.045*

Point Gap (in.) *N/A*

Dwell Angle (°) *N/A*

Ignition Timing (°) *8° BTDC*

Vacuum (Connected/Disconnected) *17-22 IN. Hg.*

Valve Clearance (in.)

Intake _____ **Exhaust** _____

IDLE SPEED 650 RPM

CAPACITIES

Engine Oil (qts)

With Filter Change *5 QTS.*

Without Filter Change *4. QTS.*

Cooling System (qts) *11.75 QTS.*

Manual Transaxle (pts) _____

Type _____

Automatic Transaxle (pts) *10.0 PINTS*

Type _____

Differential (pts) _____

Type _____

COMMONLY FORGOTTEN PART NUMBERS

Use these spaces to record the part numbers of frequently replaced parts.

PCV VALVE

Manufacturer *AC / FRAM*

Part No. *CV-789C FV-191*

CANISTER FILTER
FRAM - CA357

OIL FILTER

Manufacturer *AC*

Part No. *PF-51*

GAS FILTER
AC - GF-471
FRAM - CG -3389

AIR FILTER

Manufacturer *AC*

Part No. *A735C*

FRAM
CA3537

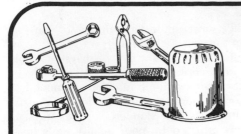

General Information and Maintenance

HOW TO USE THIS BOOK

All General Motors 1980 X-Body cars—the Chevrolet Citation, Oldsmobile Omega, Pontiac Phoenix, and Buick Skylark—are covered in this book, with procedures specifically labeled as to the particular division when it makes a difference. The purpose of this book is to cover maintenance and repair procedures that the owner can perform without special tools or equipment. A lot of attention is given to the type of jobs on which the owner can save labor charges and time by doing it him or her self. Jobs which absolutely require special tools, such as transaxle overhaul, or which the beginner is unlikely to get right the first time, such as differential adjustment, are purposely not covered.

To use the book properly, each operation must be approached logically, with a clear understanding of the theory behind the work involved. The procedures should be read completely and understood thoroughly before any work is begun. The required tools and supplies should be on hand and a clean, uncluttered place to work should be available. There is nothing more frustrating than finding yourself one metric bolt short in the middle of your Sunday afternoon repair. So read ahead and plan ahead. To avoid confu-

sion, it is best to complete one job at a time, so that results can be independently evaluated.

When reference is made in this book to the "right side" or "left side" of the car, it should be understood that these positions are to be viewed from the front seat. Thus, the left side of the car is always the driver's side, even when one is facing the car, as when working on the engine.

We have attempted to eliminate the use of special tools wherever possible, substituting more readily available hand tools. However, in some cases the special tools are necessary. These can be purchased from your G.M. dealer, or from an automotive parts store.

Always be conscious of the need for safety in your work. Never crawl under your car unless it is firmly supported by jackstands or ramps. Never smoke near or allow flame to get near the battery or fuel system. Keep your clothing, hands and hair clear of the fan and pulleys when working near the engine, if it is running. Most importantly, try to be patient, even in the midst of a problem such as a particularly stubborn bolt; reaching for the largest hammer in the garage is usually a cause for later regret and more extensive repair. As you gain confidence and experience, working on your car will become a source of pride and satisfaction.

TOOLS AND EQUIPMENT

The service procedures in this book presuppose a familiarity with hand tools and their proper use. However, it is possible that you may have a limited amount of experience with the sort of equipment needed to work on an automobile. This section is designed to help you assemble a basic set of tools that will handle most of the jobs you may undertake.

In addition to the normal assortment of screwdrivers and pliers, automotive service work requires an investment in wrenches, sockets and the handles needed to drive them, and various measuring tools such as torque wrenches and feeler gauges.

You will find that virtually every nut and bolt on your X-Body car is metric. Therefore, despite various close size similarities, standard inch-size tools will not fit and must not be used. You will need a set of metric wrenches as your most basic tool kit, ranging from about 6 mm to 17 mm in size. High quality forged wrenches are available in three styles: open end, box end, and combination open/box end. The combination tools are generally the most desirable as a starter set; the wrenches shown in the accompanying illustration are of the combination type.

The other set of tools inevitably required is a ratchet handle and socket set. This set should have the same size range as your wrench set. The ratchet, extension, and flex drives for the sockets are available in many sizes; it is advisable to choose a ⅜ inch drive set initially. One break in the inch/metric sizing war is that metric-sized sockets sold in the U.S. have inch-sized drive (¼, ⅜, ½, etc.). Thus, if you already have an inch-size socket set, you need only buy new metric sockets in the sizes needed. Sockets are available in six and twelve point versions; six point types are generally cheaper and are a good choice for a first set. The choice of a drive handle for the sockets should be made with some care. If this is your first set, take the plunge and invest in a flex-head ratchet; it will get into many places otherwise accessible only through a long chain of universal joints, extensions, and adapters. An alternative is a flex handle, which lacks the ratcheting feature but has a head which pivots 180°; such a tool is shown below the ratchet handle in the illustration. In addition to the range of sockets mentioned, a rubber-lined spark plug socket should be purchased. The correct size

for the plugs in your X-Body car's engine is ⅝ inch.

The most important thing to consider when purchasing hand tools is quality. Don't be misled by the low cost of "bargain" tools. Forged wrenches, tempered screwdriver blades, and fine tooth ratchets are much better investments than their less expensive counterparts. The skinned knuckles and frustration inflicted by poor quality tools make any job an unhappy chore. Another consideration is that quality tools come with an on-the-spot replacement guarantee—if the tool breaks, you get a new one, no questions asked.

Most jobs can be accomplished using the tools on the accompanying lists. There will be an occasional need for a special tool, such as snap ring pliers; that need will be mentioned in the text. It would not be wise to buy a large assortment of tools on the premise that someday they will be needed. Instead, the tools should be acquired one at a time, each for a specific job, both to avoid unnecessary expense and to be certain that you have the right tool.

The tools needed for basic maintenance jobs, in addition to the wrenches and sockets mentioned, include:
1. Jackstands, for support;
2. Oil filter wrench;
3. Oil filler spout or funnel;
4. Grease gun;
5. Battery terminal and clamp cleaner;
6. Container for draining oil;
7. Many rags for the inevitable spills.

In addition to these items there are several others which are not absolutely necessary, but handy to have around. These include a transmission funnel and filler tube, a drop (trouble) light on a long cord, an adjustable wrench (crescent wrench), and slip joint pliers.

A more advanced list of tools suitable for tune-up work, can be drawn up easily. While the tools involved are slightly more sophisticated, they need not be outrageously expensive. The key to these purchases is to make them with an eye towards adaptability and wide range. A basic list of tune-up tools could include:
1. Tachometer;
2. Spark plug gauge and gapping tool;
3. Timing light.

In this list, the choice of a timing light should be made carefully. A light which

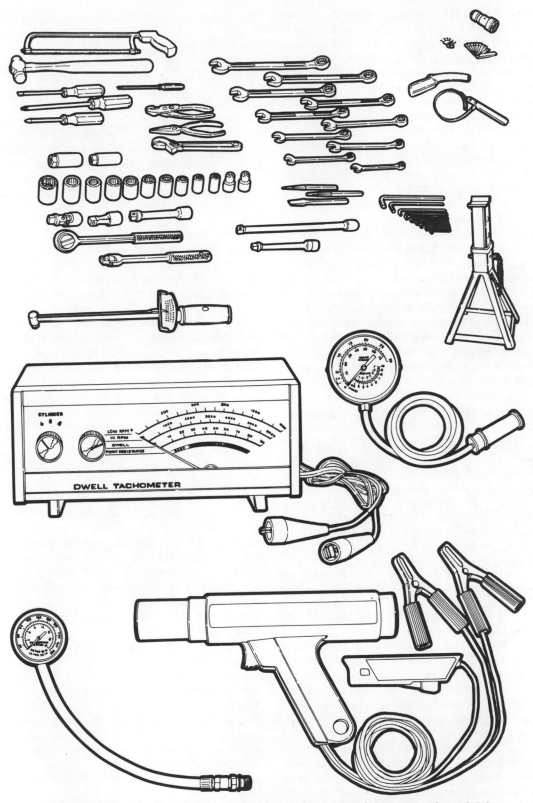

You need only a basic assortment of hand tools for most maintenance and repair jobs

works on the DC current supplied by the car battery is the best choice; it should have a xenon tube for brightness. The X-Body cars have electronic ignition, and thus the light should have an inductive pick-up (the timing light illustrated has one of these).

In addition to these basic tools, there are several other tools and gauges you may find useful. These include:

1. A compression gauge. The screw-in type is slower to use, but eliminates the possibility of a faulty reading due to escaping pressure;

2. A manifold vacuum gauge;

3. A test light;

4. An induction meter. This is used to determine whether or not there is current flowing in a wire, and thus is extremely helpful in electrical troubleshooting.

Finally, you will probably find a torque wrench necessary for all but the most basic of work. The beam type models are perfectly adequate. The newer click (breakaway) type torque wrenches are more accurate, but are much more expensive, and must be periodically recalibrated.

SERVICING YOUR CAR SAFELY

It is virtually impossible to anticipate all of the hazards involved with automotive maintenance and service, but care and common sense will prevent most accidents.

The rules of safety for mechanics range from "don't smoke around gasoline," to "use the proper tool for the job." The trick to avoiding injuries is to develop safe work habits and take every possible precaution.

DOs

• Do keep a fire extinguisher and first aid kit within easy reach.

• Do wear safety glasses or goggles when cutting, drilling, grinding or prying, even if you have 20–20 vision. If you wear glasses for the sake of vision, they should be made of hardened glass that can serve also as safety glasses, or wear safety goggles over your regular glasses.

• Do shield your eyes whenever you work around the battery. Batteries contain sulphuric acid. In case of contact with the eyes or skin, flush the area with water or a mixture of water and baking soda and get medical attention immediately.

• Do use safety stands for any undercar

Always support the car securely with jackstands; don't use cinder blocks, tire-changing jacks, or the like

service. Jacks are for raising vehicles; safety stands are for making sure the vehicle stays raised until you want to come down. Whenever the car is raised, block the wheels remaining on the ground and set the parking brake.

• Do use adequate ventilation when working with any chemicals or hazardous materials. Like carbon monoxide, the asbestos dust resulting from brake lining wear can be poisonous in sufficient quantities.

• Do disconnect the negative battery cable when working on the electrical system. The secondary ignition system can contain up to 40,000 volts.

• Do follow manufacturer's directions whenever working with potentially hazardous materials. Both brake fluid and antifreeze are poisonous if taken internally.

• Do properly maintain your tools. Loose hammerheads, mushroomed punches and chisels, frayed or poorly grounded electrical cords, excessively worn screwdrivers, spread wrenches (open end), cracked sockets, slipping ratchets, or faulty droplight sockets can cause accidents.

• Do use the proper size and type of tool for the job being done.

• Do when possible, pull on a wrench handle rather than push on it, and adjust your stance to prevent a fall.

• Do be sure that adjustable wrenches are tightly closed on the nut or bolt and pulled so that the face is on the side of the fixed jaw.

• Do select a wrench or socket that fits the nut or bolt. The wrench or socket should sit straight, not cocked.

• Do strike squarely with a hammer; avoid glancing blows.

• Do set the parking brake and block the drive wheels if the work requires the engine running.

DON'Ts

• Don't run an engine in a garage or anywhere else without proper ventilation— EVER! Carbon monoxide is poisonous; it takes a long time to leave the human body and you can build up a deadly supply of it in your system by simply breathing in a little every day. You may not realize you are slowly poisoning yourself. Always use power vents, windows, fans or open the garage doors.

• Don't work around moving parts while wearing a necktie or other loose clothing. Short sleeves are much safer than long, loose sleeves; hard-toed shoes with neoprene soles protect your toes and give a better grip on slippery surfaces. Jewelry such as watches, fancy belt buckles, beads or body adornment of any kind is not safe working around a car. Long hair should be hidden under a hat or cap.

• Don't use pockets for toolboxes. A fall or bump can drive a screwdriver deep into your body. Even a wiping cloth hanging from the back pocket can wrap around a spinning shaft or fan.

• Don't smoke when working around gasoline, cleaning solvent or other flammable material.

• Don't smoke when working around the battery. When the battery is being charged, it gives off explosive hydrogen gas.

• Don't use gasoline to wash your hands; there are excellent soaps available. Gasoline may contain lead, and lead can enter the body through a cut, accumulating in the body until you are very ill. Gasoline also removes all the natural oils from the skin so that bone dry hands will suck up oil and grease.

• Don't service the air conditioning system unless you are equipped with the necessary tools and training. The refrigerant, R-12, is extremely cold when compressed, and when released into the air will instantly freeze any surface it contacts, including your eyes. Although the refrigerant is normally non-toxic, R-12 becomes a deadly poisonous gas in the presence of an open flame. One good whiff of the vapors from burning refrigerant can be fatal.

HISTORY

Planning for the 1980 G.M. X-Body cars began in the Chevrolet advance design studios in April, 1974. Five principal objectives were outlined: the car would have to be fuel-efficient, roomy, comfortable, safe, and durable.

Four months later, in August, 1974, a group met to consider the proposals advanced. From the beginning, it was decided that a front wheel drive, transverse-engined car would be the most efficient design possible, and could most easily meet the objectives established. Work began on prototypes, mostly re-worked versions of front-drive Volkswagens and Fiats. Soon it was decided to make the X-Body car a corporate undertaking. Pontiac joined the project in the latter half of 1975, and Buick and Oldsmobile divisions began work in February, 1976. By this time, the Chevrolet pre-prototype Citations were nearly completed (each at a cost of over $650,000) and ready for evaluation. Styling was finalized in July, 1976, four phases of prototypes were built between February, 1977, and January, 1978, and 141 pilotline cars were built between February and July, 1978.

The X-Body car was originally scheduled to make its debut at the start of the 1979 model year, but this introduction was postponed to iron out final wrinkles (mostly problems with supply of never before produced components). The April, 1979, introduction of the car as a certified 1980 model also meant that it could be produced for seventeen months before having to undergo emissions recertification with the Environmental Protection Agency, a costly and time-consuming process. Finally, of course, the 1980 designation was a symbolic one—as the "first G.M. car for the '80s," the new X-Body models demonstrated the efficient and thoughtful direction for the corporation over the next difficult decade.

The result of all this work is a car which is almost 800 pounds lighter than the car it replaces, but has more interior space and luggage room, and better fuel economy, performance, and handling.

Most of these improvements can be credited to the use of the transverse-engine, front wheel drive configuration. By packaging the entire drive train in the front "box" of the car, the rest is left for people and their possessions, an eminently sensible arrangement, although one which had been the exclusive province of European and Japanese carmakers until the introduction of the X-car.

The do-it-yourselfer should be pleased to

discover that designing a completely new car gave G.M. engineers an opportunity to either reduce or eliminate most servicing headaches. For example, the X-Bodies have a self-adjusting clutch, a "maintenance-free" battery, and sealed and lubricated for life front and rear wheel bearings which require no periodic adjustment. There are many other aids to scheduled maintenance which make working on these cars a much more enjoyable and less time-consuming task than it has been in the past.

The X-Bodies are the first of a new range of G.M. front-drive cars. They will be followed by larger and smaller versions, each to suit specific needs and whims. But the X-Bodies are truly the first G.M. cars of the '80s, and, as the owner of one of these cars, you are helping to create a little bit of history yourself.

A Note About Terminology

There are a few descriptive words used in connection with the X-Body cars which may be new to you.

First, of course, is the term "X-Body" itself. The explanation for this, used to collectively describe the Citation, Omega, Phoenix, and Skylark, is quite simple. All General Motors cars have code names, used within the corporation to designate a body size series. For example, the full-size Impala, Eighty-Eight, LeSabre, and Bonneville are known within G.M. as "B-Bodies." The 1972 Nova was the first "X-Body," and all cars built on that floorpan since have been known by the term.

If this is your first front wheel drive car, you may not be familiar with the terms "transaxle," "halfshaft," or "constant velocity joint."

In a front wheel drive car, the transmission and differential share a common housing, and the front axles (halfshafts) are driven directly by this unit. Thus, a "transaxle" is a combination transmission/differential/drive axle. The X-Body cars use a manual transaxle as standard equipment and an automatic transaxle as an option.

"Halfshafts" are drive axles. The term came about as a way to describe the two shafts which emerge from the transaxle case and connect to the front wheels, transmitting power from one to the other. In a conventional front engine/rear drive car, a driveshaft is used to transmit power from the transmis-

sion to the drive axle. Thus, in a front wheel drive car, where there are two driveshafts, each one becomes half of a driveshaft, or a halfshaft. The halfshafts are also known as "drive axles."

A "constant velocity joint" is a variation on a conventional universal joint. Differences between them lie in the greater flexibility of the constant velocity joint, and its ability to transmit power at an angle without fluctuations in speed (thus, "constant velocity"). Two constant velocity joints are used on each halfshaft.

Because the X-Body is an all-metric car, there are a few metric terms with which you should be familiar, if only so that you won't become annoyed by the constant references to them in this book. Newton-meters are the metric equivalent of foot-pounds, a measurement of torque. Thus, the "Nm."s you see in these pages are torque values in Newton-meters. Millimeters are abbreviated to "mm"; liters are "L". Celcius temperature measurements are of course abbreviated to "C." In all cases, conventional English equivalents are given in the text along with the metric value.

MODEL IDENTIFICATION

Chevrolet Citation

Oldsmobile Omega

Pontiac Phoenix

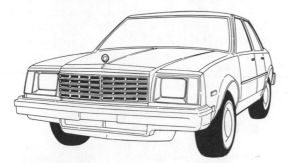

Buick Skylark

SERIAL NUMBER IDENTIFICATION

Vehicle

The vehicle identification number is a 13 place sequence stamped on a plate attached to the left front of the instrument panel, visible through the windshield. The number can be interpreted as follows:

The first number indicates which division manufactured the car. 1 is for Chevrolet, 2 is Pontiac, 3 is Oldsmobile, and 4 is Buick.

The first letter (X) is the series. All X-Body

The V.I.N. plate is visible through the windshield

cars are (obviously) series X. The second and third number are the body style codes. The fourth number is the engine VIN code: 5 for the 2.5 liter (151 cubic inch) four cylinder built by Pontiac, 7 for the 2.8 liter (173 cubic inch) V6 built by Chevrolet.

The second letter is the model year, A for 1980. Next may be a letter or a number. A letter "W" indicates the car was built at the Willow Run, Michigan plant; a number 6 indicates the car was built in Oklahoma City. The last six numbers are the plant sequence (serial) number.

Engine

The four cylinder engine VIN code is stamped on a pad at the right front of the cylinder block below the cylinder head. The V6 VIN code is stamped on a pad at the left front of the cylinder block below the cylinder head.

Transaxle

The manual transaxle identification number is stamped on a pad on the forward side of the transaxle case, next to the middle transaxle-to-engine attaching bolt. The automatic transaxle identification number is stamped on the oil flange pad to the right of the oil dipstick, at the rear of the transaxle. The automatic transaxle model code tag is on top of the case, next to the shift lever.

ROUTINE MAINTENANCE

Routine maintenance is the self-explanatory term used to describe the sort of periodic work necessary to keep a car in safe and reliable working order. A regular program aimed at monitoring essential systems ensures that the car's components are functioning correctly (and will continue to do so until the next inspection, one hopes), and can prevent small problems from developing into major headaches. Routine maintenance also pays off big dividends in keeping major repair costs at a minimum, extending the life of the car, and enhancing resale value, should you ever desire to part with your X-car.

The Citation, Omega, Phoenix, and Skylark require less in the way of routine maintenance than any cars in recent memory. However, a very definite maintenance schedule is provided by General Motors, and must be

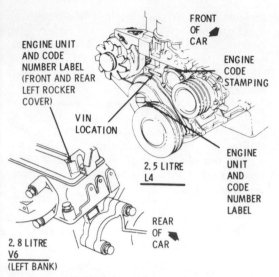

ENGINE UNIT AND CODE NUMBER LABEL (FRONT AND REAR LEFT ROCKER COVER)

FRONT OF CAR

ENGINE CODE STAMPING

VIN LOCATION

2.5 LITRE L4

ENGINE UNIT AND CODE NUMBER LABEL

REAR OF CAR

2.8 LITRE V6 (LEFT BANK)

Engine serial code locations

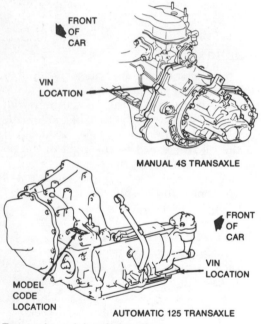

FRONT OF CAR

VIN LOCATION

MANUAL 4S TRANSAXLE

FRONT OF CAR

VIN LOCATION

MODEL CODE LOCATION

AUTOMATIC 125 TRANSAXLE

Transaxle serial code locations

followed, not only to keep the new car warranty in effect, but also to keep the car working properly. The "Maintenance Intervals" chart in this chapter outlines the routine maintenance which must be performed according to intervals based on either accumulated mileage or time. Your X-Body car also came with a maintenance schedule provided by G.M. Adherence to these schedules will result in a longer life for your car, and will, over the long run, save you money and time.

The checks and adjustments in the follow-

ing sections generally require only a few minutes of attention every few weeks; the services to be performed can be easily accomplished in a morning. The most important part of any maintenance program is regularity. The few minutes or occasional morning spent on these seemingly trivial tasks will forestall or eliminate major problems later.

Air Cleaner

The air cleaner element is a dry paper type. It should be replaced every 30,000 miles (every 15,000 miles if the car is used in extremely dusty conditions) as follows:

1. Remove the wing nut (V6) or bolts (four cylinder) on top of the air cleaner housing which sits on top of the carburetor.

2. Remove the housing lid.

3. Lift out the old filter.

4. Before installing the new filter, wipe out the housing with a damp cloth. Check the lid gasket for a tight seal.

Unscrew the wingnut on the V6 air cleaner case

Remove the two nuts on the four cylinder air cleaner case

The old filter element simply lifts out

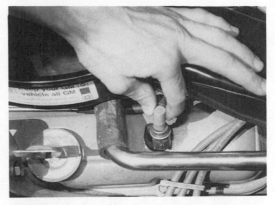

V6 PCV valve location

Wipe out the case before installing a new element

Four cylinder PCV valve location

5. Install a new filter into the housing. Replace the lid and wing nut or bolts.

PCV Valve

The Positive Crankcase Ventilation (PCV) valve must be replaced every 30,000 miles (48,000 km.). Details on the PCV system, including system tests, are given in Chapter Four.

The valve is located in a rubber grommet in the valve cover, connected to the air cleaner housing by a large diameter rubber hose. To replace the valve:

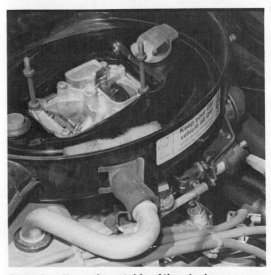

Slide the clip on the outside of the air cleaner case to the right to release the four cylinder PCV filter

1. Pull the valve (with the hose attached) from the rubber grommet in the valve cover.

2. Remove the valve from the hose.

3. Install the new valve into the hose.

4. Install the valve in the grommet.

PCV FILTER

Four cylinder engines have a PCV filter located in the air cleaner housing which must be replaced at 30,000 mile (48,000 km.) intervals.

1. Remove the air cleaner housing lid.

2. Slide back the filter retaining clip.

3. Pull the old filter from the hose.

4. Install the new filter, replace the clip, and replace the lid.

Evaporation Control System Canister Filter

All models have a charcoal canister located in the engine compartment as part of the Evaporation Control System (ECS). Details on this system can be found in Chapter Four. Every 30,000 miles, or 24 months, the filter on the bottom of the charcoal canister must be changed. Cut the interval in half if the car is driven under extremely dusty conditions.

1. Locate the canister in the right front of the engine compartment. It is held at the base by two bolts. Unbolt and lift the canister without disconnecting any of the hoses.

NOTE: *If there is not enough slack in the hoses to allow you to get at the filter, label them before removal. It is important to reconnect them properly.*

2. Turn the canister over. The filter, installed in the bottom, can be simply pulled out.

3. Install a new filter into the bottom of the canister.

4. Install the canister.

The ECS hoses should be inspected for cracks, kinks, or breaks at the time of filter replacement. If replacement hoses are necessary, use only hose designed for the purpose, which is usually marked "EVAP". This hose is available from your dealer or an automotive parts store.

Battery

The Citation, Omega, Phoenix and Skylark have a "maintenance free" battery as standard equipment, eliminating the need for fluid level checks and the possibility of specific gravity tests. Nevertheless, the battery does require some attention.

Once a year, the battery terminals and the cable clamps should be cleaned. Remove the side terminal bolts and the cables, negative cable first. Clean the cable clamps and the battery terminals with a wire brush, until all corrosion, grease, etc. is removed and the metal is shiny. It is especially important to clean the inside of the clamp thoroughly, since a small deposit of foreign material or oxidation there will prevent a sound electrical connection and inhibit either starting or charging. Special tools are available for cleaning the side terminal clamps and terminals.

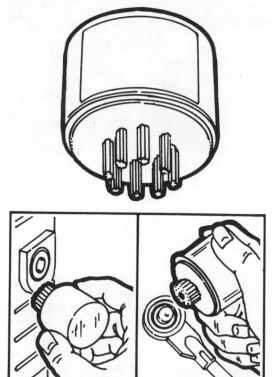

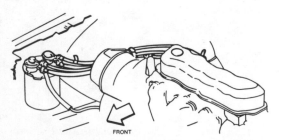

The charcoal canister is located in the right front of the engine compartment

A special tool is available for cleaning the side terminals and clamps

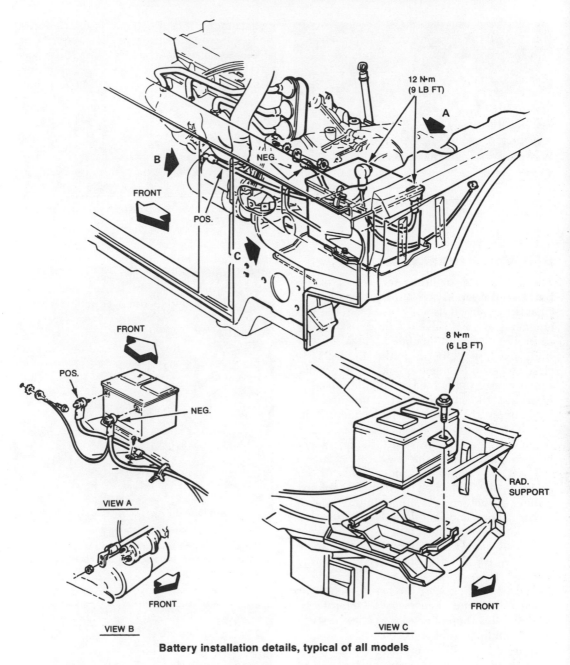

12 N•m
(9 LB FT)

A

NEG.

B

FRONT

POS.

C

FRONT

8 N•m
(6 LB FT)

POS.

NEG.

RAD.
SUPPORT

VIEW A

FRONT

FRONT

VIEW B

VIEW C

Battery installation details, typical of all models

Before installing the cables, loosen the battery hold-down clamp, remove the battery, and check the battery tray. Clear it of any debris and check it for soundness. Rust should be wire brushed away, and the metal given a coat of anti-rust paint. Replace the battery and tighten the hold-down clamp securely, but be careful not to overtighten, which will crack the battery case.

After the clamps and terminals are clean, reinstall the cables, negative cable last. Give the clamps and terminals a thin external coat of grease after installation, to retard corrosion.

Check the cables at the same time that the terminals are cleaned. If the cable insulation is cracked or broken, or if the ends are frayed, the cable should be replaced with a new cable of the same length and gauge.

NOTE: *Keep flame or sparks away from the battery; it gives off explosive hydrogen gas. Battery electrolyte contains sulphuric acid. If you should get any on your skin or in your eyes, flush the affected areas with*

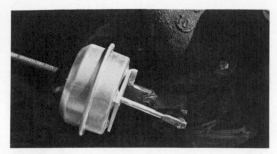

V6 EFE valve

plenty of clear water; if it lands in your eyes, get medical help immediately.

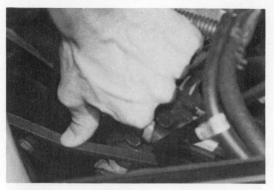

Belt tension can be checked with your thumb, but a gauge is recommended

EFE Valve (Heat Riser)

The EFE valve, or heat riser, is part of the Early Fuel Evaporation system, described in Chapter Four. If is only used on the V6 engine. The EFE valve is a thermostatically-controlled, vacuum-operated valve in the right exhaust pipe (near the firewall). It closes when the engine is cold, to direct hot exhaust gases to the intake manifold, in order to preheat the incoming air/fuel mixture. If it sticks open, the result will be frequent stalling during warmup, especially in cold and damp weather. If it sticks shut, the result will be a rough idle after the engine is warm.

The EFE valve should move freely. It can easily be checked when the engine is cold by pulling the actuating arm next to the vacuum motor to open and shut the valve. If the valve is sticking or binding, a quick shot of solvent especially made for the purpose should free it up. The EFE valve shaft is more easily reached from under the car. The solvent should be applied after the first 6 months or 7,500 miles, and then every 24 months or 30,000 miles thereafter—more often if sticking or binding problems occur.

If the valve is still stuck after application of the solvent, sometimes rapping the end of the shaft lightly with a hammer will break it loose. Otherwise, the components will have to be removed for further repairs.

All accessories have a slotted mount to adjust belt tension; this one belongs to the four cylinder's alternator

Drive Belts

BELT TENSION

Every 12 months or 15,000 miles, check the water pump, alternator, power steering pump (if equipped), and air conditioning compressor (if equipped) drive belts for proper tension. Also look for signs of wear,

The air conditioning compressor's adjusting bolt is above the left arrow. You can lever the compressor in or out by inserting a ½ in. drive rachet into the square hole above the arrow on the right

How to Spot Worn V-Belts

V-Belts are vital to efficient engine operation—they drive the fan, water pump and other accessories. They require little maintenance (occasional tightening) but they will not last forever. Slipping or failure of the V-belt will lead to overheating. If your V-belt looks like any of these, it should be replaced.

Cracking or weathering

This belt has deep cracks, which cause it to flex. Too much flexing leads to heat build-up and premature failure. These cracks can be caused by using the belt on a pulley that is too small. Notched belts are available for small diameter pulleys.

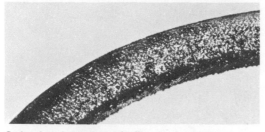

Softening (grease and oil)

Oil and grease on a belt can cause the belt's rubber compounds to soften and separate from the reinforcing cords that hold the belt together. The belt will first slip, then finally fail altogether.

Glazing

Glazing is caused by a belt that is slipping. A slipping belt can cause a run-down battery, erratic power steering, overheating or poor accessory performance. The more the belt slips, the more glazing will be built up on the surface of the belt. The more the belt is glazed, the more it will slip. If the glazing is light, tighten the belt.

Worn cover

The cover of this belt is worn off and is peeling away. The reinforcing cords will begin to wear and the belt will shortly break. When the belt cover wears in spots or has a rough jagged appearance, check the pulley grooves for roughness.

Separation

This belt is on the verge of breaking and leaving you stranded. The layers of the belt are separating and the reinforcing cords are exposed. It's just a matter of time before it breaks completely.

fraying, separation, glazing and so on, and replace the belts as required.

Belt tension should be checked with a gauge made for the purpose. If a gauge is not available, tension can be checked with moderate thumb pressure applied to the belt at its longest span midway between pulleys. If the belt has a free span less than twelve inches, it should deflect approximately ⅛–¼ inch. If the span is longer than twelve inches, deflection can range between ⅛ and ⅜ inches.

1. Loosen the driven accessory's pivot and mounting bolts.

2. Move the accessory toward or away from the engine until the tension is correct. You can use a wooden hammer handle or a broomstick as a lever, but do not use anything metallic.

3. Tighten the bolts and recheck the tension. If new belts have been installed, run the engine for a few minutes, then recheck and readjust as necessary.

It is better to have belts too loose than too tight, because overtight belts will lead to bearing failure, particularly in the water pump and alternator. However, loose belts place an extremely high impact load on the driven component due to the whipping action of the belt.

Cooling System

Once a month, the engine coolant level should be checked. This is quickly accomplished by observing the level of coolant in the recovery tank, which is the translucent tank mounted to the right of the radiator, and connected to the radiator filler neck by a length of hose. As long as coolant is visible in

You can use an inexpensive tester to check antifreeze protection

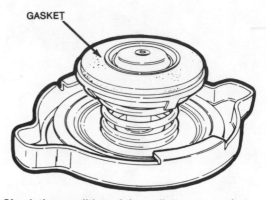

Check the condition of the radiator cap gasket

the tank between the "Full Cold" and "Full Hot" marks, the coolant level is OK.

If coolant is needed, a 50/50 mix of ethylene glycol-base antifreeze and clear water should always be used for additions, both winter and summer. This is imperative on cars with air conditioning; without the antifreeze, the heater core could freeze when the air conditioning is used. Add coolant to the recovery tank through the capped opening; make additions only when the engine is cool.

The radiator hoses, clamps, and radiator cap should be checked at the same time as the coolant level. Hoses which are brittle, cracked, or swollen should be replaced. Clamps should be checked for tightness (screwdriver tight only—do not allow the clamp to cut into the hose or crush the fitting). The radiator cap gasket should be checked for any obvious tears, cracks or

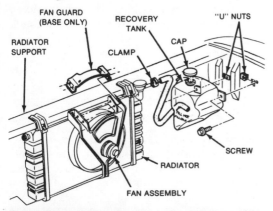

The coolant recovery tank is at the right front of the engine compartment

How to Spot Bad Hoses

Both the upper and lower radiator hoses are called upon to perform difficult jobs in an inhospitable environment. They are subject to nearly 18 psi at under hood temperatures often over 280°F., and must circulate nearly 7500 gallons of coolant an hour—3 good reasons to have good hoses.

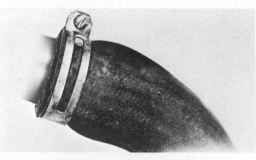

A good test for any hose is to feel it for soft or spongy spots. Frequently these will appear as swollen areas of the hose. The most likely cause is oil soaking. This hose could burst at any time, when hot or under pressure.

Swollen hose

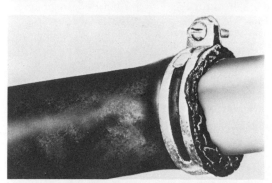

Cracked hoses can usually be seen but feel the hoses to be sure they have not hardened; a prime cause of cracking. This hose has cracked down to the reinforcing cords and could split at any of the cracks.

Cracked hose

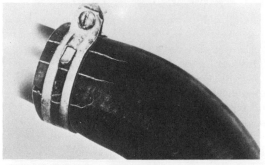

Weakened clamps frequently are the cause of hose and cooling system failure. The connection between the pipe and hose has deteriorated enough to allow coolant to escape when the engine is hot.

Frayed hose end (due to weak clamp)

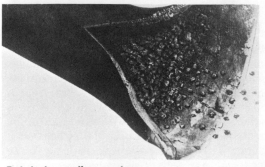

Debris, rust and scale in the cooling system can cause the inside of a hose to weaken. This can usually be felt on the outside of the hose as soft or thinner areas.

Debris in cooling system

swelling, or any signs of incorrect seating in the radiator neck.

CAUTION: *To avoid injury when working with a hot engine, cover the radiator cap with a thick cloth. Wear a heavy glove to protect your hand. Turn the radiator cap slowly to the first stop, and allow all the pressure to vent (indicated when the hissing noise stops). When the pressure has been released, press down and remove the cap the rest of the way.*

The cooling system should be drained, flushed and refilled every two years or 30,000 miles, according to the manufacturer's recommendations. However, many mechanics prefer to change the coolant every year; it is cheap insurance against corrosion, overheating or freezing.

1. Remove the radiator cap when the engine is cool. See the preceding CAUTION about removing the cap.

2. With the radiator cap removed, run the engine until heat can be felt in the upper hose, indicating that the thermostat is open. The heater should be turned on to its maximum heat position, so that the core is flushed out.

3. Shut off the engine and open the drain cock in the bottom of the radiator.

4. Close the drain cock and fill the system with clear water. A cooling system flushing additive can be added, if desired.

5. Run the engine until it is hot again.

6. Drain the system, then flush with water until it runs clear.

7. Clean out the coolant recovery tank: remove the cap leaving the hoses in place. Remove the tank and drain it of any coolant.

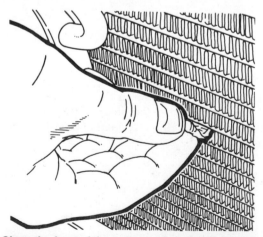

Clean the front of the radiator of any bugs, leaves, or other debris at every yearly coolant change

Clean it out with soap and water, empty it, and install it.

8. Close the drain cock and fill the radiator with a 50/50 mix of ethylene glycol base antifreeze and water to the base of the radiator filler neck. Fill the coolant recovery tank with the same stuff to the "Full Hot" mark. Install the recovery tank cap.

9. Run the engine until the upper radiator hose is hot again (radiator cap still off). With the engine idling, add the 50/50 mix of antifreeze and water to the radiator until the level reaches the bottom of the filler neck. Shut off the engine and install the radiator cap, aligning the arrows with the overflow tube. Turn off the heater.

Air Conditioning System

The air conditioning system requires no routine maintenance, except for belt tension adjustment periodically, as outlined previously. The air conditioning system should be operated for about five minutes each week, even in winter. This will circulate lubricating oil within the system to prevent the various seals from drying out.

The factory-installed air conditioning unit has no sight glass for system checks. It is recommended that all air conditioning service work be entrusted to a qualified mechanic. The system is a potentially hazardous one.

CAUTION: *Do not attempt to charge or discharge the refrigerant system unless you are thoroughly familiar with its operation and the hazards involved. The compressed refrigerant used in the air conditioning system expands and evaporates (boils) into the atmosphere at a temperature of −21.7° F (−29.8° C) or less. This will freeze any surface that it contacts, including your eyes. In addition, the refrigerant decomposes into a poisonous gas in the presence of flame.*

Windshield Wipers

For maximum effectiveness and longest element life, the windshield and wiper blades should be kept clean. Dirt, tree sap, road tar and so on will cause streaking, smearing and blade deterioration if left on the glass. It is advisable to wash the windshield carefully with a commercial glass cleaner at least once a month. Wipe off the rubber blades with the wet rag afterwards.

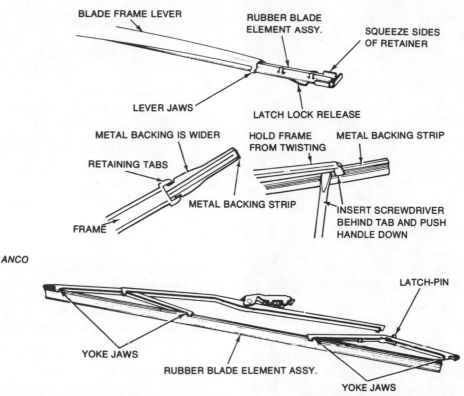

TRICO

BLADE FRAME LEVER

RUBBER BLADE ELEMENT ASSY.

SQUEEZE SIDES OF RETAINER

LEVER JAWS

LATCH LOCK RELEASE

METAL BACKING IS WIDER

RETAINING TABS

HOLD FRAME FROM TWISTING

METAL BACKING STRIP

METAL BACKING STRIP

FRAME

INSERT SCREWDRIVER BEHIND TAB AND PUSH HANDLE DOWN

ANCO

LATCH-PIN

YOKE JAWS

RUBBER BLADE ELEMENT ASSY.

YOKE JAWS

The rubber element can be changed without replacing the entire blade assembly; your X-car may have either one of these types of blades

If the blades are found to be cracked, broken or torn, they should be replaced immediately. Replacement intervals will vary with usage, although ozone deterioration usually limits blade life to about one year. If the wiper pattern is smeared or streaked, or if the blade chatters across the glass, the elements should be replaced. It is easiest and most sensible to replace the elements in pairs.

The wiper blades are retained to the wiper arms by one of two methods. One uses a press-type release tab, which, when depressed, allows the blade to be separated from the arm. The other uses a coil spring retainer. By inserting a screwdriver on top of the spring and pressing downward, the blade can be separated from the arm.

The rubber wiper element can be replaced separately from the blade, which is usually less expensive than replacing both blade and element. As with the blades, two methods are used to retain the rubber element to the blade. On one, a press-type button is used which, when depressed, releases the element, which can be slid off the blade. On the

other, a squeeze clip is used; squeezing the clip allows the element to be pulled from the blade. Replacements are simply slid back into place; be sure all the arms are engaged.

Fluid Level Checks
ENGINE OIL

The engine oil level should be checked at every fuel stop, or once a week, whichever occurs more regularly. The best time to check is when the engine is warm, although

V6 oil dipstick location

Four cylinder oil dipstick location

Four cylinder oil filler location

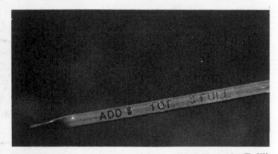

Keep the oil level between the "Add" and "Full" marks

V6 oil filler location

checking immediately after the engine has been shut off will result in an inaccurate reading, since it takes a few minutes for all of the oil to drain back down into the crankcase. If the engine is cold, the engine should not be run before the level is checked. The oil level is checked by means of a dipstick, located at the front of the engine compartment:

1. If the engine is warm, it should be allowed to sit for a few minutes after being shut off to allow the oil to drain down into the oil pan. The car should be parked on a level surface.

2. Pull the dipstick out from its holder, wipe it clean with a rag, and reinsert it firmly. Be sure it is pushed all the way home, or the reading you're about to take will be incorrect.

3. Pull the dipstick again and hold it horizontally to prevent the oil from running. The dipstick on the four cylinder engine is marked with "Add" and "Full" lines. The V6 engine dipstick is marked "Add 1 Qt." and "Full." The oil level should be above the "Add" line.

4. Reinstall the dipstick.

If oil is needed, it is added through the capped opening in the engine valve cover. One quart of oil will raise the level from "Add" to "Full". Only oils labeled "SE" should be used; select a viscosity that will be compatible with the temperatures expected until the next drain interval. See the "Oil and Fuel Recommendations" section later in this chapter if you are not sure what type of oil to use. Check the oil level again after any additions. Be careful not to overfill, which will lead to leakage and seal damage.

TRANSAXLE

Manual

The fluid level in the manual transaxle should be checked every 12 months or 7,500 miles, whichever comes first.

1. Park the car on a level surface. The transaxle should be cool to the touch. If it is hot, check the level later, when it has cooled.

2. Slowly remove the filler hole plug from the left side of the transaxle. If lubricant trickles out as the plug is removed, the fluid level is correct. If not, stick in your finger (watch out for sharp threads); the lubricant should be right up to the edge of the filler hole.

3. If lubricant is needed, add DEXRON® II automatic transmission fluid until the level is correct. The use of a manual transmission lubricant is specifically *not* recommended.

4. When the level is correct, install the filler plug and tighten until snug.

Automatic

The fluid level in the automatic transaxle should be checked every 12 months or 7,500 miles, whichever comes first. The transaxle has a dipstick for fluid level checks.

1. Drive the car until it is at normal operating temperature. The level should not be checked immediately after the car has been driven for a long time at high speed, or in city traffic in hot weather; in those cases, the transaxle should be given a half hour to cool down.

2. Stop the car, apply the parking brake, then shift slowly through all gear positions, ending in Park. Let the engine idle for about

Automatic transaxle fluid dipstick and filler hole location

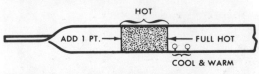

Automatic transaxle dipstick markings

five minutes with the engine in Park. The car should be on a level surface.

3. With the engine still running, remove the dipstick, wipe it clean, then reinsert it, pushing it fully home.

4. Pull the dipstick again and, holding it horizontally, read the fluid level.

5. Cautiously feel the end of the dipstick to determine the temperature. Note that on the X-Body cars the cool and warm level dimples are above the hot level area. If the fluid level is not in the correct area, more will have to be added.

6. Fluid is added through the dipstick tube. You will probably need the aid of a spout or a long-necked funnel. Be sure that whatever you pour through is perfectly clean and dry. Use an automatic transmission fluid marked "DEXRON® II." Add fluid slowly, and in small amounts, checking the level frequently between additions. Do not overfill, which will cause foaming, fluid loss, slippage, and possible transaxle damage. It takes only one pint to raise the level from "Add" to "Full" when the transaxle is hot.

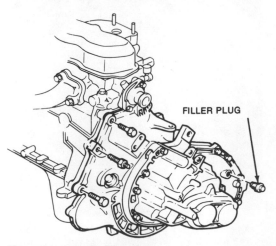

Manual transaxle filler plug

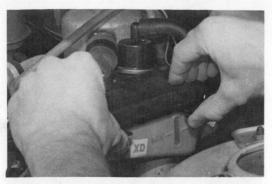

Use thumb pressure to remove the brake master cylinder cover

Proper brake fluid level; non-power brakes do not have the see-through window on the side of the reservoir

BRAKE FLUID

Once a month, the fluid level in the brake master cylinder should be checked.

1. Park the car on a level surface.

2. Clean off the master cylinder cover before removal.

3. The cover simply snaps onto the master cylinder body. Use your thumbs to press up on the two tabs on the side of the cover to unsnap it. Remove the cover, being careful not to drop or tear the rubber diaphragm underneath. Be careful also not to drip any brake fluid on painted surfaces; the stuff eats paint.

NOTE: *Brake fluid absorbs moisture from the air, which reduces effectiveness, and will corrode brake parts once in the system. Never leave the master cylinder or the brake fluid container uncovered for any longer than necessary.*

4. The fluid level should be about ¼ inch below the lip of the master cylinder well.

5. If fluid addition is necessary, use only extra heavy duty disc brake fluid meeting DOT 3 specifications. The fluid should be reasonably fresh because brake fluid deteriorates with age.

6. Replace the cover, making sure that the diaphragm is correctly seated.

If the brake fluid level is constantly low, the system should be checked for leaks. However, it is normal for the fluid level to fall gradually as the disc brake pads wear; expect the fluid level to drop not more than ⅛ inch for every 10,000 miles of wear.

STEERING GEAR

The rack and pinion steering gear used on the X-Body cars is a sealed unit; no fluid level checks or additions are ever necessary.

POWER STEERING FLUID

The power steering hydraulic fluid level is checked with a dipstick inserted into the pump reservoir. The dipstick is attached to the reservoir cap. The level can be checked with the fluid either warm or cold; the car should be parked on a level surface. Check the fluid level every 12 months or 7,500 miles, whichever comes first.

1. With the engine off, unscrew the dipstick and check the level. If the engine is warm, the level should be between the "Hot" and "Cold" marks. If the engine is cold, the level should be between the "Add" and "Cold" marks.

The power steering reservoir dipstick is attached to the cap; the four cylinder reservoir is right up front, behind the radiator

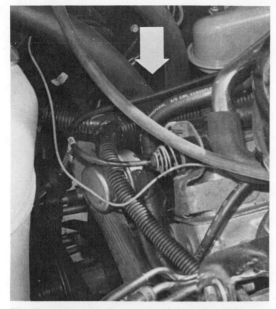

The V6 power steering reservoir is at the right rear of the engine compartment. We couldn't get a photograph of it with the engine in the car, but don't let its inaccessibility prevent you from checking it regularly

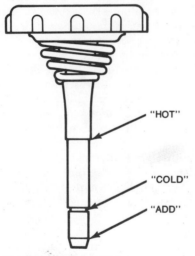

"HOT"

"COLD"

"ADD"

Power steering dipstick markings

2. If the level is low, add power steering fluid until correct. Be careful not to overfill, which will cause fluid loss and seal damage.

COOLANT LEVEL

Coolant level checks are covered earlier in this chapter, under "Cooling System." Check the coolant level every month.

BATTERY

The X-Body cars have a "Maintenance Free" battery which does not require periodic additions of water thus eliminating fluid level checks. See the "Battery" section earlier in this chapter for regular maintenance.

WINDSHIELD WASHER FLUID

Check the fluid level in the windshield washer tank at every oil level check. The fluid can be mixed in a 50% solution with water, if desired, as long as temperatures remain above freezing. Below freezing, the fluid should be used full strength. Never add engine coolant antifreeze to the washer fluid, because it will damage the car's paint.

Tires

Tires should be checked weekly for proper air pressure. A chart, located at the left front door edge, gives the recommended inflation pressures. Maximum fuel economy and tire life will result if the pressure is maintained at the highest figure given on the chart. The tires should be checked before driving since pressure can increase as much as six pounds per square inch (psi) due to heat buildup. It is a good idea to have your own accurate pressure gauge, because not all gauges on service station air pumps can be trusted. When checking pressures, do not neglect the spare tire. Note that some spare tires require pressures considerably higher than those used in the other tires.

While you are about the task of checking

Capacities

Year	Engine Displacement Cu In. (cc)	Crankcase Quarts (Liters)		Transaxle Pints (L)		Gas Tank Gal (L)	Cooling System Qts (L)	
		w/filter	wo/filter	4 speed	Auto		w/heater	w/AC
1980	151 (2500)	4.0 (3.8)	3.0 (2.8)	3.0(1.5)	10.0(4.6)	14(53)	9.5(9.0)	9.75(9.3)
	173 (2800)	5.0 (4.8)	4.0 (3.8)	3.0(1.5)	10.0(4.6)	14(53)	11.5(10.8)	11.75(11.2)

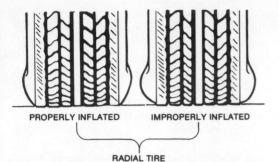

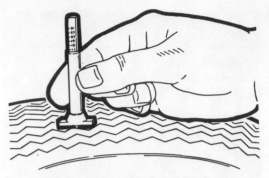

Don't judge a radial tire's pressure by its appearance. An improperly inflated radial tire looks similar to a properly inflated one

Inexpensive gauges are also available for measuring tread wear

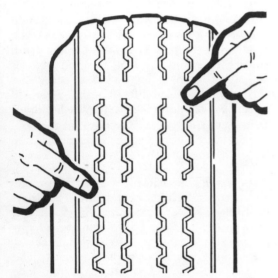

Tread wear indicators will appear as bands across the tread when the tire is due for replacement

You can use a penny for tread wear checks; if the top of Lincoln's head is visible in two adjacent grooves, the tire should be replaced

air pressure, inspect the tire treads for cuts, bruises, and other damage. Check the air valves to be sure that they are tight. Replace any missing valve caps.

Check the tires for uneven wear that might indicate the need for front end alignment or tire rotation. Tires should be replaced when a tread wear indicator appears as a solid band across the tread.

When buying new tires, give some thought to the following points, especially if you are considering a switch to larger tires or a different profile series:

1. All four tires should be of the same construction type. Radial, bias, or bias-belted tires must not be mixed.

2. The wheels must be the correct width for the tire. Tire dealers have charts of tire and wheel rim compatibility. A mismatch can cause sloppy handling and rapid tread wear. The tread width should match the rim width (inside bead to inside bead) within an inch. For radial tires, the rim width should be 80% or less of the tire (not tread) width.

3. The height (mounted diameter) of the new tires can change speedometer accuracy, engine speed per given road speed, fuel mileage, acceleration, and ground clearance. Tire manufacturers furnish full measurement specifications.

4. The spare tire should be usable, at least for low speed operation, with the new tires.

5. There shouldn't be any body interference when the car is loaded, on bumps or in turning.

All of these problems can be avoided by replacing the tires with new ones of the same type and size. The P-metric radials installed as standard equipment on the X-Bodies are particularly fuel-efficient; you can expect some reduction in fuel mileage if, when they wear out, they are replaced with conven-

How to Read Tire Wear

The way your tires wear is a good indicator of other parts of your car. Abnormal wear patterns are often caused by the need for simple tire maintenance, or for front end alignment.

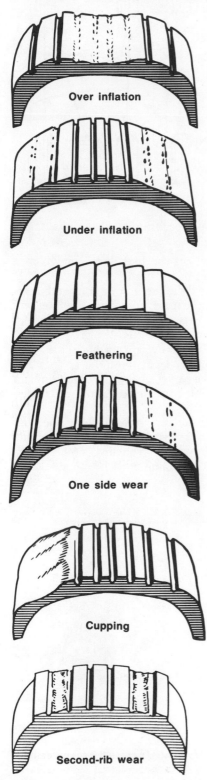

Over inflation

Under inflation

Feathering

One side wear

Cupping

Second-rib wear

Excessive wear at the center of the tread indicates that the air pressure in the tire is consistently too high. The tire is riding on the center of the tread and wearing it prematurely. Occasionally, this wear pattern can result from outrageously wide tires on narrow rims. The cure for this is to replace either the tires or the wheels.

This type of wear usually results from consistent under-inflation. When a tire is under inflated, there is too much contact with the road by the outer treads, which wear prematurely. When this type of wear occurs, and the tire pressure is known to be consistently correct, a bent or worn steering component or the need for wheel alignment could be indicated.

Feathering is a condition when the edge of each tread rib develops a slightly rounded edge on one side and a sharp edge on the other. By running your hand over the tire, you can usually feel the sharper edges before you'll be able to see them. The most common causes of feathering are incorrect toe-in setting or deteriorated bushings in the front suspension.

When an inner or outer rib wears faster than the rest of the tire, the need for wheel alignment is indicated. There is excessive camber in the front suspension, causing the wheel to lean too much putting excessive load on one side of the tire. Misalignment could also be due to sagging springs, worn ball joints, or worn control arm bushings. Be sure the vehicle is loaded the way it's normally driven when you have the wheels aligned.

Cups or scalloped dips appearing around the edge of the tread almost always indicate worn (sometimes bent) suspension parts. Adjustment of wheel alignment alone will seldom cure the problem. Any worn component that connects the wheel to the car can cause this type of wear. Occasionally, wheels that are out of balance will wear like this, but wheel imbalance usually shows up as bald spots between the outside edges and center of the tread.

Second-rib wear is normally found only in radial tires, and appears where the steel belts end in relation to the tread. Normally, it can be kept to a minimum by paying careful attention to tire pressure and frequently rotating the tires. This is frequently considered normal wear but excessive amounts indicate that the tires are too wide for the wheels.

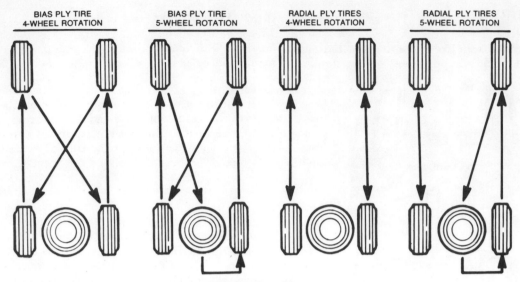

| BIAS PLY TIRE 4-WHEEL ROTATION | BIAS PLY TIRE 5-WHEEL ROTATION | RADIAL PLY TIRES 4-WHEEL ROTATION | RADIAL PLY TIRES 5-WHEEL ROTATION |

Tire rotation diagrams

tional radials, or tires of other construction types. One other thing to remember when buying new tires: always have the dealer install new valve stems. Few things are more aggravating than having a new tire go flat because of an old, leaky valve stem.

TIRE ROTATION

Tire rotation is recommended every 6,000 miles or so, to obtain maximum tire wear. The pattern you use depends on whether or not your car has a usable spare. Radial tires should not be cross-switched (from one side of the car to the other); they last longer if their direction of rotation is not changed. Snow tires sometimes have directional arrows molded into the side of the carcass; the arrow shows the direction of rotation. They will wear very rapidly if their rotation is reversed. Studded tires will lost their studs if their rotational direction is reversed. Mark the wheel position or direction of rotation on radial tires or studded snow tires before removing them to avoid these problems.

Fuel Filter

All models have a fuel filter located within the carburetor body. The fuel filter has a check valve to prevent fuel spillage in the event of an accident. When the filter is replaced, make sure the new one is of the same type. All filters are of the paper element type. Replace the filter every 15,000 miles.

1. Place a few absorbent rags underneath the fuel line where it joins the carburetor.

2. Disconnect the fuel line connection at the fuel inlet nut.

3. Unscrew the fuel inlet nut from the carburetor. As the nut is removed, the filter will be pushed partway out by spring pressure.

4. Remove the filter and spring.

5. Install the new spring and filter. The hole in the filter faces the nut.

6. Install a new gasket on the inlet nut and install the nut into the carburetor. Tighten securely.

7. Install the fuel line. Tighten the connector to 18 ft. lbs. (24 Nm.) while holding the inlet nut with a wrench.

8. Start the engine and check for leaks.

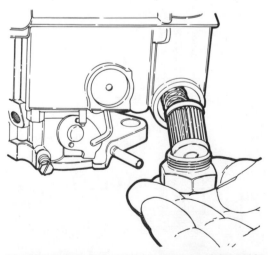

The fuel filter is located behind the fuel inlet nut in the carburetor body

LUBRICATION

Oil and Fuel Recommendations

OIL

The SAE (Society of Automotive Engineers) grade number indicates the viscosity of the engine oil, and thus its ability to lubricate at a given temperature. The lower the SAE grade number, the lighter the oil; the lower the viscosity, the easier it is to crank the engine in cold weather.

The API (American Petroleum Institute) designation indicates the classification of engine oil for use under given operating conditions. Only oils designated for use "Service SE" should be used. Oils of the SE type perform a variety of functions inside the engine in addition to the basic function as a lubricant. Through a balanced system of metallic detergents and polymeric dispersants, the oil prevents the formation of high and low temperature deposits, and also keeps sludge and dirt particles in suspension. Acids, particularly sulfuric acid, as well as other byproducts of combusion, are neutralized. Both the SAE grade number and the API designation can be found on the top of the oil can.

NOTE: *Non-detergent or straight mineral oils must never be used.*

Oil viscosities should be chosen from those oils recommended for the lowest anticipated temperatures during the oil change interval.

Multi-viscosity oils offer the important advantage of being adaptable to temperature extremes. They allow easy starting at low temperatures, yet give good protection at high speeds and engine temperatures. This is a decided advantage in changeable climates or in long distance touring.

FUEL

All G.M. X-Body cars must use unleaded fuel. The use of leaded fuel will plug the catalyst rendering it inoperative, and will increase the exhaust back pressure to the point where engine output will be severely reduced. The minimum octane for both the four cylinder and V6 engines is 91 RON. All unleaded fuels sold in the U.S. are required to meet this minimum octane rating.

Use of a fuel too low in octane (a measurement of anti-knock quality) will result in spark knock. Since many factors affect operating efficiency, such as altitude, terrain, and air temperature and humidity, knocking may result even thought the recommended fuel is being used. If persistent knocking occurs, it may be necessary to switch to a slightly higher grade of unleaded gasoline. Continuous or heavy knocking may result in serious engine damage, for which the manufacturer is not responsible.

NOTE: *Your car's engine fuel requirement can change with time, due to carbon buildup, which changes the compression ratio. If your car's engine knocks, pings, or runs on, switch to a higher grade of fuel, if possible, and check the ignition timing. Sometimes changing brands of gasoline will cure the problem. If it is necessary to retard timing from specifications, don't change it more than a few degrees. Retarded timing will reduce power output and fuel mileage, and will increase engine temperature.*

Lubricant Changes

ENGINE OIL AND FILTER

If you purchased your X-Body car new, the engine oil and filter should be changed at the first 7,500 miles or 12 months (whichever comes first), and every 7,500 miles or 12 months thereafter. You should make it a practice to change the oil filter at every oil change; otherwise, a quart of dirty oil remains in the engine every other time the oil is changed. The change interval should be halved when the car is driven under severe conditions, such as in extremely dusty weather, or when the car is used for trailer towing, prolonged high speed driving, or repeated short trips in freezing weather.

USE THESE SAE VISCOSITY GRADES

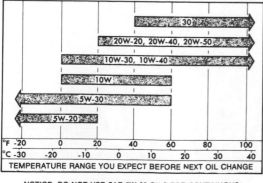

30
20W-20, 20W-40, 20W-50
10W-30, 10W-40
10W
5W-30
5W-20

°F -20   0   20   40   60   80   100
°C -30   -20   -10   0   10   20   30   40
TEMPERATURE RANGE YOU EXPECT BEFORE NEXT OIL CHANGE

NOTICE: DO NOT USE SAE 5W-20 OILS FOR CONTINUOUS HIGH-SPEED DRIVING. 5W-30 OILS MAY BE USED UP TO 100°F (38°C)

Oil viscosity chart; multi-viscosity oils offer greater temperature latitude

Maintenance Intervals Chart

Intervals are for number of months or thousands of miles, whichever comes first.

NOTE: *Heavy-duty operation (trailer towing, prolonged idling, severe stop and start driving) should be accompanied by a 50% increase in maintenance. Cut the interval in half for these conditions.*

Maintenance	*Service Interval*
Air cleaner (Replace)	30,000 mi. (48,000 km.)
PCV valve (Replace)	30,000 mi. (48,000 km.)
Carbon canister filter (Replace)	30,000 mi. (48,000 km.)
EFE system check	6 mo/7,500 mi. (12,000 km.), then every 24 mo/30,000 mi (48,000 km.)
Belt tension (Adjust)	12 mo/15,000 mi. (24,000 km.)
Engine oil and filter (Change)	12 mo/7,500 mi. (12,000 km.)
Fuel filter (Change)	15,000 mi. (24,000 km.)

Manual transaxle
  Check
  Change
	
	12 mo/7,500 mi. (12,000 km.)
	100,000 mi. (160,000 km.)

Automatic transaxle
  Check
  Change (including filter)
	
	12 mo/7,500 mi. (12,000 km.)
	100,000 mi. (160,000 km.)

Engine coolant
  Check
  Change
	
	Weekly
	12 mo/15,000 mi. (24,000 km.)

Chassis lubrication	12 mo/7,500 mi. (12,000 km.)
Rotate tires	7,500 mi. (12,000 km.)
Brake fluid (Check)	12 mo/7,500 mi. (12,000 km.)
Spark plugs and wires, ignition timing, idle speed	30,000 mi. (48,000 Km.) See Chapter Two

1. Drive the car until the engine is at normal operating temperature. A run to the parts store for oil and a filter should accomplish this. If the engine is not hot when the oil is changed, most of the acids and contaminants will remain inside the engine.

2. Shut off the engine, and slide a pan of at least six quarts capacity under the oil pan. Throw-away aluminum roasting pans can be used for this.

3. Remove the drain plug from the engine oil pan, after wiping the plug area

Recommended Lubricants

Lubricant	Classification
Engine Oil	API SE
Manual Transaxle	DEXRON® II
Automatic Transaxle	DEXRON® II
Power Steering	Power Steering Fluid
Chassis Grease	EP Grease meeting G.M. specification 6031-M
Brake Fluid	DOT 3
Antifreeze	Ethylene Glycol
Clutch Linkage Pivot points Push rod to fork joint	Engine Oil Chassis Grease
Transaxle Shift Linkage	Engine Oil

clean. The drain plug is the bolt inserted at an angle into the lowest point of the oil pan.

4. The oil from the engine will be HOT. It will probably not be possible to hold onto the drain plug. You may have to let it fall into the pan and fish it out later. Allow all the oil to drain completely. This will take a few minutes.

5. Wipe off the drain plug, removing any traces of metal particles. Pay particular attention to the threads. Replace it, and tighten it snugly.

6. The oil filter for the V6 engine is right up front, just behind the radiator. The four cylinder oil filter is at the back of the engine. It is impossible to reach from above, and almost as inaccessible from below. It may be easiest to remove the right front wheel and reach through the fender opening to get at the four cylinder oil filter. Use an oil filter strap wrench to loosen the oil filter; these are available at auto parts stores. It is recommended that you purchase one with as thin a strap as possible, to get into tight areas. Place the drain pan on the ground, under the filter. Unscrew and discard the old filter. It will be VERY HOT, so be careful.

7. If the oil filter is on so tightly that it collapses under pressure from the wrench,

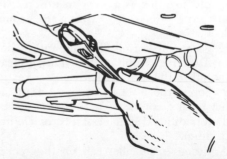

The oil drain plug is located at the lowest point of the oil pan

The V6 oil filter is right up front

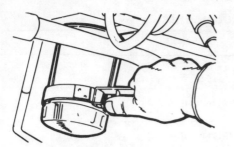

Use an oil filter strap wrench to remove the oil filter; install the new filter by hand

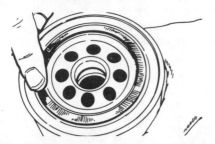

Apply a thin film of clean oil to the new filter gasket to prevent it from tearing upon installation

drive a long punch or a nail through it, across the diameter and as close to the base as possible, and use this as a lever to unscrew it. Make sure you are turning it counterclockwise.

8. Clean off the oil filter mounting surface with a rag. Apply a thin film of clean engine oil to the filter gasket.

9. Screw the filter on by hand until the gasket makes contact. Then tighten it by hand an additional ½ to ¾ of a turn. Do not overtighten.

10. Remove the filler cap on the rocker (valve) cover, after wiping the area clean.

11. Add the correct number of quarts of oil specified in the Capacities Chart. If you don't have an oil can spout, you will need a funnel. Be certain you do not overfill the engine, which can cause serious damage. Replace the cap.

12. Check the oil level on the dipstick. It is normal for the level to be a bit above the full mark. Start the engine and allow it to idle for a few minutes.

CAUTION: *Do not run the engine above idle speed until it has built up oil pressure, indicated when the oil light goes out.*

Check around the filter and drain plug for any leaks.

13. Shut off the engine, allow the oil to drain for a minute, and check the oil level.

After completing this job, you will have several quarts of filthy oil to dispose of. The best thing to do with it is to funnel it into old plastic milk containers or bleach bottles. Then, you can either pour it into the recycling barrel at the gas station (if you're on good terms with the attendant), or put the containers into the trash.

Manual Transaxle

The fluid in the manual transaxle should be changed at the interval specified in the Maintenance Intervals Chart, or more often if the car is used under severe conditions. You may also want to change it if you have purchased your X-car used, or if it has been driven in water deep enough to reach the transaxle case.

1. The fluid should be hot before it is drained. If the car is driven until the engine is at normal operating temperature, the fluid should be hot enough.

2. Remove the filler plug from the left side of the transaxle to provide a vent.

3. The drain plug is located on the bottom of the transaxle case. Place a pan under the drain plug and remove it.

CAUTION: *The fluid will be HOT. Push up against the threads as you unscrew the plug to prevent leakage.*

4. Allow the fluid to drain completely. Check the condition of the plug gasket, and replace it if necessary. It will probably be ok. Clean off the plug and replace, tightening until snug.

5. Fill the transaxle with fluid through the filler hole in the left side. Use only DEXRON® II automatic transmission fluid to fill the transaxle. DO NOT use conventional manual transmission lubricants. You will need the aid of a long necked funnel or a funnel and a hose to pour through. Lubricant capacity is only three quarts (2.8 L); do not overfill.

6. The fluid should come right up to the edge of the filler hole. You can stick your finger in to verify this. Watch out for sharp threads.

7. Replace the filler plug. Dispose of the old fluid in the same manner as old engine oil. Take a drive in your car, stop on a level surface, and check the fluid level.

Automatic Transaxle

The fluid should be changed according to the schedule in the Maintenance Intervals

Chart. If the car is normally used in severe service, such as stop and start driving, trailer towing, or the like, the interval should be halved. If the car is driven under especially nasty conditions, such as in heavy city traffic where the temperature normally reaches 90° F, or in very hilly or mountainous areas, or in police, taxi, or delivery service, the fluid should be changed every 15,000 miles (24,000 km.).

The fluid must be hot before it is drained; a 20 minute drive should accomplish this.

1. There is no drain plug; the fluid pan must be removed. Place a drain pan underneath the transaxle pan and remove the pan attaching bolts at the front and sides of the pan.

2. Loosen the rear pan attaching bolts approximately four turns each.

3. Very carefully pry the pan loose. You can use a screwdriver for this if you work CAREFULLY. Do not distort the pan flange, or score the mating surface of the transaxle case. You'll be very sorry later if you do. As the pan is pried loose, all of the fluid is going to come pouring out.

4. Remove the remaining bolts and remove the pan and gasket. Throw away the gasket.

5. Clean the pan with solvent and allow it to air dry. If you use a rag to wipe out the pan, you risk leaving bits of lint behind, which will clog the dinky hydraulic passages in the transaxle.

6. Remove and discard the filter and the O-ring seal.

7. Install a new filter and O-ring, locating the filter against the dipstick stop.

8. Install a new gasket on the pan and install the pan. Tighten the bolts evenly and in rotation to 12 ft. lbs. (16 Nm.). Do not overtighten.

9. Add approximately 4 qts. (3.8 L) of DEXRON® II automatic transmission fluid to the transaxle through the dipstick tube. You will need a long necked funnel, or a funnel and tube to do this.

10. With the transaxle in Park, put on the parking brake, block the front wheels, start the engine and let it idle. DO NOT RACE THE ENGINE. DO NOT MOVE THE LEVER THROUGH ITS RANGES.

11. With the lever in Park, check the fluid level. If it's ok, take the car out for a short drive, park on a level surface, and check the level again, as outlined earlier in this chapter. Add more fluid if necessary. Be careful

not to overfill, which will cause foaming and fluid loss.

NOTE: *If the drained fluid is discolored (brown or black), thick, or smells burnt, serious transmission troubles, probably due to overheating, should be suspected. Your car's transaxle should be inspected by a reliable transmission specialist to determine the problem.*

Chassis Greasing

There are only two areas which require regular chassis greasing: the front suspension components and the steering linkage. These parts should be greased every 12 months or 7,500 miles (12,000 Km.) with an EP grease meeting G.M. specification 6031M.

If you choose to do this job yourself, you will need to purchase a hand operated grease gun, if you do not own one already, and a long flexible extension hose to reach the various grease fittings. You will also need a cartridge of the appropriate grease.

Press the fitting on the grease gun hose onto the grease fitting on the suspension or steering linkage component. Pump a few shots of grease into the fitting, until the rubber boot on the joint begins to expand, indicating that the joint is full. Remove the gun from the fitting. Be careful not to overfill the joints, which will rupture the rubber boots, allowing the entry of dirt. You can keep the grease fittings clean by covering them with a small square of tin foil.

Grease the steering linkage at the knuckle (black arrow) and the ball joint at the lower arm (above the white arrow)

Chassis Lubrication

Every 12 months or 7,500 miles (12,000 km.), the various linkages and hinges on the chassis and body should be lubricated, as follows:

TRANSAXLE SHIFT LINKAGE

Lubricate the manual transaxle shift linkage contact points with the EP grease used for chassis greasing, which should meet G.M. specification 6031M. The automatic transaxle linkage should be lubricated with clean engine oil.

HOOD LATCH AND HINGES

Clean the latch surfaces and apply clean engine oil to the latch pilot bolts and the spring anchor. Use the engine oil to lubricate the hood hinges as well. Use a chassis grease to lubricate all the pivot points in the latch release mechanism.

DOOR HINGES

The gas tank filler door, car door, and rear hatch or trunk lid hinges should be wiped clean and lubricated with clean engine oil. Silicone spray also works well on these parts, but must be applied more often. Use engine oil to lubricate the trunk or hatch lock mechanism and the lock bolt and striker. The door lock cylinders can be lubricated easily with a shot of silicone spray or one of the many dry penetrating lubricants commercially available.

PARKING BRAKE LINKAGE

Use chassis grease on the parking brake cable where it contacts the guides, links, levers, and pulleys. The grease should be a water resistant one for durability under the car.

ACCELERATOR LINKAGE

Lubricate the carburetor stud, carburetor lever, and the accelerator pedal lever at the support inside the car with clean engine oil.

PUSHING AND TOWING

The X-Body cars may not be pushed or towed to start, because doing so may cause the catalytic converter to explode. If the battery is weak, the engine may be jump started, using the procedure outlined in the following section.

Your Citation, Omega, Phoenix, or Skylark

may be towed on all four wheels at speeds less than 35 mph (60 km/h) for distances up to 50 miles (80 km). The driveline and steering must be normally operable. If either one is damaged, the car may not be flat-towed. If the car is flat-towed (on all four wheels), the steering must be unlocked, the transaxle shifted to Neutral, and the parking brake released. Towing attachment must be made to the main structural members of the chassis, not to the bumpers or sheetmetal.

The car may be towed on its rear wheels by a wrecker; make sure that safety chains are used. X-Body cars with manual transaxles may be towed on their front wheels, for short distances and at low speeds. Be sure the transaxle is in Neutral. Cars with automatic transaxles should not be towed on their front wheels; transaxle damage may result. If it is impossible to tow the car on its rear wheels, place the front wheels on a dolly.

JUMP STARTING

Jump starting is the only way to start an automatic transaxle model with a weak battery, and the best method for a manual transaxle model.

CAUTION: *Do not attempt this procedure on a frozen battery; it will probably explode.*

The battery in the other vehicle must be a 12 volt, negatively grounded one. Do not attempt to jump start your car with a 24 volt power source; serious electrical damage will result.

1. Turn off all electrical equipment. Place the automatic transaxle in Park or the manual in Neutral and set the parking brake.

2. Make sure that the two vehicles are not touching. It is a good idea to keep the engine running in the booster vehicle.

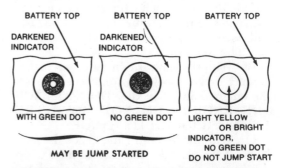

Check the appearance of the charge indicator on top of the battery before attempting a jump start; if it's not green or dark, do not jump start the car

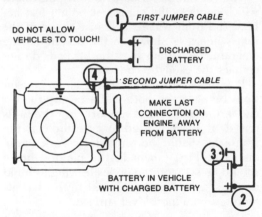

MAKE CONNECTIONS IN NUMERICAL ORDER

FIRST JUMPER CABLE

DO NOT ALLOW
VEHICLES TO TOUCH!

DISCHARGED
BATTERY

SECOND JUMPER CABLE

MAKE LAST
CONNECTION ON
ENGINE, AWAY
FROM BATTERY

BATTERY IN VEHICLE
WITH CHARGED BATTERY

Cable connections for jump starting

3. Remove the caps from both batteries and cover the openings with cloths. This step can be ignored with "maintenance free" batteries.

4. Attach one end of a jumper cable to the positive (+) terminal of the booster battery. The red cable is usually positive. Attach the other end to the positive terminal of the discharged battery.

CAUTION: *Be very careful about these connections. An alternator and regulator can be destroyed in a remarkably short time if battery polarity is reversed.*

5. Attach one end of the other cable (the black one) to the negative (−) terminal of the booster battery. Attach the other end to a ground point such as the alternator bracket on the engine of the car being started. Do not connect it to the battery.

CAUTION: *Be careful not to lean over the battery while making this last connection.*

6. If the engine will not start, disconnect the batteries as soon as possible. If this is not done, the two batteries will soon reach a state of equilibrium, with both too weak to start an engine. This is no problem if the engine of the booster vehicle is running fast enough to keep up the charge. Lengthy cranking can also damage the starter.

7. Reverse the procedure exactly to remove the jumper cables. Discard the rags, because they may have acid on them.

NOTE: *It is recognized that some or all of the precautions outlined in this procedure are often ignored with no harmful results. However, the procedure outlined is the only fully safe, foolproof one.*

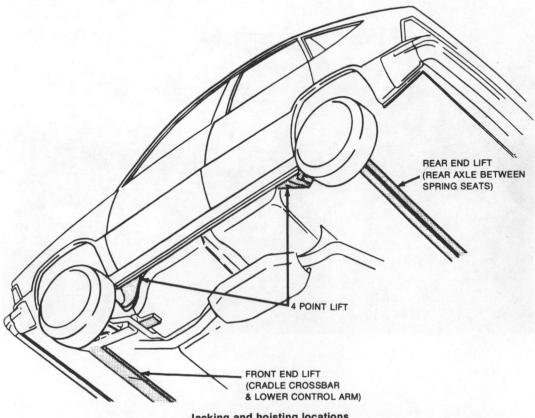

REAR END LIFT
(REAR AXLE BETWEEN
SPRING SEATS)

4 POINT LIFT

FRONT END LIFT
(CRADLE CROSSBAR
& LOWER CONTROL ARM)

Jacking and hoisting locations

JACKING AND HOISTING

The X-Body cars are supplied with a jack for changing tires. This is a bumper jack, engaging slots in the bumpers by means of a hook. This jack is satisfactory for its intended purpose; it is not meant to support the car while you go crawling around underneath it. *Never crawl under the car when it is supported by only the bumper jack.*

The car may also be jacked at the rear axle between the spring seats, or at the front end at the engine cradle crossbar or lower control arm. The car must never be lifted by the rear lower control arms.

The car can be raised on a four point hoist which contacts the chassis at points just behind the front wheels and just ahead of the rear wheels, as shown in the accompanying diagram. Be certain that the lift pads do not contact the catalytic converter.

It is imperative that strict safety precautions be observed both while raising the car and in the subsequent support after the car is raised. If a jack is used to raise the car, the transaxle should be shifted to Park (automatic) or First (manual), the parking brake should be set, and the opposite wheel should be blocked. Jacking should only be attempted on a hard level surface.

Tune-Up and Troubleshooting

TUNE-UP PROCEDURES

In order to extract the full measure of performance and economy from your car's engine it is essential that it be properly tuned at regular intervals. Although the tune-up intervals for the 1980 X-Body cars have been stretched to limits which would have been thought impossible a few years ago, periodic maintenance is still required. A regularly scheduled tune-up will keep your car's engine running smoothly and will prevent the annoying minor breakdowns and poor performance associated with an untuned engine.

A complete tune-up should be performed at the interval specified in the "Maintenance Intervals Chart" in Chapter One. This interval should be halved if the car is operated under severe conditions, such as trailer towing, prolonged idling, continual stop-and-start driving, or if starting and running problems are noticed. It is assumed that the routine maintenance described in the first chapter has been kept up, as this will have a decided effect on the results of a tune-up. All of the applicable steps should be followed in order, as the result is a cumulative one.

If the specifications on the tune-up label in the engine compartment of your X-Body disagree with the "Tune-Up Specifications" chart in this chapter, the figures on the

sticker must be used. The label often reflects changes made during the production run.

Spark Plugs

Spark plugs ignite the air and fuel mixture in the cylinder as the piston reaches the top of the compression stroke. The controlled explosion that results forces the piston down, turning the crankshaft and the rest of the drive train.

The average life of a spark plug in an X-Body car is 30,000 miles. Part of the reason for this extraordinarily long life is the exclusive use of unleaded fuel, which reduces the amount of deposits within the combustion chamber and on the spark plug electrodes themselves, compared with the deposits left by the leaded gasoline used in the past. An additional contribution to long life is made by the HEI (High Energy Ignition) System, which fires the spark plugs with over 35,000 volts of electricity. The high voltage serves to keep the electrodes clear, and because it is a "cleaner" blast of electricity than that produced by conventional breaker-points ignitions, the electrodes suffer less pitting and wear.

Nevertheless, the life of a spark plug is dependent on a number of factors, including

Tune-Up Specifications

When analyzing compression test results, look for uniformity among cylinders rather than specific pressures.

Year	ENGINE No. Cyl Displacement (cu in.)	hp	SPARK PLUGS Orig Type	Gap (in.)	DISTRIBUTOR Point Dwell (deg)	Point Gap (in.)	IGNITION TIMING (deg) ▲ ● Man Trans	Auto Trans	VALVES Intake Opens (deg) ■	Fuel Pump Pressure (psi)	IDLE SPEED (rpm) ▲ Man Trans ●	Auto Trans
1980	4—151	All	R-43TSX	.060	Electronic		10B(12B)	10B	33	6.5–8.0	1000	650
	6—173	All	R-44TS	.045	Electronic		4B(6B)	8B(10B)	25	6.0–7.5	1050(1100)	650(700)

NOTE: The underhood specifications sticker often reflects tune-up specification changes made in production. Sticker figures must be used if they disagree with those in this chart.

▲ See text for procedure

● Figure in parenthesis indicates California and High Altitude engine

■ All figures Before Top Dead Center

B Before Top Dead Center

Part numbers in this chart are not recommendations by Chilton for any product by brand name.

the mechanical condition of the engine, driving conditions, and the driver's habits.

When you remove the plugs, check the condition of the electrodes; they are a good indicator of the internal state of the engine. Since the spark plug wires must be checked every 15,000 miles, the spark plugs can be removed and examined at the same time. This will allow you to keep an eye on the mechanical status of the engine.

A small deposit of light tan or rust-red material on a spark plug that has been used for any period of time is to be considered normal. Any other color, or abnormal amounts of wear or deposits, indicates that there is something amiss in the engine.

The gap between the center electrode and the side or ground electrode can be expected to increase not more than 0.001 in. every 1,000 miles under normal conditions.

When a spark plug is functioning normally or, more accurately, when the plug is installed in an engine that is functioning properly, the plugs can be taken out, cleaned, regapped, and reinstalled in the engine without doing the engine any harm.

When, and if, a plug fouls and begins to misfire, you will have to investigate, correct the cause of the fouling, and either clean or replace the plug.

There are several reasons why a spark plug will foul and you can learn which is at fault by just looking at the plug. A few of the most common reasons for plug fouling, and a description of the fouled plug's appearance, are listed in the "Troubleshooting" section, which also offers solutions to the problems.

Spark plugs suitable for use in your car's engine are offered in a number of different heat ranges. The amount of heat which the plug absorbs is determined by the length of the lower insulator. The longer the insulator, the hotter the plug will operate; the shorter the insulator, the cooler it will operate. A spark plug that absorbs (or retains) little heat and remains too cool will accumulate deposits of oil and carbon, because it is not hot enough to burn them off. This leads to fouling and consequent misfiring. A spark plug that absorbs too much heat will have no deposits, but the electrodes will burn away quickly and, in some cases, preignition may result. Preignition occurs when the spark plug tips get so hot that they ignite the fuel/air mixture before the actual spark fires. This premature ignition will usually cause a pinging sound under conditions of low speed and heavy load. In severe cases, the heat may become high enough to start the fuel/air mixture burning throughout the combustion chamber rather than just to the front of the plug. In this case, the resultant explosion (detonation) will be strong enough to damage pistons, rings, and valves.

In most cases the factory recommended heat range is correct; it is chosen to perform well under a wide range of operating conditions. However, if most of your driving is long distance, high speed travel, you may want to install a spark plug one step colder than standard. If most of your driving is of the short trip variety, when the engine may not always reach operating temperature, a hotter plug may help burn off the deposits normally accumulated under those conditions.

REMOVAL

1. Number the wires with pieces of adhesive tape so that you won't cross them when you replace them.

2. The spark plug boots have large grips to aid in removal. Grasp the wire by the rubber boot and twist the boot ½ turn in either direction to break the tight seal between the boot and the plug. Then twist and pull on the boot to remove the wire from the spark plug. Do not pull on the wire itself or you will damage the carbon cord conductor.

3. Use a ⅝ inch spark plug socket to loosen all of the plugs about two turns. You will need an extension to reach the rear spark plugs if your car has the V6 engine. A universal joint installed at the socket end of the extension will ease the process.

If removal of the plugs is difficult, apply a few drops of penetrating oil or silicone spray

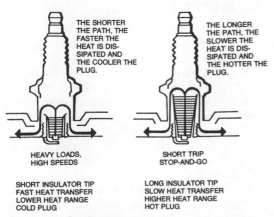

THE SHORTER THE PATH, THE FASTER THE HEAT IS DISSIPATED AND THE COOLER THE PLUG.

THE LONGER THE PATH, THE SLOWER THE HEAT IS DISSIPATED AND THE HOTTER THE PLUG.

HEAVY LOADS, HIGH SPEEDS

SHORT TRIP STOP-AND-GO

SHORT INSULATOR TIP
FAST HEAT TRANSFER
LOWER HEAT RANGE
COLD PLUG

LONG INSULATOR TIP
SLOW HEAT TRANSFER
HIGHER HEAT RANGE
HOT PLUG

Spark plug heat range

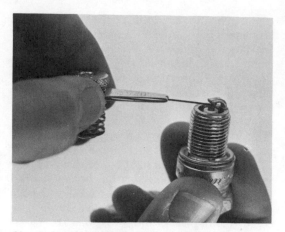

Check the electrode gap with a wire gauge

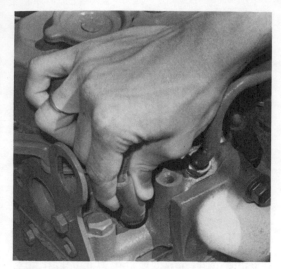

Twist and pull on the rubber boot to remove the spark plug wires

to the area around the base of the plug, and allow it a few minutes to work.

4. If compressed air is available, apply it to the area around the spark plug holes. Otherwise, use a rag or a brush to clean the area. Be careful not to allow any foreign material to drop into the spark plug holes.

5. Remove the plugs by unscrewing them the rest of the way.

INSPECTION

Check the plugs for deposits and wear. If they are not going to be replaced, clean the plugs thoroughly. Remember that any kind of deposit will decrease the efficiency of the plug. Plugs can be cleaned on a spark plug cleaning machine, which can sometimes be found in service stations, or you can do an acceptable job of cleaning with a stiff brush. If the plugs are cleaned, the electrodes must be filed flat. Use an ignition points file, not an emery board or the like, which will leave deposits. The electrodes must be filed perfectly flat with sharp edges; rounded edges reduce the spark plug voltage by as much as 50%.

Check spark plug gap before installation. The ground electrode must be parallel to the center electrode and the specified size wire gauge should pass through the gap with a slight drag. Always check the gap on new plugs, too; they are not always correctly set at the factory. Do not use a flat feeler gauge when measuring the gap, because the reading will be inaccurate. Wire gapping tools usually have a bending tool attached. Use that to adjust the side electrode until the

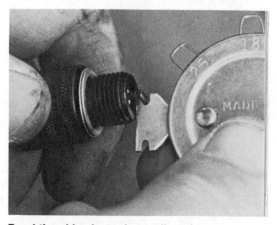

Bend the side electrode to adjust the gap

proper distance is obtained. Absolutely never bend the center electrode. Also, be careful not to bend the side electrode too far or too often; it may weaken and break off within the engine, requiring removal of the cylinder head to retrieve it.

INSTALLATION

1. Lubricate the threads of the spark plugs with a drop of oil or a shot of silicone spray. Install the plugs and tighten them hand-tight. Take care not to cross-thread them.

2. Tighten the spark plugs with the socket. Do not apply the same amount of force you would use for a bolt; just snug them in. These spark plugs do not use gaskets, and over-tightening will make future removal difficult. If a torque wrench is available, tighten to 7–15 ft lbs.

NOTE: *While over-tightening the spark plug is to be avoided, under-tightening is just as bad. If combustion gases leak past*

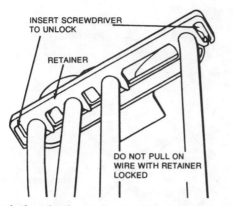

Unlock the plastic retainers to replace the plug wires

the threads, the spark plug will overheat and rapid electrode wear will result.

3. Install the wires on their respective plugs. Make sure the wires are firmly connected. You will be able to feel them click into place. Spark plug wiring diagrams are in Chapter Three if you get into trouble.

CHECKING AND REPLACING SPARK PLUG WIRES

Every 15,000 miles, inspect the spark plug wires for burns, cuts, or breaks in the insulation. Check the boots and the nipples on the distributor cap. Replace any damaged wiring.

Every 45,000 miles or so, the resistance of the wires should be checked with an ohmmeter. Wires with excessive resistance will cause misfiring, and may make the engine difficult to start in damp weather. Generally, the useful life of the cables is 45,000–60,000 miles.

To check resistance, remove the distributor cap, leaving the wires in place. Connect one lead of an ohmmeter to an electrode within the cap; connect the other lead to the corresponding spark plug terminal (remove it from the spark plug for this test). Replace any wire which shows a resistance over 30,000 ohms. A chart in the "Troubleshooting" section at the end of this chapter gives resistance values as a function of length. Generally speaking, however, resistance should not be over 25,000 ohms, and 30,000 ohms must be considered the outer limit of acceptability.

It should be remembered that resistance is also a function of length; the longer the wire, the greater the resistance. Thus, if the wires on your car are longer than the factory originals, resistance will be higher, quite possibly outside these limits.

When installing new wires, replace them one at a time to avoid mixups. Start by replacing the longest one first. Install the boot firmly over the spark plug. Route the wire over the same path as the original. Insert the nipple firmly onto the tower on the distributor cap, then install the cap cover and latches to secure the wires.

High Energy Ignition (HEI) System

The General Motors HEI system is a pulse-triggered, transistor-controlled, inductive discharge ignition system. It is a completely

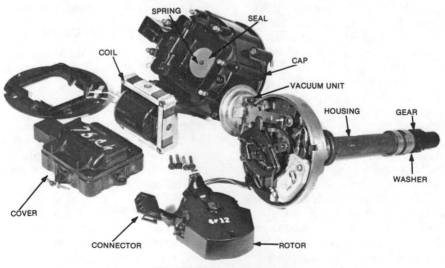

HEI distributor components

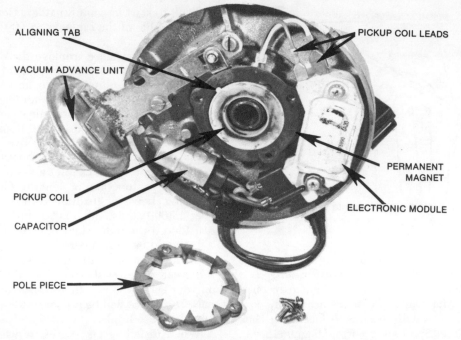

ALIGNING TAB

VACUUM ADVANCE UNIT

PICKUP COIL LEADS

PERMANENT MAGNET

ELECTRONIC MODULE

PICKUP COIL

CAPACITOR

POLE PIECE

All HEI circuitry is contained within the distributor body

self-contained unit—all parts are contained within the distributor.

The distributor, in addition to housing the mechanical and vacuum advance mechanisms, contains the ignition coil, the electronic control module, and the magnetic triggering device. The magnetic pick-up assembly contains a permanent magnet, a pole piece with internal "teeth", and a pick-up coil (not to be confused with the ignition coil).

In the HEI system, as in other electronic ignition systems, the breaker points have been replaced with an electronic switch—a transistor—which is located *within* the control module. This switching transistor performs the same function the points did in a conventional ignition system; it simply turns coil primary current on and off at the correct time. Essentially then, electronic and conventional ignition systems operate on the same principle.

The module which houses the switching transistor is controlled (turned on and off) by a magnetically generated impulse induced in the pick-up coil. When the teeth of the rotating timer align with the teeth of the pole piece, the induced voltage in the pick-up coil signals the electronic module to open the coil primary circuit. The primary current then decreases, and a high voltage is induced in the ignition coil secondary windings which is then directed through the rotor and high

voltage leads (spark plug wires) to fire the spark plugs.

In essence then, the pick-up coil module system simply replaces the conventional breaker points and condenser. The condenser found within the distributor is for radio suppression purposes only and has nothing to do with the ignition process. The module automatically controls the dwell period, increasing it with increasing engine speed. Since dwell is automatically controlled, it cannot be adjusted. The module itself is non-adjustable and non-repairable and must be replaced if found defective.

HEI SYSTEM PRECAUTIONS

Before going on to troubleshooting, it might be a good idea to take note of the following precautions:

Timing Light Use

Inductive pick-up timing lights are the best kind to use with HEI. Timing lights which connect between the spark plug and the spark plug wire occasionally (not always) give false readings.

Spark Plug Wires

The plug wires used with HEI systems are of a different construction than conventional wires. When replacing them, make sure you get the correct wires, since conventional wires won't carry the voltage. Also, handle them carefully to avoid cracking or splitting them and *never* pierce them.

Tachometer Use

Not all tachometers will operate or indicate correctly when used on a HEI system. While some tachometers may give a reading, this does not necessarily mean the reading is correct. In addition, some tachometers hook up differently from others. If you can't figure out whether or not your tachometer will work on your car, check with the tachometer manufacturer. Dwell readings, of course, have no significance at all.

HEI System Testers

Instruments designed specifically for testing HEI systems are available from several tool manufacturers. Some of these will even test the module itself. However, the tests given in the following section will require only an ohmmeter and a voltmeter.

TROUBLESHOOTING THE HEI SYSTEM

The symptoms of a defective component within the HEI system are exactly the same as those you would encounter in a conventional system. Some of these symptoms are:

Hard or no Starting

Rough Idle

Poor Fuel Economy

Engine misses under load or while accelerating

If you suspect a problem in your ignition system, there are certain preliminary checks which you should carry out before you begin to check the electronic portions of the system. First, it is extremely important to make sure the vehicle battery is in a good state of charge. A defective or poorly charged battery will cause the various components of the ignition system to read incorrectly when they are being tested. Second, make sure all wiring connections are clean and tight, not only at the battery, but also at the distributor cap, ignition coil, and at the electronic control module.

Since the only change between electronic and conventional ignition systems is in the distributor component area, it is imperative to check the secondary ignition circuit first. If the secondary circuit checks out properly, then the engine condition is probably not the fault of the ignition system. To check the secondary ignition system, perform a simple spark test. Remove one of the plug wires and insert some sort of extension in the plug socket. An old spark plug with the ground electrode removed makes a good extension. Hold the wire and extension about ¼ in. away from the block and crank the engine. If a normal spark occurs, then the problem is most likely *not* in the ignition system. Check for fuel system problems, or fouled spark plugs.

If, however, there is no spark or a weak spark, then further ignition system testing will have to be done. Troubleshooting techniques fall into two categories, depending on the nature of the problem. The categories are (1) Engine cranks, but won't start or (2) Engine runs, but runs rough or cuts out. To begin with, let's consider the first case.

Engine Fails to Start

If the engine won't start, perform a spark test as described earlier. This will narrow the problem area down considerably. If no spark occurs, check for the presence of normal battery voltage at the battery (BAT) terminal in the distributor cap. The ignition switch must be in the "on" position for this test. Either a voltmeter or a test light may be used for this test. Connect the test light wire to ground and the probe end to the BAT terminal at the distributor. If the light comes on, you have voltage to the distributor. If the light fails to come on, this indicates an open circuit in the ignition primary wiring leading to the distributor. In this case, you will have to check wiring continuity back to the ignition switch using a test light. If there is battery voltage at the BAT terminal, but no spark at the plugs,

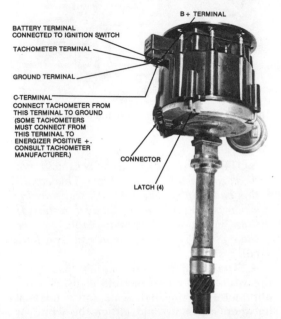

B+ TERMINAL

BATTERY TERMINAL CONNECTED TO IGNITION SWITCH

TACHOMETER TERMINAL

GROUND TERMINAL

C-TERMINAL CONNECT TACHOMETER FROM THIS TERMINAL TO GROUND (SOME TACHOMETERS MUST CONNECT FROM THIS TERMINAL TO ENERGIZER POSITIVE +. CONSULT TACHOMETER MANUFACTURER.)

CONNECTOR

LATCH (4)

Tachometer connections to the HEI distributor

HEI Plug Wire
Resistance Chart

Wire Length	Minimum	Maximum
0–15 inches	3000 ohms	10,000 ohms
15–25 inches	4000 ohms	15,000 ohms
25–35 inches	6000 ohms	20,000 ohms
Over 35 inches		25,000 ohms

then the problem lies within the distributor assembly. Go on to the distributor components test section.

Engine Runs, But Runs Rough or Cuts Out

1. Make sure the plug wires are in good shape first. There should be no obvious cracks or breaks. You can check the plug wires with an ohmmeter, but *do not* pierce the wires with a probe. Check the chart for the correct plug wire resistance.

2. If the plug wires are OK, remove the cap assembly and check for moisture, cracks, chips, or carbon tracks, or any other high voltage leaks or failures. Replace the cap if any defects are found. Make sure the timer wheel rotates when the engine is cranked. If everything is all right so far, go on to the distributor components test section following.

DISTRIBUTOR COMPONENTS TESTING

If the trouble has been narrowed down to the units within the distributor, the following tests can help pinpoint the defective component. An ohmmeter with both high and low ranges should be used. These tests are made with the cap assembly removed and the battery wire disconnected. If a tachometer is connected to the TACH terminal, disconnect it before making these tests.

1. Connect an ohmmeter between the TACH and BAT terminals in the distributor cap. The primary coil resistance should be less than one ohm.

2. To check the coil secondary resistance, connect an ohmmeter between the rotor button and the BAT terminal. Note the reading. Connect the ohmmeter between the rotor button and the TACH terminal. Note the reading. The resistance in both cases should be between 6,000 and 30,000 ohms. Be sure to test between the rotor button and both the BAT and TACH terminals.

3. Replace the coil *only* if the readings in Step 1 and Step 2 are infinite.

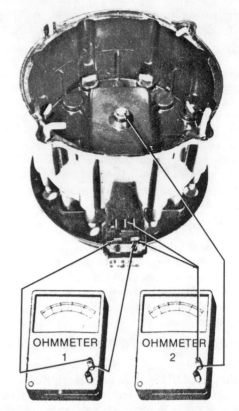

Ohmmeter 1 shows primary coil resistance connections. Ohmmeter 2 shows secondary coil resistance connections

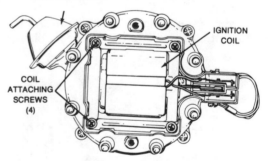

The coil is accessible by removing the four attaching screws

NOTE: *These resistance checks will not disclose shorted coil windings. This condition can only be detected with scope analysis or a suitably designed coil tester. If these instruments are unavailable, replace the coil with a known good coil as a final coil test.*

4. To test the pick-up coil, first disconnect the white and green module leads. Set the ohmmeter on the high scale and connect it between a ground and either the white or

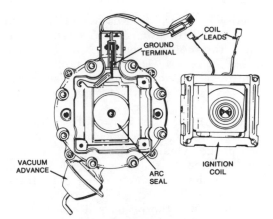

Check the condition of the arc seal under the coil

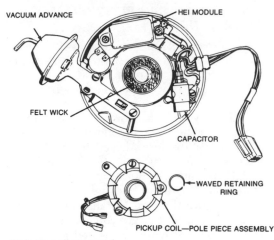

Pick-up coil removal

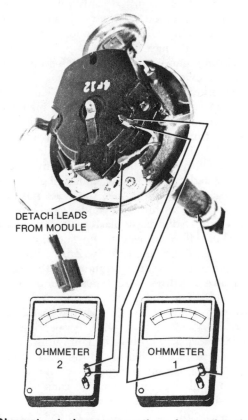

Ohmmeter 1 shows connections for testing the pick-up coil. Ohmmeter 2 shows connections for testing the pick-up coil continuity

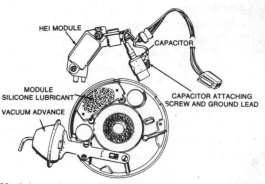

Module replacement; be sure to coat the mating surfaces with silicone lubricant

green lead. Any resistance measurement *less* than infinity requires replacement of the pick-up coil.

5. Pick-up coil continuity is tested by connecting the ohmmeter (on low range) between the white and green leads. Normal resistance is between 650 and 850 ohms. Move the vacuum advance arm while performing this test. This will detect any break in coil continuity. Such a condition can cause intermittent misfiring. Replace the pick-up coil if the reading is outside the specified limits.

6. If no defects have been found at this time, and you still have a problem, then the module will have to be checked. If you do not have access to a module tester, the only possible alternative is a substitution test. If the module fails the substitution test, replace it.

HEI SYSTEM MAINTENANCE

Except for periodic checks of the spark plug wires, and an occasional check of the distributor cap for cracks (see Steps 1 and 2 under "Engine Runs, But Runs Rough or Cuts Out" for details), no maintenance is required on the HEI System. No periodic lubrication is necessary; engine oil lubricates the lower bushing, and an oil-filled reservoir lubricates the upper bushing.

DISTRIBUTOR CAP REMOVAL AND INSTALLATION

1. Disconnect the ignition switch wire from the distributor cap. Also disconnect the tachometer wire, if so equipped.

2. Release the coil connectors from the cap.

3. Remove the distributor cap by turning the four latches counterclockwise. You will need a stubby screwdriver to get at the latches if your car has the four cylinder engine, because clearances are very tight between the distributor and the firewall.

4. Remove the cap. Installation is the reverse of removal. Be sure you get the ignition and tachometer wires connected to the correct terminals.

HEI SYSTEM TACHOMETER HOOKUP

There is a terminal marked TACH on the distributor cap. Connect one tachometer lead to this terminal and the other lead to a ground. On some tachometers, the leads must be connected to the TACH terminal and to the battery positive terminal.

CAUTION: *Never ground the TACH terminal; serious module and ignition coil damage will result. If there is any doubt as to the correct tachometer hookup, check with the tachometer manufacturer.*

Ignition Timing

Ignition timing is the measurement, in degrees of crankshaft rotation, of the point at which the spark plugs fire in each of the cylinders. It is measured in degrees before or after Top Dead Center (TDC) of the compression stroke.

Because it takes a fraction of a second for the spark plug to ignite the mixture in the cylinder, the spark plug must fire a little before the piston reaches TDC. Otherwise, the mixture will not be completely ignited as the piston passes TDC and the full power of the explosion will not be used by the engine.

The timing measurement is given in degrees of crankshaft rotation before the piston reaches TDC (BTDC). If the setting for the ignition timing is 5° BTDC, the spark plug must fire 5° before each piston reaches TDC. This only holds true, however, when the engine is at idle speed.

As the engine speed increases, the pistons go faster. The spark plugs have to ignite the fuel even sooner if it is to be completely ig-

nited when the piston reaches TDC. To do this, the distributor has two means to advance the timing of the spark as the engine speed increases. This is accomplished by centrifugal weights within the distributor, and a vacuum diaphragm mounted on the side of the distributor.

If the ignition is set too far advanced (BTDC), the ignition and expansion of the fuel in the cylinder will occur too soon and tend to force the piston down while it is still traveling up. This causes engine ping. If the ignition spark is set too far retarded, after TDC (ATDC), the piston will have already passed TDC and started on its way down when the fuel is ignited. This will cause the piston to be forced down for only a portion of its travel. This will result in poor engine performance and lack of power.

Timing marks consist of a notch on the rim of the crankshaft pulley and a scale of degrees attached to the front of the engine. The notch corresponds to the position of the piston in the number 1 cylinder. A stroboscopic (dynamic) timing light is used, which is hooked into the circuit of the No. 1 cylinder spark plug. Every time the spark plug fires, the timing light flashes. By aiming the timing light at the timing marks, the exact position of the piston within the cylinder can be read, since the stroboscopic flash makes the mark on the pulley appear to be standing still. Proper timing is indicated when the notch is aligned with the correct number on the scale.

There are three basic types of timing light available. The first is a simple neon bulb with two wire connections (one for the spark plug and one for the plug wire, connecting the light in series). This type of light is quite dim, and must be held closely to the marks to be seen, but it is quite inexpensive. The second type of light operates from the car's battery. Two alligator clips connect to the battery terminals, while a third wire connects to the spark plug with an adapter. This type of light is more expensive, but the xenon bulb provides a nice bright flash which can even be seen in sunlight. The third type replaces the battery source with 110 volt house current. Some timing lights have other functions built into them, such as dwell meters, tachometers, or remote starting switches. These are convenient, in that they reduce the tangle of wires under the hood, but may duplicate the functions of tools you already have.

Because your X-Body car has electronic ignition, you should use a timing light with an inductive pickup. This pickup simply clamps around the Number 1 spark plug wire, eliminating the adapter. It is not susceptible to crossfiring or false triggering, which may occur with a conventional light due to the greater voltages produced by HEI.

IGNITION TIMING ADJUSTMENT

1. Refer to the directions on the tune-up label inside the engine compartment. Follow all the instructions on the label.

2. Locate the timing marks on the crankshaft pulley and the front of the engine.

3. Clean off the timing marks so that you can see them. Use chalk or white paint to color the mark on the crankshaft pulley and the mark on the scale which will indicate the correct timing when aligned with the notch on the crankshaft pulley.

4. Attach a tachometer to the engine. See the preceding section, "HEI System Tachometer Hookup".

5. Attach a timing light to the engine, according to the manufacturer's instructions. If the timing light has three wires, one, usually green or blue, is attached to the No. 1 spark plug with an adapter, unless an inductive pickup is used, which simply clamps around the wire. The other wires are connected to the battery. The red wire goes to the positive side of the battery and the black wire is connected to the negative side of the battery. Do not pierce the No. 1 spark plug wire, or attempt to insert a wire between the boot and the wire. This will break the insulation and result in an ignition miss.

NOTE: *Number one spark plug is at the front of the four cylinder engine (right side of the car) and at the right front of the V6 engine (the left rear spark plug if you are*

facing the car). Firing order diagrams are in Chapter Three.

6. Disconnect and plug the vacuum hose at the distributor vacuum advance, if so directed by the tune-up label. This will be required in most cases to prevent vacuum advance to the distributor. The hose must be plugged to prevent a vacuum leak into the carburetor. A golf tee makes a good plug. Be careful not to split the hose.

7. Check to make sure that all of the wires clear the fan and then start the engine. Allow the engine to reach normal operating temperature.

CAUTION: *Block the front wheels and set the parking brake securely. Shift the manual transmission to Neutral or the automatic to Drive, as instructed on the tune-up label. Do not stand in front of the car when making adjustments!*

8. Adjust the engine speed to the correct setting (as specified on the tune-up label or given in the "Tune-Up Specifications" chart in this chapter) by means of the idle speed screw. The location of the screw is shown in the "Carburetor" section of this chapter.

9. Aim the timing light at the timing marks. If the marks which you put on the pulley and the engine are aligned when the light flashes, the timing is correct. Turn off the engine and disconnect the timing light and tachometer. If the marks are not in alignment, the timing will have to be adjusted.

10. Turn off the engine.

The V6 distributor lockbolt is at the base of the distributor shaft

Four cylinder timing marks; V6 similar

The four cylinder distributor has two lockbolts. Loosen the outer one (lower arrow) to adjust timing

11. Loosen the distributor lockbolt so that the distributor can just be turned with a little effort. The V6 engine has a conventional lockbolt and clamp. The four cylinder engine has two lockbolts. One, at the outer edge, is the one you want. This loosens the distributor hold-down clamp but does not permit removal of the distributor itself. Loosen the outer lockbolt and slide the clamp away from the distributor slightly. This will allow the distributor to rotate.

12. Start the engine. Keep the wires of the timing light clear of the fan and pulleys. While observing the timing marks with the light, turn the distributor slightly until the timing marks are aligned.

13. Turn off the engine and tighten the distributor lockbolt. Start the engine and recheck the timing. Sometimes the distributor moves slightly during the tightening process. If the ignition timing is within 1° of the correct setting, that's close enough; a tolerance of 2° is permitted by the manufacturer.

14. Shut off the engine and disconnect the timing light and tachometer. Reconnect the distributor vacuum advance hose, if removed.

Valve Adjustment

Both the Pontiac-built four cylinder engine and the Chevrolet-built V6 have hydraulic valve lifters, which do not require periodic valve adjustments. The Chevrolet engine requires an initial valve adjustment anytime

the lifters are removed or the valve train is disturbed. This procedure is covered in Chapter Three.

Carburetor

This section contains only carburetor adjustments as they normally apply to engine tune-ups. Descriptions of the carburetors and complete adjustment procedures can be found in Chapter Four.

When the engine in your car is running, air/fuel mixture from the carburetor is being drawn into the engine by a partial vacuum which is created by the downward movement of the pistons on the intake stroke of the four-stroke cycle of the engine. The amount of air/fuel mixture that enters the engine is controlled by throttle plates in the bottom of the carburetor. When the engine is not running, the throttle plates are closed, completely blocking off the bottom of the carburetor from the inside of the engine. The throttle plates are connected, through the throttle linkage, to the gas pedal. What you are actually doing when you depress the gas pedal is opening up the throttle plates in the carburetor to admit more of the fuel/air mixture to the engine. The further you open the throttle plates in the carburetor, the higher the engine speed becomes.

As previously stated, when the engine is not running, the throttle plates in the carburetor remain closed. When the engine is idling, it is necessary to open the throttle plates slightly. To prevent having to keep your foot on the gas pedal when the engine is idling, an idle speed adjusting screw was added to the carburetor. This screw has the same effect as keeping your foot slightly depressed on the gas pedal. The idle speed adjusting screw contacts a solenoid on the outside of the carburetor. When the screw is turned in, it opens the throttle plates on the carburetor, raising the idle speed of the engine. This screw is called the curb idle adjusting screw and the procedures in this section will tell you how to adjust it.

Since it is difficult for the engine to draw the air/fuel mixture from the carburetor with the small amount of throttle plate opening that is present when the engine is idling, an idle mixture passage is provided in the carburetor. This passage delivers air/fuel mixture to the engine from a hole which is located in the bottom of the carburetor below the throt-

Carburetor solenoid electrical connector

tle plates. This idle mixture passage contains an adjusting screw which restricts the amount of air/fuel mixture that enters the engine at idle.

On the X-Body cars, the idle mixture screws are concealed under staked-in plugs. Idle mixture is not considered to be a normal tune-up procedure, because of the sensitivity of emission control adjustments. Mixture adjustment requires not only special tools with which to remove the concealing plugs, but also the addition of an artificial enrichment substance (propane) which must be introduced into the carburetor by means of a finely calibrated metering valve. These tools are not generally available, and require a certain amount of expertise to use. Therefore, mixture adjustments are purposely not covered in this book. If you suspect that your car's carburetor requires a mixture adjust-

ment, it is strongly recommended that the job be referred to your dealer or a qualified mechanic with specific training in making the adjustment.

IDLE SPEED ADJUSTMENTS

There are actually two idle speed adjustments which must be made. One is an adjustment made with the idle speed screw, which is connected to the throttle plate linkage and contacts the idle speed solenoid. This is called "Curb" idle on cars with air conditioning, or "Basic" idle speed on cars without air conditioning. The second adjustment is made to the idle speed solenoid, which is mounted to the carburetor, and the plunger of which is contacted by the idle speed screw. This adjustment is called "Solenoid" rpm on cars with air conditioning, or "Curb" idle speed on cars without air conditioning. The illustrations given on these pages should help you sort out all this.

Cars Without Air Conditioning

1. The first step is to prepare the engine for these adjustments. Follow the instructions given on the tune-up label inside the engine compartment. It will usually say to warm the engine to operating temperature, make sure the choke is fully open, and place the idle speed screw on the lowest step of the fast idle cam. The fast idle cam is normally marked "H", "2", and "1" on its three steps. Open the throttle by hand and place the idle

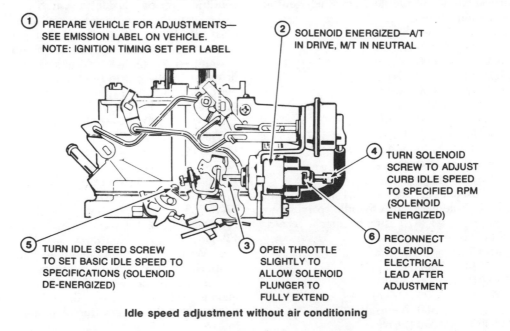

① PREPARE VEHICLE FOR ADJUSTMENTS—SEE EMISSION LABEL ON VEHICLE. NOTE: IGNITION TIMING SET PER LABEL

② SOLENOID ENERGIZED—A/T IN DRIVE, M/T IN NEUTRAL

④ TURN SOLENOID SCREW TO ADJUST CURB IDLE SPEED TO SPECIFIED RPM (SOLENOID ENERGIZED)

⑤ TURN IDLE SPEED SCREW TO SET BASIC IDLE SPEED TO SPECIFICATIONS (SOLENOID DE-ENERGIZED)

③ OPEN THROTTLE SLIGHTLY TO ALLOW SOLENOID PLUNGER TO FULLY EXTEND

⑥ RECONNECT SOLENOID ELECTRICAL LEAD AFTER ADJUSTMENT

Idle speed adjustment without air conditioning

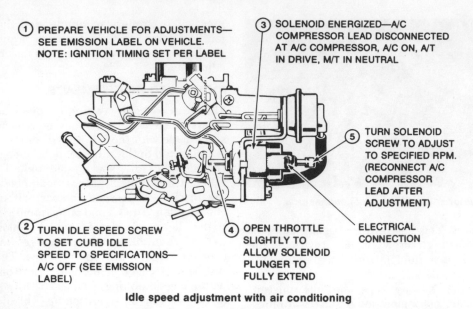

① PREPARE VEHICLE FOR ADJUSTMENTS—
SEE EMISSION LABEL ON VEHICLE.
NOTE: IGNITION TIMING SET PER LABEL

③ SOLENOID ENERGIZED—A/C
COMPRESSOR LEAD DISCONNECTED
AT A/C COMPRESSOR, A/C ON, A/T
IN DRIVE, M/T IN NEUTRAL

⑤ TURN SOLENOID
SCREW TO ADJUST
TO SPECIFIED RPM.
(RECONNECT A/C
COMPRESSOR
LEAD AFTER
ADJUSTMENT)

② TURN IDLE SPEED SCREW
TO SET CURB IDLE
SPEED TO SPECIFICATIONS—
A/C OFF (SEE EMISSION
LABEL)

④ OPEN THROTTLE
SLIGHTLY TO
ALLOW SOLENOID
PLUNGER TO
FULLY EXTEND

ELECTRICAL
CONNECTION

Idle speed adjustment with air conditioning

speed screw on step "1". Connect a tachometer to the engine.

2. Place the automatic transaxle in Drive, or the manual transaxle in Neutral. Make sure the solenoid is energized (plunger extended).

3. Open the throttle slightly to allow the solenoid plunger to fully extend.

4. Turn the solenoid screw to adjust the engine speed to the following "Curb" idle speed, according to carburetor number (the carburetor number is stamped on the flat vertical surface of the float bowl, adjacent to the vacuum tube):

Carb. No.	Curb rpm
17059614	650 (Drive)
17059615	1000 (Neutral)
17059714	650 (Drive)
17059715	1000 (Neutral)
17059650	700 (Drive)
17059651	750 (Neutral)
17059760	700 (Drive)
17059763	750 (Neutral)
17059618	650 (Drive)
17059619	1000 (Neutral)

5. Disconnect the electrical connector from the solenoid. Turn the idle speed screw in or out to set the basic idle speed, according to carburetor number:

Carb No.	Basic rpm
17059614	500 (Drive)
17059615	500 (Neutral)
17059714	500 (Drive)
17059715	500 (Neutral)
17059650	800 (Drive)
17059651	1200 (Neutral)
17059760	800 (Drive)
17059763	800 (Neutral)
17059618	500 (Drive)
17059619	500 (Neutral)

Cars With Air Conditioning

1. Follow Step 1 given for "Cars Without Air Conditioning."

2. Disconnect the electrical lead from the air conditioning compressor. Turn the air conditioning "off" inside the car.

3. Turn the idle speed screw to set the curb idle to specifications, according to the carburetor number (the carburetor number is stamped on the flat vertical surface of the float bowl, adjacent to the vacuum tube):

Carb. No.	Curb rpm
17059616	900 (Drive)
17059617	1300 (Neutral)
17059716	850 (Drive)
17059717	1200 (Neutral)
17059652	850 (Drive)
17059653	1200 (Neutral)
17059762	800 (Drive)
17059763	800 (Neutral)
17059620	900 (Drive)
17059621	1300 (Neutral)

4. With the air conditioning lead still disconnected, turn the air conditioning "On", put the automatic transaxle in Drive, or the manual transaxle in Neutral, and open the throttle slightly to allow the solenoid plunger to extend.

5. Turn the solenoid screw to adjust the engine speed to following figure, according to carburetor number:

Carb. No.	Solenoid rpm
17059616	650 (Drive)
17059617	1000 (Neutral)
17059716	650 (Drive)
17059717	1000 (Neutral)
17059652	700 (Drive)
17059653	750 (Neutral)
17059762	700 (Drive)
17059763	750 (Neutral)
17059620	650 (Drive)
17059621	1000 (Neutral)

Troubleshooting

The following section is designed to aid in the rapid diagnosis of engine problems. The systematic format is used to diagnose problems ranging from engine starting difficulties to the need for engine overhaul. It is assumed that the user is equipped with basic hand tools and test equipment (tachdwell meter, timing light, voltmeter, and ohmmeter).

Troubleshooting is divided into two sections. The first, *General Diagnosis*, is used to locate the problem area. In the second, *Specific Diagnosis*, the problem is systematically evaluated.

General Diagnosis

Problem: Symptom	Begin at Specific Diagnosis, Number _____
Engine Won't Start:	
Starter doesn't turn	1.1, 2.1
Starter turns, engine doesn't	2.1
Starter turns engine very slowly	1.1, 2.4
Starter turns engine normally	3.1, 4.1
Starter turns engine very quickly	6.1
Engine fires intermittently	4.1
Engine fires consistently	5.1, 6.1
Engine Runs Poorly:	
Hard starting	3.1, 4.1, 5.1, 8.1
Rough idle	4.1, 5.1, 8.1
Stalling	3.1, 4.1, 5.1, 8.1
Engine dies at high speeds	4.1, 5.1
Hesitation (on acceleration from standing stop)	5.1, 8.1
Poor pickup	4.1, 5.1, 8.1
Lack of power	3.1, 4.1, 5.1, 8.1
Backfire through the carburetor	4.1, 8.1, 9.1
Backfire through the exhaust	4.1, 8.1, 9.1
Blue exhaust gases	6.1, 7.1
Black exhaust gases	5.1
Running on (after the ignition is shut off)	3.1, 8.1
Susceptible to moisture	4.1
Engine misfires under load	4.1, 7.1, 8.4, 9.1
Engine misfires at speed	4.1, 8.4
Engine misfires at idle	3.1, 4.1, 5.1, 7.1, 8.4

Engine Noise Diagnosis

Problem: Symptom	Probable Cause
Engine Noises:①	
Metallic grind while starting	Starter drive not engaging completely
Constant grind or rumble	* Starter drive not releasing, worn main bearings
Constant knock	Worn connecting rod bearings
Knock under load	Fuel octane too low, worn connecting rod bearings
Double knock	Loose piston pin
Metallic tap	* Collapsed or sticky valve lifter, excessive valve clearance, excessive end play in a rotating shaft
Scrape	* Fan belt contacting a stationary surface
Tick while starting	S.U. electric fuel pump (normal), starter brushes
Constant tick	* Generator brushes, shreaded fan belt
Squeal	* Improperly tensioned fan belt
Hiss or roar	* Steam escaping through a leak in the cooling system or the radiator overflow vent
Whistle	* Vacuum leak
Wheeze	Loose or cracked spark plug

①—It is extremely difficult to evaluate vehicle noises. While the above are general definitions of engine noises, those starred (*) should be considered as possibly originating elsewhere in the car. To aid diagnosis, the following list considers other potential sources of these sounds.

Metallic grind:
 Throwout bearing; transmission gears, bearings, or synchronizers; differential bearings, gears; something metallic in contact with brake drum or disc.

Metallic tap:
 U-joints; fan-to-radiator (or shroud) contact.

Scrape:
 Brake shoe or pad dragging; tire to body contact; suspension contacting undercarriage or exhaust; something non-metallic contacting brake shoe or drum.

Tick:
 Transmission gears; differential gears; lack of radio suppression; resonant vibration of body panels; windshield wiper motor or transmission; heater motor and blower.

Squeal:
 Brake shoe or pad not fully releasing; tires (excessive wear, uneven wear, improper inflation); front or rear wheel alignment (most commonly due to improper toe-in).

Hiss or whistle:
 Wind leaks (body or window); heater motor and blower fan.

Roar:
 Wheel bearings; wind leaks (body and window).

Index

Sample Section

Test and Procedure	Results and Indications	Proceed to
4.1—Check for spark: Hold each spark plug wire approximately ¼" from ground with gloves or a heavy, dry rag. Crank the engine and observe the spark.	If no spark is evident:	4.2
	If spark is good in some cases:	4.3
	If spark is good in all cases:	4.6

Specific Diagnosis

This section is arranged so that following each test, instructions are given to proceed to another, until a problem is diagnosed.

1.1—Inspect the battery visually for case condition (corrosion, cracks) and water level.	If case is cracked, replace battery:	1.4
	If the case is intact, remove corrosion with a solution of baking soda and water (**CAUTION:** *do not get the solution into the battery*), and fill with water:	1.2

1.2—Check the battery cable connections: Insert a screwdriver between the battery post and the cable clamp. Turn the headlights on high beam, and observe them as the screwdriver is gently twisted to ensure good metal to metal contact.

Testing battery cable connections using a screwdriver

If the lights brighten, remove and clean the clamp and post; coat the post with petroleum jelly, install and tighten the clamp: **1.4**

If no improvement is noted: **1.3**

1.3—Test the state of charge of the battery using an individual cell tester or hydrometer.

Spec. Grav. Reading	Charged Condition
1.260–1.280	Fully Charged
1.230–1.250	Three Quarter Charged
1.200–1.220	One Half Charged
1.170–1.190	One Quarter Charged
1.140–1.160	Just About Flat
1.110–1.130	All The Way Down

State of battery charge

Electrolyte temperature (°F) / Specific gravity correction

+120	+016
+100	+012 / +008 / +004 ADD to reading
+80	no correction
+60	−004 / −008
+40	−012 / −016
+20	−020 / −024 SUBTRACT from reading
0	−028 / −032 / −036
−20	−040

The effect of temperature on the specific gravity of battery electrolyte

If indicated, charge the battery. **NOTE:** *If no obvious reason exists for the low state of charge (i.e., battery age, prolonged storage), the charging system should be tested:* **1.4**

1.4—Visually inspect battery cables for cracking, bad connection to ground, or bad connection to starter.	If necessary, tighten connections or replace the cables:	2.1

Tests in Group 2 are performed with coil high tension lead disconnected to prevent accidental starting.

2.1—Test the starter motor and solenoid: Connect a jumper from the battery post of the solenoid (or relay) to the starter post of the solenoid (or relay).

If starter turns the engine normally: **2.2**

If the starter buzzes, or turns the engine very slowly: **2.4**

If no response, replace the solenoid (or relay). **3.1**

If the starter turns, but the engine doesn't, ensure that the flywheel ring gear is intact. If the gear is undamaged, replace the starter drive. **3.1**

Test and Procedure	Results and Indications	Proceed to
2.2—Determine whether ignition override switches are functioning properly (clutch start switch, neutral safety switch), by connecting a jumper across the switch(es), and turning the ignition switch to "start".	If starter operates, adjust or replace switch:	**3.1**
	If the starter doesn't operate:	**2.3**
2.3—Check the ignition switch "start" position: Connect a 12V test lamp between the starter post of the solenoid (or relay) and ground. Turn the ignition switch to the "start" position, and jiggle the key.	If the lamp doesn't light when the switch is turned, check the ignition switch for loose connections, cracked insulation, or broken wires. Repair or replace as necessary:	**3.1**
	If the lamp flickers when the key is jiggled, replace the ignition switch.	**3.3**

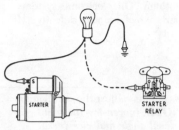
Checking the ignition switch "start" position

2.4—Remove and bench test the starter, according to specifications in the car section.	If the starter does not meet specifications, repair or replace as needed:	**3.1**
	If the starter is operating properly:	**2.5**
2.5—Determine whether the engine can turn freely: Remove the spark plugs, and check for water in the cylinders. Check for water on the dipstick, or oil in the radiator. Attempt to turn the engine using an 18″ flex drive and socket on the crankshaft pulley nut or bolt.	If the engine will turn freely only with the spark plugs out, and hydrostatic lock (water in the cylinders) is ruled out, check valve timing:	**9.2**
	If engine will not turn freely, and it is known that the clutch and transmission are free, the engine must be disassembled for further evaluation:	**Next Chapter**
3.1—Check the ignition switch "on" position: Connect a jumper wire between the distributor side of the coil and ground, and a 12V test lamp between the switch side of the coil and ground. Remove the high tension lead from the coil. Turn the ignition switch on and jiggle the key.	If the lamp lights:	**3.2**
	If the lamp flickers when the key is jiggled, replace the ignition switch:	**3.3**
	If the lamp doesn't light, check for loose or open connections. If none are found, remove the ignition switch and check for continuity. If the switch is faulty, replace it:	**3.3**

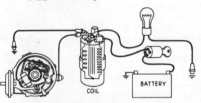
Checking the ignition switch "on" position

Test and Procedure	Results and Indications	Proceed to
3.2—Check the ballast resistor or resistance wire for an open circuit, using an ohmmeter. On HEI systems, connect a test light between a good ground and the BAT terminal at the distributor. If the light fails to come on, this indicates an open circuit in the ignition primary wiring. HEI systems do not use a resistance wire in the primary wiring.	Replace the resistor or resistance wire if the resistance is zero or, if the test lamp fails to light, check the primary wiring.	3.3
3.3—On point-type ignition systems, visually inspect the breaker points for burning, pitting or excessive wear. Gray coloring of the point contact surfaces is normal. Rotate the crankshaft until the contact heel rests on a high point of the distributor cam and adjust the point gap to specifications.	If the breaker points are intact, clean the contact surfaces with fine emery cloth, and adjust the point gap to specifications. If the points are worn, replace them. On electronic systems, replace any parts which appear defective. If condition persists:	3.4
3.4—On point-type ignition systems, connect a dwell-meter between the distributor primary lead and ground. Crank the engine and observe the point dwell angle.	On point-type systems, adjust the dwell angle if necessary. **NOTE:** *Increasing the point gap decreases the dwell angle and vice-versa.*	3.6
	If the dwell meter shows little or no reading:	3.5
3.5—On point-type ignition systems, check the condenser for short: connect an ohmmeter across the condenser body and the pigtail lead.	If any reading other than infinite is noted, replace the condenser:	3.6

Checking the condenser for short

Test and Procedure	Results and Indications	Proceed to
3.6—Test the coil primary resistance: On point-type ignition systems, connect an ohmmeter across the coil primary terminals, and read the resistance on the low scale. Note whether an external ballast resistor or resistance wire is utilized. To test coil primary resistance on HEI systems, connect an ohmmeter between the TACH and BAT terminals in the distributor cap.	Coils utilizing ballast resistors or resistance wires should have approximately 1.0 ohms resistance. Coils with internal resistors should have approximately 4.0 ohms resistance. If values far from the above are noted, replace the coil. Coil primary resistance on HEI systems should be less than one ohm.	4.1
4.1—Check for spark: Hold each spark plug wire approximately ¼" from ground with gloves or a heavy, dry rag. Crank the engine, and observe the spark.	If no spark is evident:	4.2
	If spark is good in some cylinders:	4.3
	If spark is good in all cylinders:	4.6

Test and Procedure	Results and Indications	Proceed to
4.2—Check for spark at the coil high tension lead: Remove the coil high tension lead from the distributor and position it approximately ¼″ from ground. Crank the engine and observe spark. **CAUTION:** *This test should not be performed on cars equipped with transistorized ignition.*	If the spark is good and consistent:	**4.3**
	If the spark is good but intermittent, test the primary electrical system starting at 3.3:	**3.3**
	If the spark is weak or non-existent, replace the coil high tension lead, clean and tighten all connections and retest. If no improvement is noted:	**4.4**
4.3—Visually inspect the distributor cap and rotor for burned or corroded contacts, cracks, carbon tracks, or moisture. Also check the fit of the rotor on the distributor shaft (where applicable).	If moisture is present, dry thoroughly, and retest per 4.1:	**4.1**
	If burned or excessively corroded contacts, cracks, or carbon tracks are noted, replace the defective part(s) and retest per 4.1:	**4.1**
	If the rotor and cap appear intact, or are only slightly corroded, clean the contacts thoroughly (including the cap towers and spark plug wire ends) and retest per 4.1: If the spark is good in all cases:	**4.6**
	If the spark is poor in all cases:	**4.5**
4.4—Check the coil secondary resistance: On point-type systems, connect an ohmmeter across the distributor side of the coil and the coil tower. Read the resistance on the high scale of the ohmmeter. On HEI systems, connect an ohmmeter between the rotor button in the cap and either the TACH or BAT terminals. 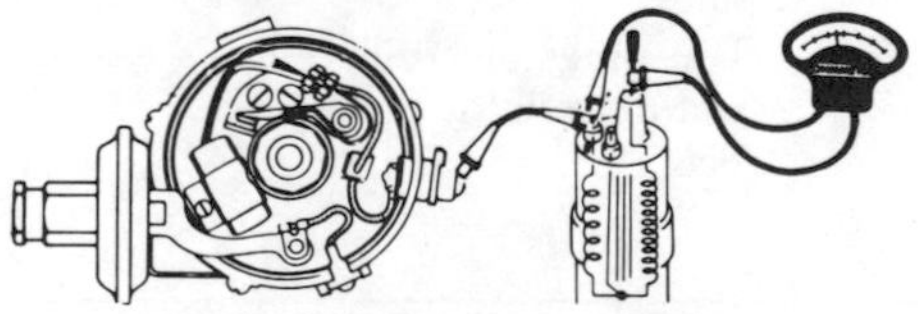	The resistance of a satisfactory coil should be between 4,000 and 10,000 ohms. If resistance is considerably higher (i.e. 40,000 ohms) replace the coil and retest per 4.1. **NOTE:** *this does not apply to high performance coils.* On HEI systems, resistance should be between 6000 and 30,000 ohms.	

Testing the coil secondary resistance

Test and Procedure	Results and Indications	Proceed to
4.5—Visually inspect the spark plug wires for cracking or brittleness. Ensure that no two wires are positioned so as to cause induction firing (adjacent and parallel). Remove each wire, one by one, and check resistance with an ohmmeter.	Replace any cracked or brittle wires. If any of the wires are defective, replace the entire set. Replace any wires with excessive resistance (over 8000Ω per foot for suppression wire), and separate any wires that might cause induction firing. On HEI systems, resistance ratings vary with length, and are: 0–15 inches—3000–10,000 Ω; 15–25 inches—4000–15,000 Ω; 25–35 inches—6000–20,000 Ω; Over 35 inches—25,000 Ω.	**4.6**
4.6—Remove the spark plugs, noting the cylinders from which they were removed, and evaluate according to the chart below.	See following	**See following.**

	Condition	Cause	Remedy	Proceed to
	Electrodes eroded, light brown deposits.	Normal wear. Normal wear is indicated by approximately .001″ wear per 1000 miles.	Clean and regap the spark plug if wear is not excessive: Replace the spark plug if excessively worn:	4.7
	Carbon fouling (black, dry, fluffy deposits).	If present on one or two plugs:		
		Faulty high tension lead(s).	Test the high tension leads:	4.5
		Burnt or sticking valve(s).	Check the valve train: (Clean and regap the plugs in either case.)	9.1
		If present on most or all plugs: Overly rich fuel mixture, due to restricted air filter, improper carburetor adjustment, improper choke or heat riser adjustment or operation.	Check the fuel system:	5.1
	Oil fouling (wet black deposits)	Worn engine components. **NOTE:** *Oil fouling may occur in new or recently rebuilt engines until broken in.*	Check engine vacuum and compression: Replace with new spark plug	6.1
	Lead fouling (gray, black, tan, or yellow deposits, which appear glazed or cinder-like).	Combustion by-products.	Clean and regap the plugs: (Use plugs of a different heat range if the problem recurs.)	4.7
	Gap bridging (deposits lodged between the electrodes).	Incomplete combustion, or transfer of deposits from the combustion chamber.	Replace the spark plugs:	4.7
	Overheating (burnt electrodes, and extremely white insulator with small black spots).	Ignition timing advanced too far.	Adjust timing to specifications:	8.2
		Overly lean fuel mixture.	Check the fuel system:	5.1
		Spark plugs not seated properly.	Clean spark plug seat and install a new gasket washer: (Replace the spark plugs in all cases.)	4.7

	Condition	Cause	Remedy	Proceed to
	Fused spot deposits on the insulator.	Combustion chamber blow-by.	Clean and regap the spark plugs:	**4.7**
	Pre-ignition (melted or severely burned electrodes, blistered or cracked insulators, or metallic deposits on the insulator).	Incorrect spark plug heat range.	Replace with plugs of the proper heat range:	**4.7**
		Ignition timing advanced too far.	Adjust timing to specifications:	**8.2**
		Spark plugs not being cooled efficiently.	Clean the spark plug seat, and check the cooling system:	**11.1**
		Fuel mixture too lean.	Check the fuel system:	**5.1**
		Poor compression.	Check compression:	**6.1**
		Fuel grade too low.	Use higher octane fuel:	**4.7**

Test and Procedure	Results and Indications	Proceed to
4.7—Determine the static ignition timing. Using the crankshaft pulley timing marks as a guide, locate top dead center on the compression stroke of the number one cylinder.	The rotor should be pointing toward the no. 1 tower in the distributor cap, and the points should be just opening or the armature spoke for that cylinder should be lined up with the stator.	**4.8**
4.8—Check coil polarity: Connect a voltmeter negative lead to the coil high tension lead, and the positive lead to ground (**NOTE:** *reverse the hook-up for positive ground cars*). Crank the engine momentarily. Checking coil polarity	If the voltmeter reads up-scale, the polarity is correct:	**5.1**
	If the voltmeter reads down-scale, reverse the coil polarity (switch the primary leads):	**5.1**
5.1—Determine that the air filter is functioning efficiently: Hold paper elements up to a strong light, and attempt to see light through the filter.	Clean permanent air filters in gasoline (or manufacturer's recommendation), and allow to dry. Replace paper elements through which light cannot be seen:	**5.2**
5.2—Determine whether a flooding condition exists: Flooding is identified by a strong gasoline odor, and excessive gasoline present in the throttle bore(s) of the carburetor.	If flooding is not evident:	**5.3**
	If flooding is evident, permit the gasoline to dry for a few moments and restart. If flooding doesn't recur:	**5.6**
	If flooding is persistent:	**5.5**
5.3—Check that fuel is reaching the carburetor: Detach the fuel line at the carburetor inlet. Hold the end of the line in a cup (not styrofoam), and crank the engine.	If fuel flows smoothly:	**5.6**
	If fuel doesn't flow (**NOTE:** *Make sure that there is fuel in the tank*), or flows erratically:	**5.4**

Test and Procedure	Results and Indications	Proceed to
5.4—Test the fuel pump: Disconnect all fuel lines from the fuel pump. Hold a finger over the input fitting, crank the engine (with electric pump, turn the ignition or pump on); and feel for suction.	If suction is evident, blow out the fuel line to the tank with low pressure compressed air until bubbling is heard from the fuel filler neck. Also blow out the carburetor fuel line (both ends disconnected):	**5.6**
	If no suction is evident, replace or repair the fuel pump: **NOTE:** *Repeated oil fouling of the spark plugs, or a no-start condition, could be the result of a ruptured vacuum booster pump diaphragm, through which oil or gasoline is being drawn into the intake manifold (where applicable).*	**5.6**
5.5—Check the needle and seat: Tap the carburetor in the area of the needle and seat.	If flooding stops, a gasoline additive (e.g., Gumout) will often cure the problem:	**5.6**
	If flooding continues, check the fuel pump for excessive pressure at the carburetor (according to specifications). If the pressure is normal, the needle and seat must be removed and checked, and/or the float level adjusted:	**5.6**
5.6—Test the accelerator pump by looking into the throttle bores while operating the throttle.	If the accelerator pump appears to be operating normally:	**5.7**
	If the accelerator pump is not operating, the pump must be reconditioned. Where possible, service the pump with the carburetor(s) installed on the engine. If necessary, remove the carburetor. Prior to removal:	**5.7**
5.7—Determine whether the carburetor main fuel system is functioning: Spray a commercial starting fluid into the carburetor while attempting to start the engine.	If the engine starts, runs for a few seconds, and dies:	**5.8**
	If the engine doesn't start:	**6.1**
5.8—Uncommon fuel system malfunctions: See below:	If the problem is solved:	**6.1**
	If the problem remains, remove and recondition the carburetor.	

Condition	Indication	Test	Usual Weather Conditions	Remedy
Vapor lock	Car will not re-start shortly after running.	Cool the components of the fuel system until the engine starts.	Hot to very hot	Ensure that the exhaust manifold heat control valve is operating. Check with the vehicle manufacturer for the recommended solution to vapor lock on the model in question.
Carburetor icing	Car will not idle, stalls at low speeds.	Visually inspect the throttle plate area of the throttle bores for frost.	High humidity, 32–40°F.	Ensure that the exhaust manifold heat control valve is operating, and that the intake manifold heat riser is not blocked.

Condition	Indication	Test	Usual Weather Conditions	Remedy
Water in the fuel	Engine sputters and stalls; may not start.	Pump a small amount of fuel into a glass jar. Allow to stand, and inspect for droplets or a layer of water.	High humidity, extreme temperature changes.	For droplets, use one or two cans of commercial gas dryer. For a layer of water, the tank must be drained, and the fuel lines blown out with compressed air.

Test and Procedure	Results and Indications	Proceed to
6.1—Test engine compression: Remove all spark plugs. Insert a compression gauge into a spark plug port, crank the engine to obtain the maximum reading, and record.	If compression is within limits on all cylinders:	7.1
	If gauge reading is extremely low on all cylinders:	6.2
	If gauge reading is low on one or two cylinders: (If gauge readings are identical and low on two or more adjacent cylinders, the head gasket must be replaced.)	6.2

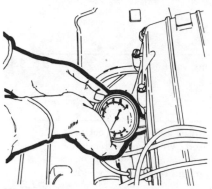

Check compression at the spark plug hole

Compression pressure limits
(© Buick Div. G.M. Corp.)

Maxi. Press. Lbs. Sq. In.	Min. Press. Lbs. Sq. In.	Maxi. Press. Lbs. Sq. In.	Min. Press. Lbs. Sq. In.	Max. Press. Lbs. Sq. In.	Min. Press. Lbs. Sq. In.	Max. Press. Lbs. Sq. In.	Min. Press. Lbs. Sq. In.
134	101	162	121	188	141	214	160
136	102	164	123	190	142	216	162
138	104	166	124	192	144	218	163
140	105	168	126	194	145	220	165
142	107	170	127	196	147	222	166
146	110	172	129	198	148	224	168
148	111	174	131	200	150	226	169
150	113	176	132	202	151	228	171
152	114	178	133	204	153	230	172
154	115	180	135	206	154	232	174
156	117	182	136	208	156	234	175
158	118	184	138	210	157	236	177
160	120	186	140	212	158	238	178

Test and Procedure	Results and Indications	Proceed to
6.2—Test engine compression (wet): Squirt approximately 30 cc. of engine oil into each cylinder, and retest per 6.1.	If the readings improve, worn or cracked rings or broken pistons are indicated:	Next Chapter
	If the readings do not improve, burned or excessively carboned valves or a jumped timing chain are indicated: NOTE: A jumped timing chain is often indicated by difficult cranking.	7.1
7.1—Perform a vacuum check of the engine: Attach a vacuum gauge to the intake manifold beyond the throttle plate. Start the engine, and observe the action of the needle over the range of engine speeds.	See below.	See below

	Reading	Indications	Proceed to
	Steady, from 17–22 in. Hg.	Normal:	8.1

	Reading	Indications	Proceed to
	Low and steady.	Late ignition or valve timing, or low compression:	6.1
	Very low.	Vacuum leak:	7.2
	Needle fluctuates as engine speed increases.	Ignition miss, blown cylinder head gasket, leaking valve or weak valve spring:	6.1, 8.3
	Gradual drop in reading at idle.	Excessive back pressure in the exhaust system:	10.1
	Intermittent fluctuation at idle.	Ignition miss, sticking valve:	8.3, 9.1
	Drifting needle.	Improper idle mixture adjustment, carburetors not synchronized (where applicable), or minor intake leak. Synchronize the carburetors, adjust the idle, and retest. If the condition persists:	7.2
	High and steady.	Early ignition timing:	8.2

Test and Procedure	Results and Indications	Proceed to
7.2—Attach a vacuum gauge per 7.1, and test for an intake manifold leak. Squirt a small amount of oil around the intake manifold gaskets, carburetor gaskets, plugs and fittings. Observe the action of the vacuum gauge.	If the reading improves, replace the indicated gasket, or seal the indicated fitting or plug:	8.1
	If the reading remains low:	7.3
7.3—Test all vacuum hoses and accessories for leaks as described in 7.2. Also check the carburetor body (dashpots, automatic choke mechanism, throttle shafts) for leaks in the same manner.	If the reading improves, service or replace the offending part(s):	8.1
	If the reading remains low:	6.1
8.1—Remove the distributor cap and check to make sure that the armature turns when the engine is cranked. Visually inspect the distributor components.	Clean, tighten or replace any components which appear defective.	8.2

Test and Procedure	Results and Indications	Proceed to
8.2—Connect a timing light (per manufacturer's recommendation) and check the dynamic ignition timing. Disconnect and plug the vacuum hose(s) to the distributor if specified, start the engine, and observe the timing marks at the specified engine speed.	If the timing is not correct, adjust to specifications by rotating the distributor in the engine: (Advance timing by rotating distributor opposite normal direction of rotor rotation, retard timing by rotating distributor in same direction as rotor rotation.)	**8.3**
8.3—Check the operation of the distributor advance mechanism(s): To test the mechanical advance, disconnect all but the mechanical advance, and observe the timing marks with a timing light as the engine speed is increased from idle. If the mark moves smoothly, without hesitation, it may be assumed that the mechanical advance is functioning properly. To test vacuum advance and/or retard systems, alternately crimp and release the vacuum line, and observe the timing mark for movement. If movement is noted, the system is operating.	If the systems are functioning: If the systems are not functioning, remove the distributor, and test on a distributor tester:	**8.4** **8.4**
8.4—Locate an ignition miss: With the engine running, remove each spark plug wire, one by one, until one is found that doesn't cause the engine to roughen and slow down.	When the missing cylinder is identified:	**4.1**
9.1—Evaluate the valve train: Remove the valve cover, and ensure that the valves are adjusted to specifications. A mechanic's stethoscope may be used to aid in the diagnosis of the valve train. By pushing the probe on or near push rods or rockers, valve noise often can be isolated. A timing light also may be used to diagnose valve problems. Connect the light according to manufacturer's recommendations, and start the engine. Vary the firing moment of the light by increasing the engine speed (and therefore the ignition advance), and moving the trigger from cylinder to cylinder. Observe the movement of each valve.	See below.	**See below**

Observation	Probable Cause	Remedy	Proceed to
Metallic tap heard through the stethoscope.	Sticking hydraulic lifter or excessive valve clearance.	Adjust valve. If tap persists, remove and replace the lifter:	**10.1**

Observation	Probable Cause	Remedy	Proceed to
Metallic tap through the stethoscope, able to push the rocker arm (lifter side) down by hand.	Collapsed valve lifter.	Remove and replace the lifter:	**10.1**
Erratic, irregular motion of the valve stem.*	Sticking valve, burned valve.	Recondition the valve and/or valve guide:	**Next Chapter**
Eccentric motion of the pushrod at the rocker arm.*	Bent pushrod.	Replace the pushrod:	**10.1**
Valve retainer bounces as the valve closes.*	Weak valve spring or damper.	Remove and test the spring and damper. Replace if necessary:	**10.1**

*—When observed with a timing light.

Test and Procedure	Results and Indications	Proceed to
9.2—Check the valve timing: Locate top dead center of the No. 1 piston, and install a degree wheel or tape on the crankshaft pulley or damper with zero corresponding to an index mark on the engine. Rotate the crankshaft in its direction of rotation, and observe the opening of the No. 1 cylinder intake valve. The opening should correspond with the correct mark on the degree wheel according to specifications.	If the timing is not correct, the timing cover must be removed for further investigation:	
10.1—Determine whether the exhaust manifold heat control valve is operating: Operate the valve by hand to determine whether it is free to move. If the valve is free, run the engine to operating temperature and observe the action of the valve, to ensure that it is opening.	If the valve sticks, spray it with a suitable solvent, open and close the valve to free it, and retest. If the valve functions properly:	**10.2**
	If the valve does not free, or does not operate, replace the valve:	**10.2**
10.2—Ensure that there are no exhaust restrictions: Visually inspect the exhaust system for kinks, dents, or crushing. Also note that gasses are flowing freely from the tailpipe at all engine speeds, indicating no restriction in the muffler or resonator.	Replace any damaged portion of the system:	**11.1**

Test and Procedure	Results and Indications	Proceed to
11.1—Visually inspect the fan belt for glazing, cracks, and fraying, and replace if necessary. Tighten the belt so that the longest span has approximately ½″ play at its midpoint under thumb pressure.	Replace or tighten the fan belt as necessary:	**11.2**

Checking the fan belt tension

Test and Procedure	Results and Indications	Proceed to
11.2—Check the fluid level of the cooling system.	If full or slightly low, fill as necessary:	**11.5**
	If extremely low:	**11.3**
11.3—Visually inspect the external portions of the cooling system (radiator, radiator hoses, thermostat elbow, water pump seals, heater hoses, etc.) for leaks. If none are found, pressurize the cooling system to 14–15 psi.	If cooling system holds the pressure:	**11.5**
	If cooling system loses pressure rapidly, reinspect external parts of the system for leaks under pressure. If none are found, check dipstick for coolant in crankcase. If no coolant is present, but pressure loss continues:	**11.4**
	If coolant is evident in crankcase, remove cylinder head(s), and check gasket(s). If gaskets are intact, block and cylinder head(s) should be checked for cracks or holes.	
	If the gasket(s) is blown, replace, and purge the crankcase of coolant:	**12.6**
	NOTE: *Occasionally, due to atmospheric and driving conditions, condensation of water can occur in the crankcase. This causes the oil to appear milky white. To remedy, run the engine until hot, and change the oil and oil - filter.*	

Test and Procedure	Results and Indications
11.4— Check for combustion leaks into the cooling system: Pressurize the cooling system as above. Start the engine, and observe the pressure gauge. If the needle fluctuates, remove each spark plug wire, one by one, noting which cylinder(s) reduce or eliminate the fluctuation.	Cylinders which reduce or eliminate the fluctuation, when the spark plug wire is removed, are leaking into the cooling system. Replace the head gasket on the affected cylinder bank(s).

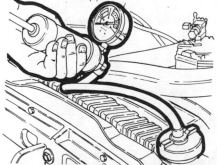

Radiator pressure testing

Test and Procedure	Results and Indications	Proceed to
11.5—Check the radiator pressure cap: Attach a radiator pressure tester to the radiator cap (wet the seal prior to installation). Quickly pump up the pressure, noting the point at which the cap releases.	If the cap releases within ± 1 psi of the specified rating, it is operating properly:	**11.6**
	If the cap releases at more than ± 1 psi of the specified rating, it should be replaced:	**11.6**

Radiator cap pressure testing.

Test and Procedure	Results and Indications	Proceed to
11.6—Test the thermostat: Start the engine cold, remove the radiator cap, and insert a thermometer into the radiator. Allow the engine to idle. After a short while, there will be a sudden, rapid increase in coolant temperature. The temperature at which this sharp rise stops is the thermostat opening temperature.	If the thermostat opens at or about the specified temperature:	**11.7**
	If the temperature doesn't increase: (If the temperature increases slowly and gradually, replace the thermostat.)	**11.7**
11.7—Check the water pump: Remove the thermostat elbow and the thermostat, disconnect the coil high tension lead (to prevent starting), and crank the engine momentarily.	If coolant flows, replace the thermostat and re-test per 11.6:	**11.6**
	If coolant doesn't flow, reverse flush the cooling system to alleviate any blockage that might exist. If system is not blocked, and coolant will not flow, recondition the water pump.	—
12.1—Check the oil pressure gauge or warning light: If the gauge shows low pressure, or the light is on, for no obvious reason, remove the oil pressure sender. Install an accurate oil pressure gauge and run the engine momentarily.	If oil pressure builds normally, run engine for a few moments to determine that it is functioning normally, and replace the sender.	—
	If the pressure remains low:	**12.2**
	If the pressure surges:	**12.3**
	If the oil pressure is zero:	**12.3**
12.2—Visually inspect the oil: If the oil is watery or very thin, milky, or foamy, replace the oil and oil filter.	If the oil is normal:	**12.3**
	If after replacing oil the pressure remains low:	**12.3**
	If after replacing oil the pressure becomes normal:	—
12.3—Inspect the oil pressure relief valve and spring, to ensure that it is not sticking or stuck. Remove and thoroughly clean the valve, spring, and the valve body.	If the oil pressure improves:	—
	If no improvement is noted:	**12.4**

Oil pressure relief valve
(© British Leyland Motors)

Test and Procedure	Results and Indications	Proceed to
12.4—Check to ensure that the oil pump is not cavitating (sucking air instead of oil): See that the crankcase is neither over nor underfull, and that the pickup in the sump is in the proper position and free from sludge.	Fill or drain the crankcase to the proper capacity, and clean the pickup screen in solvent if necessary. If no improvement is noted:	**12.5**
12.5—Inspect the oil pump drive and the oil pump:	If the pump drive or the oil pump appear to be defective, service as necessary and retest per 12.1:	**12.1**
	If the pump drive and pump appear to be operating normally, the engine should be disassembled to determine where blockage exists:	**Next Chapter**
12.6—Purge the engine of ethylene glycol coolant: Completely drain the crankcase and the oil filter. Obtain a commercial butyl cellosolve base solvent, designated for this purpose, and follow the instructions precisely. Following this, install a new oil filter and refill the crankcase with the proper weight oil. The next oil and filter change should follow shortly thereafter (1000 miles).		

3

Engine and
Engine Rebuilding

ENGINE ELECTRICAL

Distributor

REMOVAL AND INSTALLATION

1. Disconnect the ignition switch wire from the distributor cap. Also remove the tachometer lead from the cap, if equipped.

2. Release the coil connectors from the cap.

3. Remove the distributor cap by turning the four latches counterclockwise. You will need a stubby screwdriver to get at the latches if your X-Body has the four cylinder engine, because there isn't much room between the distributor and the firewall. Remove the distributor cap and set it aside without disconnecting any of the wires.

4. Remove the vacuum hose from the vacuum advance unit. Mark the position of the vacuum advance unit in relation to the engine, so that the distributor goes back into the engine the same way.

5. Remove the hold-down clamp and bolt at the base of the V6 distributor. The four cylinder engine has two bolts and a clamp. Remove the outer bolt first, then loosen, but do not remove, the inner bolt. Slide the clamp back and remove it.

6. Before removing the distributor, note the position of the rotor. Scribe a mark on the distributor body indicating the initial position of the rotor.

7. Remove the distributor from the engine. The drive gear on the distributor shaft is helical, and the shaft will rotate slightly as the distributor is removed. Note and mark the position of the rotor at this second position. Do not crank the engine with the distributor removed.

8. To install the distributor, rotate the distributor shaft until the rotor aligns with the second mark you made (when the shaft stopped moving). Lubricate the drive gear with clean engine oil, then install the distributor into the engine, aligning the vacuum advance unit with the mark made before. As the distributor is installed, the rotor should move to the mark you made first, indicating rotor position before the distributor was removed. This will ensure proper timing. If the marks do not align properly, remove the distributor and try again.

9. Install the clamp and hold-down bolt. Tighten them until the distributor can just be moved with a little effort.

10. Connect the ignition wire and tachometer wire, and install the distributor cap. Plug the vacuum advance hose. Set the ignition timing (see Chapter Two). Connect the vacuum hose.

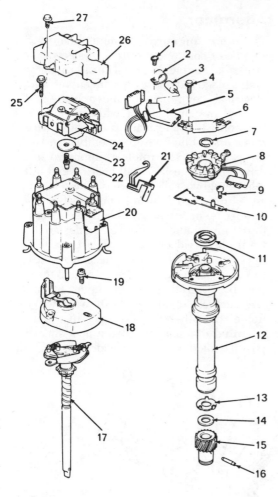

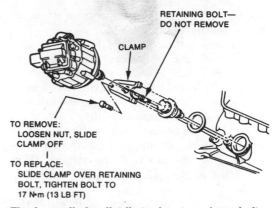

TO REMOVE:
LOOSEN NUT, SLIDE
CLAMP OFF

TO REPLACE:
SLIDE CLAMP OVER RETAINING
BOLT, TIGHTEN BOLT TO
17 N•m (13 LB FT)

The four cylinder distributor has two clamp bolts

INSTALLATION IF THE ENGINE WAS DISTURBED

If the engine was cranked while the distributor was removed, you will have to place the

Firing Order

NOTE: *To avoid confusion, replace the spark plug wires one at a time.*

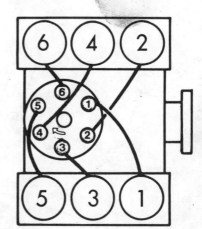

V6

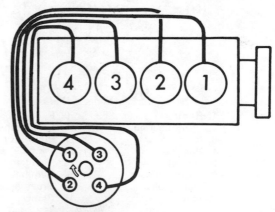

1. Screw
2. Bracket
3. Capacitor
4. Screw
5. Wiring harness
6. Module assembly
7. Retainer
8. Pole piece and plate assembly (Pick-up coil)
9. Screw
10. Plastic retainer
11. Grease retainer seal
12. Housing assembly
13. Thrust washer
14. Shim
15. Gear
16. Roll pin
17. Distributor shaft
18. Rotor
19. Screw
20. Distributor cap
21. Ground Wire
22. Resistor brush and spring
23. Seal
24. Coil
25. Screw
26. Cover
27. Screw

Exploded view of the HEI distributor

Four cylinder

engine on TDC of the compression stroke to obtain proper ignition timing.

1. Remove the No. 1 spark plug.

2. Place your thumb over the spark plug hole. Crank the engine slowly until compression is felt. It will be easier if you have someone rotate the engine by hand, using a wrench on the crankshaft pulley.

3. Align the timing mark on the crankshaft pulley with the 0° mark on the timing scale attached to the front of the engine. This places the engine at TDC of the compression stroke.

4. Turn the distributor shaft until the rotor points between the No. 1 and No. 3 spark plug towers on the cap for the four cylinder engine, or between the No. 1 and No. 6 spark plug towers for the V6.

5. Install the distributor into the engine, aligning the vacuum advance unit with the mark made before. Follow Steps 9 and 10 of the preceding removal and installation procedure.

Alternator

The alternating current generator (alternator) supplies a continuous output of electrical energy at all engine speeds. The alternator generates electrical energy for the engine and all electrical components, and recharges the battery by supplying it with current. This unit consists of four main assemblies: two end frame assemblies, a rotor assembly, and a stator assembly. The rotor is supported in the drive end frame by a ball bearing and at the other end by a roller bearing. These bearings are lubricated during manufacture and require no maintenance. There are six diodes in the end frame assembly. Diodes are electrical check valves that change the alternating current supplied from the stator windings to a direct current (DC), delivered to the output (BAT) terminal. Three diodes are negative and are mounted flush with the end frame; the other three are positive and are mounted into a strip called a heat sink. The positive diodes are easily identified as the

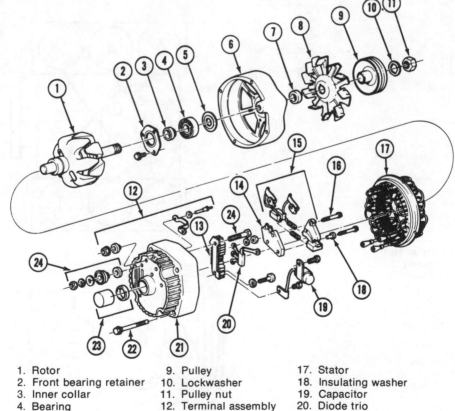

1. Rotor	9. Pulley	17. Stator
2. Front bearing retainer	10. Lockwasher	18. Insulating washer
3. Inner collar	11. Pulley nut	19. Capacitor
4. Bearing	12. Terminal assembly	20. Diode trio
5. Washer	13. Rectifier bridge	21. Rear housing
6. Front housing	14. Regulator	22. Through bolt
7. Outer collar	15. Brush assembly	23. Bearing and seal assembly
8. Fan	16. Screw	24. Terminal assembly

Exploded view of the 10-SI alternator

ones within small cavities or depressions. A capacitor, or condenser, mounted on the end frame protects the rectifier bridge and diode trio from high voltages, and suppresses radio noise. This capacitor requires no maintenance.

Two models of the SI series alternator are used on X-Body cars. The 10 SI and 15 SI are of similar construction; the 15 SI is slightly larger, uses different stator windings, and produces more current. Several different output ratings are used in the X-Body cars.

ALTERNATOR PRECAUTIONS

1. When installing a battery, make sure that the positive and negative cables are not reversed.

2. When jump-starting the car, be sure that like terminals are connected. This also applies to using a battery charger. Reversed polarity will burn out the alternator and regulator in a matter of seconds.

3. Never operate the alternator with the battery disconnected or on an otherwise uncontrolled open circuit.

4. Do not short across or ground any alternator or regulator terminals.

5. Do not try to polarize the alternator.

6. Do not apply full battery voltage to the field (brown) connector.

7. Always disconnect the battery ground cable before disconnecting the alternator lead.

8. Always disconnect the battery (negative cable first) when charging it.

9. Never subject the alternator to excessive heat or dampness. If you are steam-cleaning the engine, cover the alternator.

10. Never use arc-welding equipment on the car with the alternator connected.

REMOVAL AND INSTALLATION

1. Disconnect the negative battery cable at the battery.

CAUTION: *Failure to disconnect the negative cable may result in injury from the positive battery lead at the alternator, and may short the alternator and regulator during the removal process.*

2. Disconnect and label the two terminal plug and the battery leads from the rear of the alternator.

3. Loosen the mounting bolts. Push the alternator inwards and slip the drive belt off the pulley.

4. Remove the mounting bolts and remove the alternator.

5. To install, place the alternator in its brackets and install the mounting bolts. Do not tighten them yet.

6. Slip the belt back over the pully. Pull outwards on the unit and adjust the belt tension (see Chapter One). Tighten the mounting and adjusting bolts.

7. Install the electrical leads.

8. Install the negative battery cable.

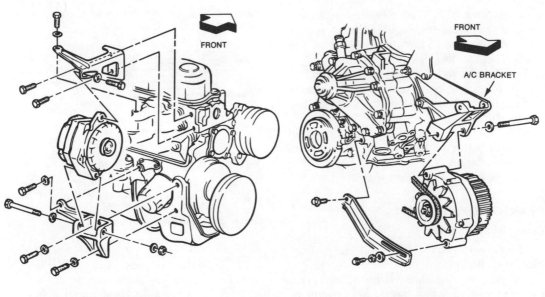

4 WITH A/C   V-6 WITH A/C

Alternator installation details; models without air conditioning similar

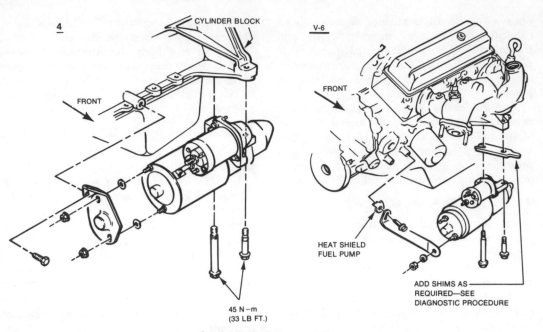

Starter installation details

Regulator

A solid state regulator is mounted within the alternator. All regulator components are enclosed in a solid mold. The regulator is non-adjustable and requires no maintenance.

Starter

REMOVAL AND INSTALLATION

1. Disconnect the negative battery cable at the battery.
2. Remove the starter-to-engine brace. On the four cylinder engine, there are two nuts securing the brace to the end of the starter; on the V6, there is one nut.
3. Working under the car, remove the two starter-to-engine bolts, and allow the starter to drop down. Note the location and number of any shims.
4. Label and disconnect the solenoid wires and battery cable. Remove the starter.
5. Installation is the reverse. Tighten the mounting bolts to 25–35 ft lbs.

STARTER OVERHAUL

Drive Replacement

1. Disconnect the field coil straps from the solenoid.
2. Remove the through bolts, and separate communtator end frame, field frame assembly, drive housing, and armature assembly from each other.

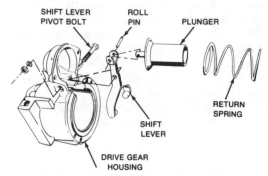

Starter shift lever and drive end housing disassembled

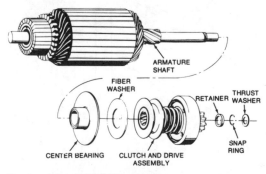

Starter drive assembly details

3. Slide the two piece thrust collar off the end of the armature shaft.
4. Slide a suitably sized metal cylinder, such as a standard half-inch pipe coupling, or an old pinion, on the shaft so that the end of

the coupling or pinion butts up against the edge of the pinion retainer.

5. Support the lower end of the armature securely on a soft surface, such as a wooden block, and tap the end of the coupling or pinion, driving the retainer towards the armature end of the snap ring.

6. Remove the snap ring from the groove in the armature shaft with a pair of pliers. Then, slide the retainer and starter drive from the shaft.

7. To reassemble, lubricate the drive end of the armature shaft with silicone lubricant, and then slide the starter drive onto shaft with pinion facing outward. Slide the retainer onto the shaft with cupped surface facing outward.

8. Again support the armature on a soft surface, with the pinion at upper end. Center the snap ring on the top of the shaft (use a new snap ring if the original was damaged during removal). Gently place a block of wood flat on top of the snap ring so as not to move it from a centered position. Tap the wooden block with a hammer in order to

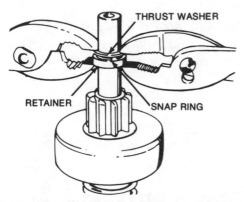

Starter drive retainer, thrust washer and snap ring installation

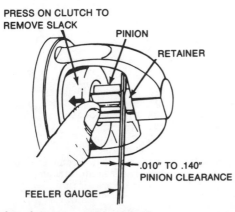

Pinion clearance measurement

force the snap ring around the shaft. Then, slide the ring down into the snap ring groove.

9. Lay the armature down flat on the surface you're working on. Slide the retainer close up on to the shaft and position it and the thrust collar next to the snap ring. Using two pairs of pliers on opposite sides of the shaft, squeeze the thrust collar and the retainer together until the snap ring is forced into the retainer.

10. Lube the drive housing bushing with a silicone lubricant. Then, install armature and clutch assembly into drive housing, engaging the solenoid shift lever with the clutch, and positioning front end of armature shaft into bushing.

11. Apply a sealing compound approved for this application onto the drive housing; then position field frame around armature shaft and against the drive housing. Work slowly and carefully to prevent damaging the starter brushes.

12. Lubricate the bushing in the commutator end frame with a silicone lubricant, place leather brake washer onto the armature shaft, and then slide the commutator end frame over the shaft and into position against the field frame. Line up bolt holes, and then install and tighten through bolts.

13. Reconnect the field coil straps to the "motor" terminal of the solenoid.

NOTE: *If replacement of the starter drive fails to cure improper engagement of starter pinion to flywheel, there are probably defective parts in the solenoid and/or shift lever. The best procedure would probably be to take the assembly to a shop where a pinion clearance check can be made by energizing the solenoid on a test bench. If the pinion clearance is incorrect, disassemble the solenoid and shift lever, inspect, and replace worn parts.*

Brush Replacement

1. After removing the starter from the engine, disconnect the field coil from the motor solenoid terminal.

2. Remove the starter through bolts and remove the commutator end frame and washer.

3. Remove the field frame and the armature assembly from the drive housing.

4. Remove the brush holder pivot pin which positions one insulated and one grounded brush.

5. Remove the brush springs.

6. Remove the brushes.

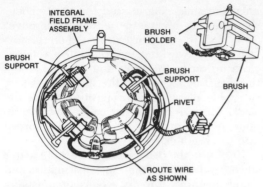

5-MT starter brush replacement detail

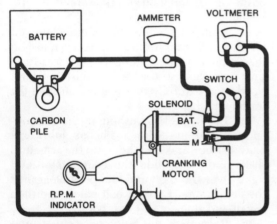

No-load test connections

7. Installation is in the reverse order of removal.

STARTER SOLENOID REMOVAL AND INSTALLATION

1. Remove the screw and washer from the motor connector strap terminal.

2. Remove the two screws which retain the solenoid housing to the end frame assembly.

3. Twist the solenoid clockwise to remove the flange key from the keyway slot in the housing.

4. Remove the solenoid assembly.

5. With the solenoid return spring installed on the plunger, position the solenoid body on the drive housing and turn it counterclockwise to engage the flange key in the keyway slot.

6. Install the two screws which retain the solenoid housing to the end frame.

Battery

Refer to Chapter One for details on battery maintenance.

REMOVAL AND INSTALLATION

1. Disconnect the negative (ground) cable first, then the positive cable. The side termi-

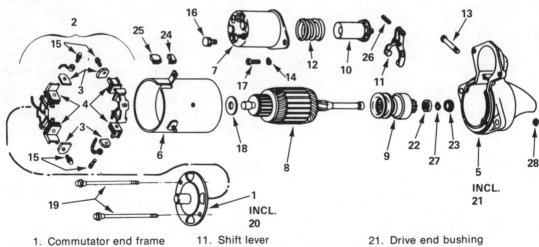

1. Commutator end frame	11. Shift lever	21. Drive end bushing
2. Brush and holder	12. Plunger return spring	22. Pinion stop collar
3. Brush	13. Shift lever shaft	23. Thrust collar
4. Brush holder	14. Lock washer	24. Grommet
5. Drive end housing	15. Brush attaching screw	25. Grommet
6. Frame and field assembly	16. Field lead to switch screw	26. Plunger pin
7. Solenoid switch	17. Switch attaching screw	27. Pinion stop retainer ring
8. Armature	18. Brake washer	28. Lever shaft retaining ring
9. Drive assembly	19. Through bolt	
10. Plunger	20. Commutator end bushing	

Exploded view of the 5-MT starter

Starter Specifications

| Engine | Starter Part No. | Series | No-Load Test @ 9 Volts | | | | Solenoid Part No. |
| | | | Amps | | RPM | | |
			Min	Max	Min	Max	
All	1109526	5 MT	45	70	7,000	11,900	1114488

nal cables are retained only by the center bolt.

CAUTION: *To avoid sparks, always disconnect the negative cable first, and connect it last.*

2. Remove the battery hold-down clamp.

3. Remove the battery.

4. Before installing the battery, clean the battery terminals and the cables thoroughly.

5. Check the battery tray to be sure it is clear of any debris. If it is rusty, it should be wire-brushed clean and given a coat of anti-rust paint, or replaced.

6. Install the battery in the tray, being sure it is centered in the lip.

7. Install the hold-down clamp. Tighten to 6 ft lbs, which is tight enough to hold the battery in place, but loose enough to prevent the case from cracking.

8. Connect the positive, then the negative battery cables. Installation torque for the cables is 9 ft lbs. Give the terminals a light external coat of grease after installation to retard corrosion.

CAUTION: *Make absolutely sure that the battery is connected properly before you turn on the ignition switch. Reversed polarity can burn out the alternator and regulator in a matter of seconds.*

ENGINE MECHANICAL

Design

The Citation, Omega, Phoenix and Skylark use two different engines, an inline four cylinder built by Pontiac as standard equipment, and a V6 built by Chevrolet as optional equipment.

The 2.5 liter (151 cu. in.) four cylinder has been in production for many years. The cylinder head and block are lightweight iron castings. Five main bearings support the crankshaft, which is made from cast nodular iron. In 1979, Pontiac updated the cylinder head design to a crossflow configuration; in the X-Body cars, the intake manifold is at the rear of the car and the exhaust manifold is at the front. A crossflow design permits better scavenging of gases and more efficient combustion. The intake manifold is made from cast aluminum, and has an integral passage through which engine coolant circulates, providing faster warmup and lower exhaust emissions. An EGR port is cast into the manifold, receiving exhaust gases from an internal passage in the head. The cylinder head has integrally-cast straight valve guides. Ball-pivot rocker arms are operated by pushrods driven by the camshaft through hydraulic lifters. Zero lash is maintained by the lifters, which require no periodic adjustment. Three ring cast aluminum pistons are connected to the crankshaft by Armasteel connecting rods. Camshaft drive is taken from the crankshaft by a bakelite fabric composition gear; the crankshaft gear is cast iron. One feature of the engine appreciated by do-it-yourselfers is the inclusion of pushrod covers on the side of the engine, which permit lifter replacement without removal of the cylinder head.

The Chevrolet 2.8 liter (173 cu. in.) V6 is an entirely new design. Most striking is the 60° bank angle of the cylinders. This design creates a more compact engine layout than the conventional 90° V bank arrangement. A 60° layout is also inherently better balanced when used with six cylinders, since a 120° firing order results naturally, providing harmonic balancing without the need for special and less satisfactory crankshaft configurations. In other respects, the Chevrolet V6 follows the conventional design of the highly respected small-block Chevrolet V8. The cylinder block and head are cast from iron. The cast nodular iron crankshaft is supported by four main bearings; number three is the thrust bearing. Camshaft drive is taken from the crankshaft by a conventional ⅜ inch pitch chain and sintered iron sprockets. Ball-pivot rocker arms are used, mounted on individually-threaded studs. The rocker arms are driven by pushrods actuated by zero-lash hydraulic lifters. Push rods are located by a guide plate held under the rocker arm stud.

General Engine Specifications

Year	Engine No. Cyl Displacement (cu in.)	Carburetor Type	Horsepower @ rpm	Torque @ rpm (ft lbs)	Bore x Stroke (in.)	Compression Ratio	Oil Pressure @ 2000 rpm
1980	4—151	2 bbl	90 @ 4000	134 @ 2400	4.000 x 3.000	8.2 : 1	37.5
	4—151 Calif.	2 bbl	90 @ 4400	128 @ 2400	4.000 x 3.000	8.2 : 1	37.5
	6—173	2 bbl	115 @ 4800	145 @ 2400	3.500 x 3.000	8.5 : 1	30–45
	6—173 Calif.	2 bbl	110 @ 4800	140 @ 2400	3.500 x 3.000	8.5 : 1	30–45

Torque Specifications
All readings in ft lbs

Year	Engine No. Cyl Displacement (cu in.)	Cylinder Head Bolts	Rod Bearing Bolts	Main Bearing Bolts	Crankshaft Bolt	Flywheel to Crankshaft Bolts	MANIFOLD	
							Intake	Exhaust
1980	4—151	75	32	70	200	44	29	44
	6—173	70	37	68	75	50	22	25

Ring Side Clearance
All measurements are given in inches

Year	Engine	Top Compression	Bottom Compression	Oil Control
1980	4—151	.0030	.0030	.0000
	6—173	.0012–.0032	.0012–.0032	.002–.007

Ring Gap
All measurements are given in inches

Year	Engine	Top Compression	Bottom Compression	Oil Control
1980	4—151	.015–.025	.009–.019	.015–.055
	6—173	.010–.020	.010–.020	.015–.055

Valve Specifications

Year	Engine No. Cyl Displacement (cu in.)	Seat Angle (deg)	Face Angle (deg)	Spring Test Pressure (lbs @ In.)	Spring Installed Height (in.)	STEM TO GUIDE Clearance (in.)		STEM Diameter (in.)	
						Intake	Exhaust	Intake	Exhaust
1980	4—151	46	45	176 @ 1.25	1.66	.0010–.0027	.0010–.0027	.3421	.3421
	6—173	46	45	195 @ 1.16	1.61	.0010–.0027	.0010–.0027	.3413	.3413

Crankshaft and Connecting Rod Specifications

All measurements are given in inches

Year	Engine No. Cyl Displacement (cu in.)	CRANKSHAFT				CONNECTING ROD		
		Main Brg Journal Dia	Main Brg Oil Clearance	Shaft End-Play	Thrust on No.	Journal Diameter	Oil Clearance	Side Clearance
1980	4—151	2.3000	.0005–.0022	.0035–.0085	5	2.0000	.0005–.0026	.006–.022
	6—173	2.4940	.0005–.0015	.0020–.0079	3	2.0000	.0005–.0020	.006–.017

Piston Clearance

All measurements are given in inches

Year	Engine	Piston to Bore Clearance
1980	4—151	.0029
	6—173	.0022

The intake manifold is cast from aluminum, as are the water pump and pistons. Connecting rods are made from forged steel.

Engine Removal and Installation

Follow Steps 1–9 for all models.

1. Disconnect the battery cables at the battery, negative cable first.
2. Remove the air cleaner.
3. Drain the cooling system.
4. Disconnect and label the distributor, starter and alternator wires, the engine-to-ground strap, the oil pressure and engine temperature wires, and all other engine electrical connections.
5. Disconnect and label all vacuum hose connections.
6. Disconnect the throttle and transaxle linkage (automatic) at the carburetor.
7. Disconnect the radiator and heater hoses.
8. Remove the power steering pump and air conditioning compressor from their mounting brackets and set them aside, without disconnecting any hoses.
9. Remove the front engine strut assembly.

ALL FOUR CYLINDER MODELS, AND SIX CYLINDER WITH AUTOMATIC TRANSAXLE

10. Remove the engine front mount-to-engine cradle nuts.
11. Remove the forward exhaust pipe or crossover pipe.
12. Disconnect and plug the fuel lines. Disconnect the battery cables from the starter and transaxle housing.
13. Remove the flywheel cover. Remove the starter on four cylinder models. Remove the torque converter-to-flywheel bolts on all automatic models.
14. On the four cylinder, remove the transaxle-to-engine bolts, leaving the upper two in place. Remove the two rear transaxle support bracket bolts. Place a block of wood under the transaxle and raise the engine and transaxle unit with a jack until the engine front mount studs clear the engine cradle. Support the engine with a lifting chain. Remove the two transaxle-to-engine bolts. Slide the engine forward and lift from the car.
15. On the six cylinder, remove the transaxle case-to-engine support bracket bolts. Place a support under the transaxle rear extension. Remove the transaxle-to-engine retaining bolts. Install a lifting chain on the engine and remove the engine from the car.

ALL SIX CYLINDER WITH MANUAL TRANSAXLE

10. Disconnect the clutch cable, shift linkage cables, and speedometer cable from the transaxle.
11. Attach a lifting chain to the engine and raise it until the engine weight is off the mounts.
12. Remove all the transaxle-to-engine bolts except one.
13. Unlock the steering column. Raise the car. Remove the stabilizer-to-lower control arm bolts. Remove the stabilizer bar plate on the left side, and loosen the plate bolts on the right side. Remove the left side crossmember assembly-to-side member bolts.
14. Remove the exhaust crossover pipe.
15. Remove all front, side and rear engine/transaxle-to-cradle nuts.
16. Remove the left wheel.
17. Remove the front crossmember-to-right side member bolts.
18. Pull the axle shafts from the transaxle using G.M. special tool J-28468 or equivalent.
19. Remove the engine cradle-to-body mount bolts on the left side.
20. Swing the side member and crossmember assembly to the left. Secure it outside the fender well.
21. Lower the left side of the engine/transaxle assembly. Place a block of wood under the transaxle and support the transaxle with a jack. Remove the last transaxle-to-engine bolt and separate and lower the transaxle out of the car. Lift the engine from the car.

Installation
ALL FOUR CYLINDER MODELS

1. Lower the engine into the cradle, aligning the transaxle and engine bellhousing.

2. With the engine still supported, install two upper transaxle-to-engine bolts. Do not lower the engine completely while the transaxle is still supported by the jack.

3. Remove the transaxle jack.

4. Lower the engine. Install the rest of the transaxle-to-engine bolts. Install the front mount-to-chassis nuts. The remainder of installation is the reverse of removal.

SIX CYLINDER WITH AUTOMATIC TRANSAXLE

1. Lower the engine into the cradle. Check that the engine front mount studs are properly located. Line up the transaxle, install, and tighten the transaxle-to-engine bolts to 55 ft lbs. The rest of installation is the reverse of removal.

SIX CYLINDER WITH MANUAL TRANSAXLE

1. Lower the engine into place. Check that the engine front mount studs are properly located.

2. Support the engine with the lifting chain. Allow the left side to drop slightly.

3. Install the forward strut bracket to the radiator support.

4. Raise the car. Raise the transaxle into the car, align with the engine, and install at least one transaxle-to-engine bolt. Start the right side axle shaft into the transaxle as the transaxle is installed.

5. Raise the left side of the engine/transaxle unit with the lifting chain.

6. Swing the side member and crossmember assembly into place, starting the left axle shaft into the transaxle as the assembly is installed. Assemble the cradle.

7. The rest of installation is the reverse of removal.

Cylinder Head

REMOVAL AND INSTALLATION

NOTE: *The engine should be "overnight" cold before removing the cylinder head.*

Four Cylinder

1. Drain the cooling system into a clean container; the coolant can be reused if it is still good.

2. Remove the air cleaner.

3. Remove the intake and exhaust manifolds. Removal of these parts is covered later in this chapter.

4. Remove the alternator bracket bolts.

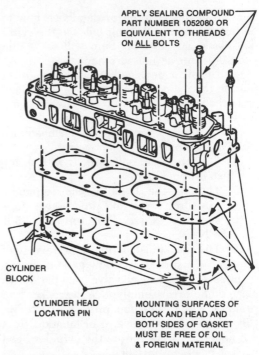

APPLY SEALING COMPOUND PART NUMBER 1052080 OR EQUIVALENT TO THREADS ON ALL BOLTS

CYLINDER BLOCK

CYLINDER HEAD LOCATING PIN

MOUNTING SURFACES OF BLOCK AND HEAD AND BOTH SIDES OF GASKET MUST BE FREE OF OIL & FOREIGN MATERIAL

Four cylinder head installation

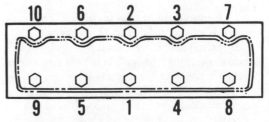

Four cylinder head torque sequence

5. If the car has air conditioning, remove the A/C compressor bracket bolts and position the compressor to one side. *Do not disconnect any of the refrigerant lines.*

6. Disconnect and label all the vacuum and electrical connections from the cylinder head.

7. Disconnect the upper radiator hose.

8. Label and disconnect the spark plug wires. Remove the plugs.

9. Remove the rocker arm cover (valve cover), rocker arms and pushrods. Their removal is covered later in this chapter. Keep these parts in order; they must be returned to their original locations.

10. Remove the cylinder head bolts and carefully lift off the cylinder head.

11. Thoroughly clean the cylinder block and head mating surfaces. Check the block and head for flatness before installing the head. See the Engine Rebuilding section at

the end of this chapter for details on how to do this. Clean out the bolt holes in the cylinder block; any dirt in them will affect the head bolt torque measurement.

12. Install a new gasket over the dowel pins on the cylinder block. The gasket, block and head must be absolutely free of any grease, oil, or other foreign matter.

13. Carefully lower the cylinder head into place on the block.

14. Coat the head bolt threads with sealer and install finger tight.

15. Tighten the bolts in the sequence shown, in three equal and progressive steps to the specified torque. Final torque is 85 ft lbs (155 Nm.).

16. The rest of installation is the reverse of removal. Be sure to use new gaskets on the manifolds. Lubricate all valve train parts with clean oil before assembly. See the rocker arm removal and installation procedure later in this chapter for rocker arm installation. It is not necessary to re-torque the cylinder head once it has been installed.

V6

1. Remove the intake manifold. This procedure is covered later in this chapter.

2. Disconnect the exhaust pipe from the exhaust manifold flange. You will need new bolts to reconnect these parts if you are working on the right cylinder head; see the exhaust manifold removal procedure later in this chapter.

3. If you are working on the left cylinder head, remove the alternator bracket and stud. Remove the heat stove pipe and the PULSAIR pipe. Remove the oil dipstick tube bracket from the head.

5. Remove the valve covers. Loosen the

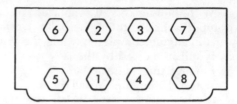
V6 cylinder head torque sequence

rocker arms until they can be pivoted aside, and remove the pushrods. Keep the pushrods in order; they must be returned to their original positions.

6. Remove the cylinder head bolts. Carefully lift off the cylinder head.

7. Thoroughly clean the cylinder block and head mating surfaces. Check the block and head for flatness before installing the head. See the Engine Rebuilding section at the end of this chapter for details on how to do this. Clean out the bolt holes in the cylinder block. Any dirt in them will affect the head bolt torque readings.

8. Place a new gasket in position over the dowel pins. The words "This Side Up" should be showing. Do not use sealer on the gasket.

9. Carefully lower the cylinder head into position.

10. Coat the head bolt threads with sealer and install them finger tight. Torque the cylinder head bolts in three progressive steps to the specified torque, using the pattern shown here. Final torque is 70 ft lbs (90 Nm.).

11. Install the pushrods into their original locations, pivot the rocker arms into place and tighten them just enough to hold the pushrods in place. Be sure the pushrods are correctly seated in the lifters.

12. Install the intake manifold.

13. Install the dipstick tube bracket, heat stove pipe, PULSAIR pipe, and alternator bracket and stud to the left cylinder head.

14. Install the exhaust pipe to the manifold.

15. Adjust the valve lash to zero clearance, as described later in this chapter.

VALVE GUIDES AND SEATS

Valve guides are integral with the cylinder head on both the four and six cylinder engines. Valves with oversize stems are available; the guides must be reamed oversize to accept these valves. As an alternative, some shops will install replacement valve guides that fit standard size valve stems. Discuss

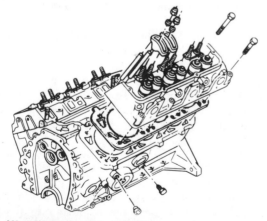
V6 cylinder head installation

these procedures with your dealer or machine shop.

Valve seats can be reground. This procedure requires special equipment; consult a machine shop or engine rebuilding shop for this service.

OVERHAUL

Cylinder head overhaul is covered in the Engine Rebuilding section at the end of this chapter.

Rocker Arms

REMOVAL AND INSTALLATION

1. Remove the valve cover.
2. Remove the rocker arm nut and ball.
3. Lift the rocker arm off the stud. Always keep the rocker arm assemblies together and install them on the same stud.
4. Lubricate the parts with clean engine oil before installation. Install the rocker arm, then the ball and nut. On the four cylinder engine, tighten the rocker arm nut to 20 ft lbs with the lifter on the base circle of the camshaft: rotate the crankshaft with a wrench on the crankshaft pulley until the rocker arm is all the way down, then tighten the nut. On the V6, adjust the valve lash, as outlined in the following section.
5. Clean all the old sealant from the rocker arm cover. Apply a thin (⅛″) bead of silicone

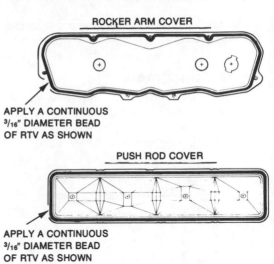

ROCKER ARM COVER

APPLY A CONTINUOUS
³/₁₆″ DIAMETER BEAD
OF RTV AS SHOWN

PUSH ROD COVER

APPLY A CONTINUOUS
³/₁₆″ DIAMETER BEAD
OF RTV AS SHOWN

Four cylinder rocker arm and pushrod cover sealer application

NOTE: AT TIME OF INSTALLATION FLANGES MUST BE FREE OF OIL. A 2–3 MM BEAD OF SEALANT MUST BE APPLIED TO FLANGES & SEALANT MUST BE SET TO TOUCH WHEN BOLTS ARE TORQUED.

RTV SEALANT

V6 rocker arm cover sealer application

sealer to the rocker cover; run the bead to the inside of the bolt holes. Install the rocker cover, and tighten the retaining bolts to 8 ft lbs while the sealer is still wet.

Rocker Arm Studs

Rocker arm studs that have damaged threads or which are loose in the cylinder heads may be replaced with new studs. Studs are available in oversizes, or the bores may be tapped and replacement studs used, on the V6 engine. The standard studs in the V6 are a press fit. The studs in the four cylinder engine are threaded into the head. Old studs can be removed with a deep socket. New

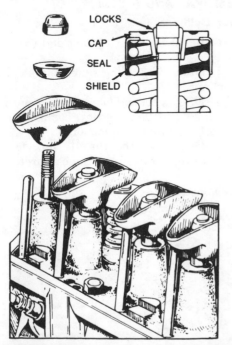

LOCKS
CAP
SEAL
SHIELD

Rocker arm, pivot and nut, and valve lock details

studs should be threaded in and tightened to 75 ft lbs (100 Nm.).

Valve Adjustment

No valve lash adjustment is required on the four cylinder engine. Tighten the rocker arm

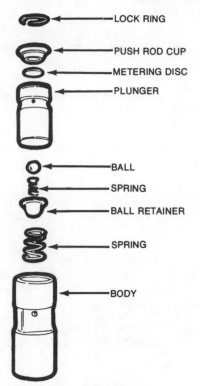

LOCK RING

PUSH ROD CUP

METERING DISC

PLUNGER

BALL

SPRING

BALL RETAINER

SPRING

BODY

Exploded view of a hydraulic lifter

V6 valve adjustment; tighten the rocker arm nut until the pushrod cannot be rotated between your fingers

nuts to 20 ft lbs, as outlined in the rocker arm removal and installation procedure given previously.

Anytime the V6 valve train is disturbed, the valve lash must be adjusted, as follows:

Crank the engine until the timing mark aligns with the "0" mark on the timing scale, and both valves in the No. 1 cylinder are closed. If the valves are moving as the timing marks align, the engine is in the No. 4 firing position. Turn the crankshaft one more revolution. With the engine in the No. 1 firing position, adjust the following valves:

Exhaust—1,2,3

Intake—1,5,6

Rotate the crankshaft one full revolution, until it is in the No. 4 firing position. Adjust the following valves:

Exhaust—4,5,6

Intake—2,3,4

Adjustment is made by backing off the rocker arm adjusting nut until there is play in the pushrod. Tighten the nut to remove the pushrod clearance (this can be determined by rotating the pushrod with your fingers while tightening the adjusting nut). When the pushrod cannot be freely turned, tighten the nut 1½ additional turns to place the hydraulic lifter in the center of its travel. No further adjustment is required.

Intake Manifold

REMOVAL AND INSTALLATION

Four Cylinder

1. Remove the air cleaner and the PCV valve.

2. Drain the cooling system into a clean container.

3. Disconnect and label the fuel and vacuum lines and the electrical connections at the carburetor and the manifold.

4. Disconnect the throttle linkage and the transaxle downshift at the carburetor.

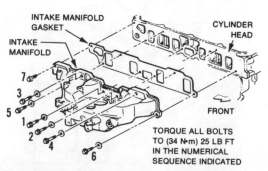

INTAKE MANIFOLD GASKET

INTAKE MANIFOLD

CYLINDER HEAD

FRONT

TORQUE ALL BOLTS TO (34 N·m) 25 LB FT IN THE NUMERICAL SEQUENCE INDICATED

Four cylinder intake manifold installation

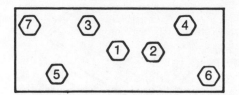

Four cylinder intake manifold torque sequence

5. Remove the carburetor and the spacer.

6. Remove the bell crank and the throttle linkage. Position to the side for clearance.

7. Remove the heater hose at the intake manifold.

8. Remove the PULSAIR check valve bracket from the manifold.

9. Remove the manifold attaching bolts and remove the manifold.

10. To install, reverse the removal procedure. Always use a new gasket. Tighten all the bolts in two stages to 25 ft lbs in the proper sequence.

V6

1. Remove the rocker covers.

2. Drain the cooling system.

3. Remove the distributor cap. Mark the position of the ignition rotor in relation to the distributor body, and remove the distributor. Do not crank the engine with the distributor removed.

4. Remove the heater and radiator hoses from the intake manifold.

5. Remove the power brake vacuum hose.

6. Disconnect and label the vacuum hoses. Remove the EFE pipe from the rear of the manifold.

7. Remove the carburetor linkage. Disconnect and plug the fuel line.

8. Remove the manifold retaining bolts and nuts.

9. Remove the intake manifold. Remove and discard the gaskets, and scrape off the old silicone seal from the front and rear ridges.

To install:

1. The gaskets are marked for right and left side installation; do not interchange them. Clean the sealing surface of the engine block, and apply a 3/16 in. bead of silicone sealer to each ridge.

2. Install the new gaskets onto the heads. The gaskets will have to be cut slightly to fit past the center pushrods. Do not cut any more material than necessary. Hold the gaskets in place by extending the ridge bead of sealer ¼ in. onto the gasket ends.

Cut the V6 intake manifold gasket as necessary to slip it past the inner pushrods

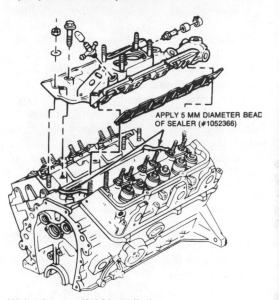

V6 intake manifold installation

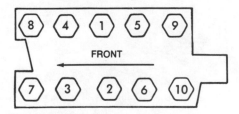

V6 intake manifold torque sequence

3. Install the intake manifold. The area between the ridges and the manifold should be completely sealed.

4. Install the retaining bolts and nuts, and tighten in sequence to 23 ft lbs. Do not overtighten; the manifold is made from aluminum, and can be warped or cracked with excessive force.

5. The rest of installation is the reverse of removal. Adjust the ignition timing after installation, and check the coolant level after the engine has warmed up.

Exhaust Manifold

REMOVAL AND INSTALLATION

Four Cylinder

1. Remove the air cleaner and the carburetor pre-heat tube.

2. Remove the manifold strut bolts from the radiator support panel and the cylinder head.

3. If equipped with air conditioning, remove the A/C compressor bracket bolts and position the compressor to one side. Do not disconnect any of the refrigerant lines.

4. Remove the dipstick tube attaching bolt.

5. Raise the car and disconnect the exhaust pipe from the manifold.

6. Remove the manifold attaching bolts and remove the manifold.

7. To install, place a new gasket into position and install the exhaust manifold over it. Install the retaining bolts finger tight, then tighten in two stages to 44 ft lbs (60 Nm.) in the sequence shown. The remainder of installation is the reverse of removal.

V6

LEFT SIDE

1. Remove the air cleaner. Remove the carburetor heat stove pipe.

2. Remove the PULSAIR pipes from the exhaust manifold.

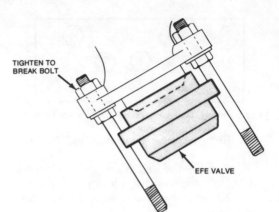

TIGHTEN TO BREAK BOLT

EFE VALVE

Tighten the right side exhaust flange bolts until they break on the V6

3. Raise and support the car. Unbolt and remove the exhaust pipe at the manifold.

4. Unbolt and remove the manifold.

To install:

1. Clean the mating surfaces of the cylinder head and manifold. Install the manifold onto the head, and install the retaining bolts finger tight.

2. Tighten the manifold bolts in a circular pattern, working from the center to the ends, to 25 ft lbs in two stages.

3. Connect the exhaust pipe to the manifold.

4. The remainder of installation is the reverse of removal.

RIGHT SIDE

1. Raise and support the car.

2. Tighten the exhaust pipe-to-manifold flange bolts until they break off. Remove the pipe from the manifold.

3. Lower the car. Remove the spark plug wires from the plugs. Number them first if they are not already labeled.

4. Remove the PULSAIR pipes from the manifold. Remove the PULSAIR bracket bolt from the rocker cover, then remove the pipe assembly.

5. Remove the manifold retaining bolts and remove the manifold.

To install:

1. Clean the mating surfaces of the cylinder head and manifold. Position the manifold against the head and install the retaining bolts finger tight.

2. Tighten the bolts in a circular pattern, working from the center to the ends, to 25 ft lbs in two stages.

3. Install the PULSAIR system.

4. Install the spark plug wires.

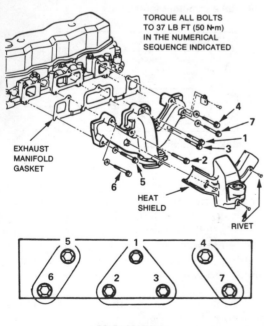

TORQUE ALL BOLTS TO 37 LB FT (50 N·m) IN THE NUMERICAL SEQUENCE INDICATED

EXHAUST MANIFOLD GASKET

HEAT SHIELD

RIVET

BOLT LOCATIONS

Four cylinder exhaust manifold installation

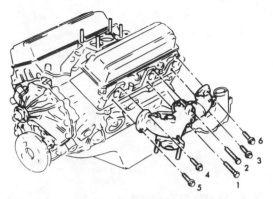

V6 exhaust manifold installation

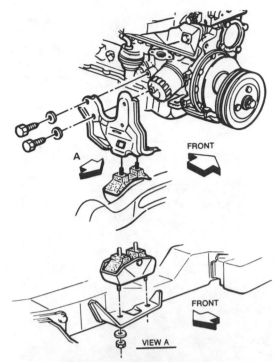

5. Raise and support the car. Connect the exhaust pipe to the manifold and install new flange bolts.

Timing Cover

REMOVAL AND INSTALLATION

Four Cylinder

1. Remove the engine drive belts.
2. Remove the right front inner fender splash shield.
3. Remove the center bolt from the crankshaft pulley and slide the hub from the shaft.
4. Remove the alternator lower bracket.
5. Remove the front engine mounts.
6. Using a floor jack, raise the engine.
7. Remove the engine mount mounting bracket-to-cylinder block bolts. Remove the bracket and mount as an assembly.
8. Remove the oil pan-to-front cover bolts.
9. Remove the front cover-to-block bolts.
10. Pull the cover slightly forward, just enough to allow cutting of the oil pan front seal flush with the block on both sides.
11. Remove the front cover and attached portion of the oil pan seal.
12. Clean the gasket surfaces thoroughly.
13. Cut the tabs from the new oil pan front seal.
14. Install the seal on the front cover, pressing the tips onto the holes provided.
15. Coat the new gasket with sealer and position it on the front cover.
16. Apply a ⅛ in. bead of silicone sealer to the joint formed at the oil pan and block.
17. Align the front cover seal with a centering tool and install the front cover. Tighten the cover with the centering tool installed, then remove the tool.
18. Install the front mount bracket assem-

Four cylinder engine mount bracket

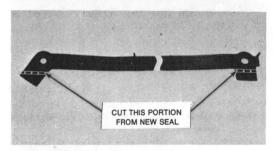

Cut the oil pan front seal flush with the front cover

Cut the tabs from a new oil seal

bly and lower alternator bracket. Lower the engine. Install the mount-to-engine cradle nuts.
19. Coat the front cover oil seal contact area on the hub with clean engine oil. Position the hub on the crankshaft and slide it on until it bottoms against the crankshaft gear.

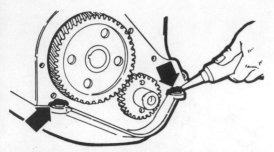

Apply sealer to the oil pan and block joint

Install the front cover bolts with the centering tool installed

Install the hub retaining bolt and tighten to 160 ft. lbs. (212 Nm.). Install the belts and adjust their tension. Install the fender shield.

V6

1. Remove the water pump. The procedure for this is given later in this chapter.

2. If the car has air conditioning, remove the compressor from its brackets and move it aside. *Do not disconnect any of the hoses.*

3. Remove the torsional damper: remove the negative battery cable at the battery, remove the engine drive belts, raise the car, remove the right inner fender splash shield, remove the drive pulley, then remove the damper retaining bolt. Install a puller onto the damper and remove the damper.

NOTE: *The outer ring (weight) of the torsional damper is bonded to the hub with rubber. The balancer must be removed with a puller which acts on the inner hub only. Pulling on the outer portion of the balancer will break the rubber bond or destroy the tuning of the damper.*

4. Remove the front cover retaining bolts and remove the cover.

5. To install, clean the front cover mating

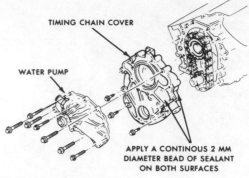

V6 front cover installation

surfaces of all old sealer. Apply a $^3/_{32}$ inch bead of silicone sealer to the front cover sealing surface.

6. Place the front cover on the engine, install the water pump, then install the retaining bolts and tighten the small bolts to 6–9 ft lbs, the medium size bolts to 13–18 ft lbs, and the large bolts to 20–30 ft lbs (8–12, 18–24, and 27–41 Nm., respectively).

7. Connect the lower radiator hose.

8. Install the torsional damper: coat the front cover seal contact area on the damper with clean engine oil. Place the damper on the crankshaft with the keyway aligned. Install the damper using a press which acts on the inner ring of the hub only. The press should thread into the crankshaft with at least ¼ inch of thread engagement.

9. Install the pulley onto the hub, and install both the pulley and the hub bolts. Tighten the pulley bolts to 20–30 ft lbs (27–41 Nm.) and the hub (damper) bolt to 66–84 ft lbs (90–115 Nm.).

10. Install the inner fender splash shield. Install the drive belts and adjust their tension. Install the air conditioning compressor, if removed, and its drive belt; adjust the tension. Connect the negative battery cable. Fill the cooling system as outlined in Chapter One.

TIMING COVER OIL SEAL

The oil seal on both engines can be replaced with the cover either on or off the engine. If the cover is on the engine, remove the crankshaft pulley and hub first. Pry out the seal using a large screwdriver, being careful not to distort the seal mating surface. Install the new seal so that the open side or helical side is towards the engine. Press it into place with a seal driver made for the purpose. Install the hub if removed.

Timing Chain or Gear

REMOVAL AND INSTALLATION

Four Cylinder

The four cylinder camshaft gear must be pressed from the camshaft, requiring camshaft removal. See the following section for that procedure.

V6

1. Remove the timing cover.
2. Place the No. 1 piston at TDC with the marks on the camshaft and crankshaft sprockets aligned as shown.
3. Remove the camshaft sprocket bolts and remove the sprocket and chain together. If the sprocket does not slide from the camshaft easily, a light blow with a soft mallet at the lower edge of the sprocket will dislodge it.
4. To install, hold the sprocket vertically with the chain hanging down. Align the marks as shown. Align the dowel in the camshaft with the hole in the sprocket, then install the sprocket and chain.
5. Install the camshaft sprocket bolts. Tighten to 15–20 ft lbs (20–27 Nm.). Lubricate the chain and sprocket with clean engine oil. Install the timing cover.

Camshaft

REMOVAL AND INSTALLATION

Four Cylinder

1. Remove the engine from the car.
2. Remove the valve cover, loosen the

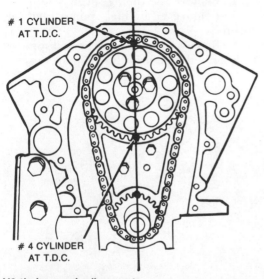

1 CYLINDER AT T.D.C.

4 CYLINDER AT T.D.C.

V6 timing mark alignment

The V6 timing chain rubber damper bolts to the front of the engine

rocker arms and pivot them aside, and remove the pushrods. Keep them in order.
3. Remove the distributor and fuel pump.
4. Remove the pushrod cover from the side of the engine. Remove the lifters. Keep them in order.
5. Remove the alternator and its bracket, and remove the front engine mount bracket assembly.
6. Remove the oil pan. Remove the oil pump and gear assembly.
7. Remove the crankshaft hub and the front cover.
8. Remove the two camshaft thrust plate screws by working through the holes in the gear.
9. Remove the camshaft and gear assembly by pulling it through the front of the block. Be very careful not to damage the bearings.

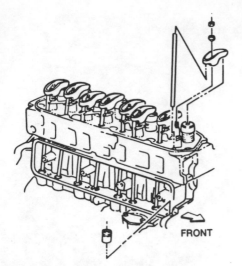

Four cylinder rocker arm, pushrod and valve lifter removal

Four cylinder camshaft thrust plate screw removal

10. If the timing gear must be removed, support the camshaft on a press, install press plates under the gear, and press off the gear.

CAUTION: *Position the thrust plate so that the woodruff key in the camshaft does not damage the plate when the gear is pressed off.*

11. To press on the gear, support the camshaft behind the front journal with press plates. Place the gear spacer ring and thrust plate over the end of the camshaft, and install the woodruff key. Press the gear onto the camshaft until it bottoms against the gear spacer ring.

The end clearance of the thrust plate should be between 0.0015 and 0.0050 in. If more, the thrust plate should be replaced. If less, replace the spacer ring.

12. Coat the camshaft and gear with clean engine oil supplement. Install the camshaft into the block, being extremely careful not to contact the bearings with the cam lobes.

13. Align the timing marks. The engine should then be in the No. 4 firing position. Install the thrust plate-to-block bolts and tighten to 75 in. lbs (10 Nm.).

14. Install the timing cover, crankshaft pulley, valve lifters (in original positions), pushrods (in original positions) the oil pump shaft and gear assembly and the oil pan and fuel pump. Install the pushrod side cover with a thin bead of silicone seal running to the inside of the bolt holes. Be sure all the old sealer is removed before applying the new sealer.

15. Install the distributor: rotate the crankshaft until No. 1 cylinder is in firing position. The number one valves will both be closed, and the timing marks will be at "0". Install the distributor in its original position, with the rotor pointing toward the No. 1 spark plug tower.

16. Pivot the rocker arms over the pushrods, and tighten the rocker arm nuts to 20 ft lbs (27 Nm.) with the lifters on the base circle of the cam lobe as described under rocker arm removal earlier in this chapter. The rest of installation is the reverse of removal.

V6

1. Remove the engine.
2. Remove the intake manifold.
3. Remove the rocker covers, pivot the rocker arms to the sides, and remove the pushrods, keeping them in order. Remove the valve lifters, keeping them in order. There are special tools which make lifter removal easier.
4. Remove the timing cover.
5. Remove the fuel pump and its pushrod.
6. Remove the timing chain and sprocket as described earlier in this chapter.

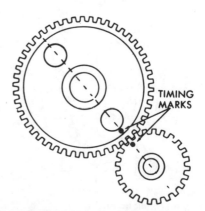

Four cylinder timing mark alignment

7. Carefully pull the camshaft from the block, being sure that the camshaft lobes do not contact the bearings.

8. To install, lubricate the camshaft journals with clean engine oil. Lubricate the lobes with "molykote" or the equivalent. Install the camshaft into the engine, being extremely careful not to contact the bearings with the cam lobes.

9. Install the timing chain and sprocket. Install the fuel pump and pushrod. Install the timing cover.

10. Install the valve lifters. If a new camshaft has been installed, new lifters should be used to ensure durability of the cam lobes.

11. Install the pushrods and rocker arms and the intake manifold. Adjust the valve lash after installing the engine. Install the valve covers.

Pistons and Connecting Rods

REMOVAL AND INSTALLATION

1. Drain the crankcase and remove the oil pan and oil pump, as described later in this chapter.

2. Drain the cooling system and remove the cylinder head(s).

3. Remove any ridge or deposits from the upper end of the cylinder bores with a ridge reamer. Do this with piston in Bottom Dead Center position and a clean rag on top of the piston to collect cuttings.

4. Check the rods and pistons for identification numbers and, if necessary, number them.

5. Remove the connecting rod cap nuts and caps. Push the rods away from the crankshaft and install the caps and nuts loosely to their respective rods.

6. Push the piston and rod assemblies up and out of the cylinders.

7. Before replacing the rings, inspect the cylinder bores. If the cylinder bore is in satisfactory condition, place each ring in its bore in turn and square it in the bore with the head of the piston. Measure the ring end-gap. If the gap is incorrect get a new ring. Do not file the end of the ring to obtain the correct gap.

8. Check the ring side clearance by installing the rings on the piston, and inserting a feeler gauge of the correct dimension between the ring and the lower land. The gauge should slide freely around the circumference of the ring without binding. Any wear will form a step on the lower land. Replace any pistons having high steps. Before checking

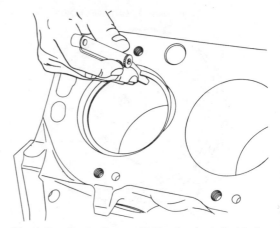

Check the ring end gap with the ring installed in its cylinder

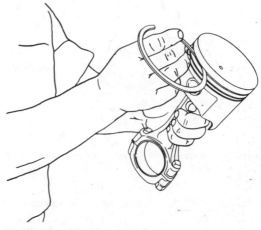

Check ring side clearance

the ring side clearance be sure the ring grooves are clean and free of carbon, sludge, or grit.

9. Install piston rings with a ring expander. Compression rings have a mark which must face the top of the piston. The top ring is chrome or molybdenum faced. When installing oil rings, do the following: first, install the oil ring in the ring groove and insert the anti-rotation tang into the oil hole; then, holding the ends of the spacer so they butt up against one another, install the lower steel oil ring rail; repeat this procedure to install the upper rail so that the gap will line up with that of the lower rail; flex the oil ring assembly to make sure it is free—if it binds, the ring groove must be dressed at a narrow point, or a distorted ring must be replaced; install lower compression ring with gap 120 degrees (one third of a circle) away from oil ring gap; install top ring with its gap 120 degrees away from that of the second ring. Be sure to install the piston in its original

FRONT OF ENGINE

NOTCH

Install the pistons with the notch facing the front of the engine

bore. Install the piston and rod assembly with the notch in the piston facing the front of the engine. Install short lengths of rubber tubing over the connecting rod bolts to prevent damage to the rod journals. Lubricate pistons and rod bearings with light engine oil. Install a ring compressor over the rings on the piston. Lower the piston and rod assembly into the bore until the ring compressor contacts the block. Using the wooden handle of a hammer, push the piston into the bore while guiding the rod onto the journal.

ENGINE LUBRICATION

Oil Pan

REMOVAL AND INSTALLATION

Four Cylinder

1. Raise and support the car. Drain the oil.
2. Remove the engine cradle-to-front engine mounts.
3. Disconnect the exhaust pipe at both the exhaust manifold and at the rear transaxle mount.
4. Disconnect and remove the starter. Remove the flywheel housing or torque converter cover.
5. Remove the alternator upper bracket.
6. Install an engine lifting chain and raise the engine.
7. Remove the lower alternator bracket. Remove the engine support bracket.
8. Remove the oil pan retaining bolts and remove the pan.
9. Reverse the procedure to install. Clean all gasket surfaces thoroughly. Install the rear oil pan gasket into the rear main bearing cap, then apply a thin bead of silicone sealer to the pan gasket depressions. Install the front pan gasket into the timing cover. Install the side gaskets onto the block, not the oil pan. They can be retained in place with grease. Apply a thin bead of silicone seal to the mating joints of the gaskets. Install the oil pan; install the timing gear bolts last, after the other bolts have been snugged down.

V6

1. Drain the oil. Disconnect the negative battery cable.
2. Remove the oil dipstick and tube.
3. Raise and support the car.
4. Remove the exhaust crossover pipe.
5. On cars with an automatic transaxle,

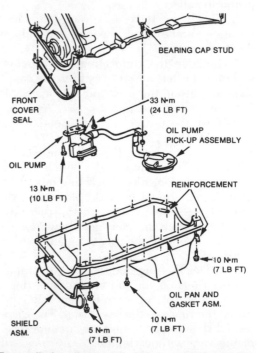

BEARING CAP STUD

FRONT COVER SEAL

33 N·m (24 LB FT)

OIL PUMP PICK-UP ASSEMBLY

OIL PUMP

13 N·m (10 LB FT)

REINFORCEMENT

SHIELD ASM.

5 N·m (7 LB FT)

10 N·m (7 LB FT)

OIL PAN AND GASKET ASM.

10 N·m (7 LB FT)

Four cylinder oil pan and pump installation details

remove the converter housing underpan. On X-Cars with a manual transaxle, remove the clutch housing cover, then remove the engine mounting bracket-to-engine mount nuts and raise the front of the engine ¾ in.

6. Remove the starter.

7. Remove the oil pan and discard the gaskets and seals.

8. Before installing the pan, make sure that all the mating surfaces are free of oil and dirt, and remove any traces of old silicone seal.

9. Apply a ⅛ in. bead of silicone seal to the oil pan sealing flange.

10. Use a new oil pan rear seal. Install the pan against the cylinder case and attach with the retaining bolts. Tighten the smaller oil pan bolts to 6–9 ft lbs, and the larger bolts to 14–22 ft lbs (8–12 and 19–30 Nm., respectively).

11. Lower the front of the engine, if it was raised (manual transaxle cars only), and install the retaining nuts.

12. Install the starter, converter or clutch housing cover, the exhaust crossover, and lower the car. Fill the crankcase with oil, connect the negative battery cable, start the engine and check for leaks.

Rear Main Oil Seal
REMOVAL AND INSTALLATION
Four Cylinder

The rear main oil seal is a one piece unit, and is removed or installed without removal of the oil pan or crankshaft.

1. Remove the transaxle, the flywheel or torque converter bellhousing, and the flywheel or flexplate.

2. Remove the rear main oil seal with a screwdriver. Be extremely careful not to scratch the crankshaft.

3. Oil the lips of the new seal with clean engine oil. Install the new seal by hand onto the rear crankshaft flange. The helical lip of the seal should face the engine. Make sure that the seal is firmly and evenly installed.

4. Replace the flywheel or flexplate, bellhousing and transaxle.

V6

1. Remove the oil pan and pump.

2. Remove the rear main bearing cap.

3. Gently pack the upper seal into the groove approximately ¼ inch on each side.

4. Measure the amount the seal was driven in on one side and add ¹/₁₆ in. Cut this

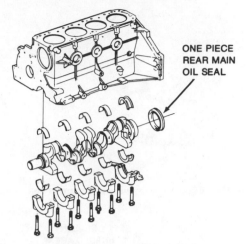

The four cylinder has a one piece ring type rear main seal

length from the old lower cap seal. Be sure to get a sharp cut. Repeat for the other side.

5. Place the piece of cut seal into the groove and pack the seal into the block. Do this for each side.

6. Install a new lower seal in the rear main cap.

7. Install a piece of Plastigage or the equivalent on the bearing journal. Install the rear cap and tighten to 75 ft lbs. Remove the cap and check the gauge for bearing clearance. If out of specification, the ends of the seal may be frayed or not flush, preventing the cap from proper seating. Correct as required.

8. Clean the journal, and apply a thin film

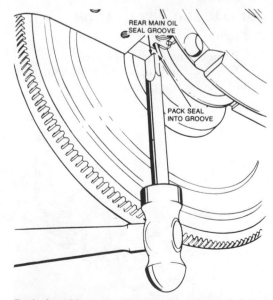

Pack the old upper seal into its groove ¼ in. on each side

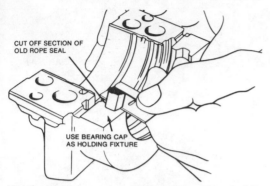

Use the bearing cap to hold the old lower seal while you cut it

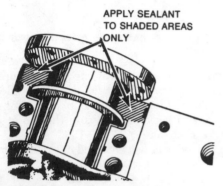

APPLY SEALANT TO SHADED AREAS ONLY

Sealer application on the V6 block

of sealer to the mating surfaces of the cap and block. Do not allow any sealer to get onto the journal or bearing. Install the bearing cap and tighten to 70 ft lbs. Install the pan and pump.

Oil Pump

REMOVAL AND INSTALLATION

All Engines

1. Remove the engine oil pan.
2. Remove the pump attaching bolts and carefully lower the pump.

3. Install in reverse order. To ensure immediate oil pressure on start-up, the oil pump gear cavity should be packed with petroleum jelly. Installation torque is 22 ft lbs (30 Nm.) for the four cylinder, 26–35 ft lbs (35–47 Nm.) for the V6.

ENGINE COOLING

Radiator

REMOVAL AND INSTALLATION

All Models

1. Disconnect the negative battery cable.
2. Drain the cooling system.
3. Remove the forward strut brace for the engine at the radiator. Loosen the bolt to prevent shearing the rubber bushing, then swing the strut rearward.
4. Disconnect the headlamp wiring harness from the fan frame. Unplug the fan electrical connector.
5. Remove the attaching bolts for the fan.
6. Scribe the hood latch location on the radiator support, then remove the latch.
7. Disconnect the coolant hoses from the radiator. Remove the coolant recovery tank hose from the radiator neck. Disconnect and plug the automatic transaxle fluid cooler lines from the radiator, if so equipped.
8. Remove the radiator attaching bolts and remove the radiator. If the car has air conditioning, it first may be necessary to raise the left side of the radiator so that the radiator neck will clear the compressor.

To install:

1. Install the radiator in the car, tightening the mounting bolts to 7 in. lbs. Connect the transaxle cooler lines and hoses. Install the coolant recovery hose.

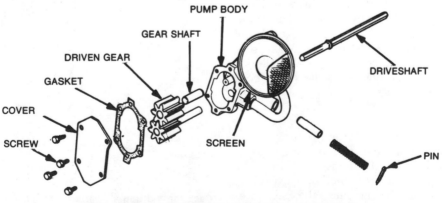

Exploded view of the V6 oil pump; four cylinder similar

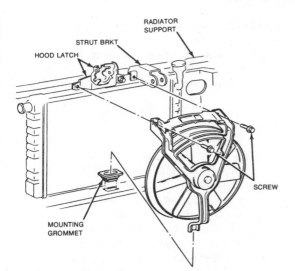

Coolant fan installation details. Heavy-duty units are similar; the only real difference is the presence of a shroud

Apply sealer to the water pump mating surfaces (V6 shown)

2. Install the hood latch. Tighten to 6 ft. lbs.

3. Install the fan, making sure the bottom leg of the frame fits into the rubber grommet at the lower support. Install the fan wires and the headlamp wiring harness. Swing the strut and brace forward, tightening to 11 ft. lbs. Connect the engine ground strap to the strut brace. Install the negative battery cable, fill the cooling system, and check for leaks.

Water Pump

REMOVAL AND INSTALLATION

All Models

1. Disconnect the negative battery cable.
2. Remove the drive belts for the water pump and accessories.
3. Disconnect the coolant hoses from the pump.
4. Remove the pump mounting bolts and remove the pump.
5. To install, if a new pump is being installed, transfer the pulley from the old pump to the new one.
6. No gasket is used. Clean the mating surfaces thoroughly, then apply a ⅛ in. bead of silicone sealer to the water pump sealing surface.
7. While the sealer is still wet, install the pump onto the engine. Tighten the bolts to 25 ft lbs (30 Nm.) on the four cylinder. On the V6, tighten the small bolts to 8 ft lbs (10 Nm.), the medium size bolts to 16 ft lbs (21 Nm.) and the large bolts to 25 ft lbs (30 Nm.). The remainder of installation is the reverse of

removal. Adjust the drive belt tension after installation.

Thermostat

The factory-installed thermostat is designed to open at 195° F (91° C).

REMOVAL AND INSTALLATION

All Models

The thermostat is located inside a housing on the front of the cylinder head on the four cyl-

Four cylinder thermostat housing

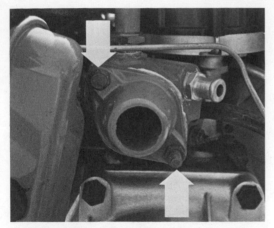

V6 thermostat housing bolt locations

thermostat housing when removing the thermostat.

1. Remove the two retaining bolts from the thermostat housing and lift up the housing with the hose attached. Remove the thermostat.

2. Insert the new thermostat, spring end down. Apply a thin bead of silicone sealer to the housing mating surface and install the housing while the sealer is still wet. Tighten the housing retaining bolts to 6 ft lbs (8 Nm.).

NOTE: *Poor heater output and slow warm-up is often caused by a thermostat stuck in the open position; occasionally one sticks shut causing immediate overheating. Do not attempt to correct a chronic overheating condition by permanently removing the thermostat. Thermostat flow restriction is designed into the system; without it, localized overheating (due to coolant turbulence) may occur, causing expensive troubles.*

inder engine, and inside the front of the intake manifold casting on the V6. It is not necessary to remove the radiator hose from the

ENGINE REBUILDING

Most procedures involved in rebuilding an engine are fairly standard, regardless of the type of engine involved. This section is a guide to accepted rebuilding procedures. Examples of standard rebuilding practices are illustrated and should be used along with specific details concerning your particular engine, found earlier in this chapter.

The procedures given here are those used by any competent rebuilder. Obviously some of the procedures cannot be performed by the do-it-yourself mechanic, but are provided so that you will be familiar with the services that should be offered by rebuilding or machine shops. As an example, in most instances, it is more profitable for the home mechanic to remove the cylinder heads, buy the necessary parts (new valves, seals, keepers, keys, etc.) and deliver these to a machine shop for the necessary work. In this way you will save the money to remove and install the cylinder head and the mark-up on parts.

On the other hand, most of the work involved in rebuilding the lower end is well within the scope of the do-it-yourself mechanic. Only work such as hot-tanking, actually boring the block or Magnafluxing (invisible crack detection) need be sent to a machine shop.

Tools

The tools required for basic engine rebuilding should, with a few exceptions, be those included in a mechanic's tool kit. An accurate torque wrench, and a dial indicator (reading in thousandths) mounted on a universal base should be available. Special tools, where required, are available from the major tool suppliers. The services of a competent automotive machine shop must also be readily available.

Precautions

Aluminum has become increasingly popular for use in engines, due to its low weight and excellent heat transfer characteristics. The following precautions must be observed when handling aluminum (or any other) engine parts:
—Never hot-tank aluminum parts.
—Remove all aluminum parts (identification tags, etc.) from engine parts before hot-tanking (otherwise they will be removed during the process).

—Always coat threads lightly with engine oil or anti-seize compounds before installation, to prevent seizure.
—Never over-torque bolts or spark plugs in aluminum threads. Should stripping occur, threads can be restored using any of a number of thread repair kits available (see next section).

Inspection Techniques

Magnaflux and Zyglo are inspection techniques used to locate material flaws, such as stress cracks. Magnaflux is a magnetic process, applicable only to ferrous materials. The Zyglo process coats the material with a fluorescent dye penetrant, and any material may be tested using Zyglo. Specific checks of suspected surface cracks may be made at lower cost and more readily using spot check dye. The dye is sprayed onto the suspected area, wiped off, and the area is then sprayed with a developer. Cracks then will show up brightly.

Overhaul

The section is divided into two parts. The first, Cylinder Head Reconditioning, assumes that the cylinder head is removed from the engine, all manifolds are removed, and the cylinder head is on a workbench. The camshaft should be removed from overhead cam cylinder heads. The second section, Cylinder Block Reconditioning, covers the block, pistons, connecting rods and crankshaft. It is assumed that the engine is mounted on a work stand, and the cylinder head and all accessories are removed.

Procedures are identified as follows:
Unmarked—Basic procedures that must be performed in order to successfully complete the rebuilding process.
Starred (*)—Procedures that should be performed to ensure maximum performance and engine life.
Double starred (**)—Procedures that may be performed to increase engine performance and reliability.

When assembling the engine, any parts that will be in frictional contact must be pre-lubricated, to provide protection on initial start-up. Any product specifically formulated for this purpose may be used. NOTE: *Do not use engine oil*. Where semi-permanent (locked but removable) installation of bolts or nuts is desired, threads should be cleaned and located with Loctite® or a similar product (non-hardening).

Repairing Damaged Threads

Several methods of repairing damaged threads are available. Heli-Coil® (shown here), Keenserts® and Microdot® are among the most widely used. All involve basically the same principle—drilling out stripped threads, tapping the hole and installing a pre-wound insert—making welding, plugging and oversize fasteners unnecessary.

Two types of thread repair inserts are usually supplied—a standard type for most Inch Coarse, Inch Fine, Metric Coarse and Metric Fine thread sizes and a spark plug type to fit most spark plug port sizes. Consult the individual manufacturer's catalog to determine exact applications. Typical thread repair kits will contain a selection of pre-wound threaded inserts, a tap (corresponding to the outside diameter threads of the insert) and an installation tool. Spark plug inserts usually differ because they require a tap equipped with pilot threads and a combined reamer/tap section. Most manufacturers also supply blister-packed thread repair inserts separately in addition to a master kit containing a variety of taps and inserts plus installation tools.

Before effecting a repair to a threaded hole, remove any snapped, broken or damaged bolts or studs. Penetrating oil can be used to free frozen threads; the offending item can be removed with locking pliers or with a screw or stud extractor. After the hole is clear, the thread can be repaired, as follows:

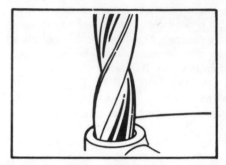

Drill out the damaged threads with specified drill. Drill completely through the hole or to the bottom of a blind hole

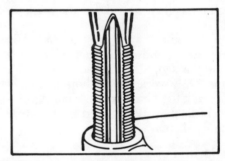

With the tap supplied, tap the hole to receive the thread insert. Keep the tap well oiled and back it out frequently to avoid clogging the threads

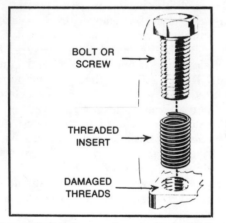

Damaged bolt holes can be repaired with thread repair inserts

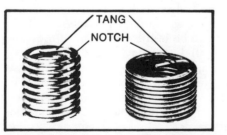

Standard thread repair insert (left) and spark plug thread insert (right)

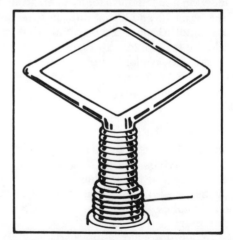

Screw the threaded insert onto the installation tool until the tang engages the slot. Screw the insert into the tapped hole until it is ¼–½ turn below the top surface. After installation break off the tang with a hammer and punch

Standard Torque Specifications and Fastener Markings

The Newton-metre has been designated the world standard for measuring torque and will gradually replace the foot-pound and kilogram-meter. In the absence of specific torques, the following chart can be used as a guide to the maximum safe torque of a particular size/grade of fastener.

- There is no torque difference for fine or coarse threads.
- Torque values are based on clean, dry threads. Reduce the value by 10% if threads are oiled prior to assembly.
- The torque required for aluminum components or fasteners is considerably less.

U. S. BOLTS

SAE Grade Number	1 or 2			5			6 or 7		

Bolt Markings

Manufacturer's marks may vary—number of lines always 2 less than the grade number.

Usage	Frequent			Frequent			Infrequent		
Bolt Size (inches)—(Thread)	Maximum Torque			Maximum Torque			Maximum Torque		
	Ft-Lb	kgm	Nm	Ft-Lb	kgm	Nm	Ft-Lb	kgm	Nm
¼—20	5	0.7	6.8	8	1.1	10.8	10	1.4	13.5
—28	6	0.8	8.1	10	1.4	13.6			
5⁄16—18	11	1.5	14.9	17	2.3	23.0	19	2.6	25.8
—24	13	1.8	17.6	19	2.6	25.7			
3⁄8—16	18	2.5	24.4	31	4.3	42.0	34	4.7	46.0
—24	20	2.75	27.1	35	4.8	47.5			
7⁄16—14	28	3.8	37.0	49	6.8	66.4	55	7.6	74.5
—20	30	4.2	40.7	55	7.6	74.5			
½—13	39	5.4	52.8	75	10.4	101.7	85	11.75	115.2
—20	41	5.7	55.6	85	11.7	115.2			
9⁄16—12	51	7.0	69.2	110	15.2	149.1	120	16.6	162.7
—18	55	7.6	74.5	120	16.6	162.7			
5⁄8—11	83	11.5	112.5	150	20.7	203.3	167	23.0	226.5
—18	95	13.1	128.8	170	23.5	230.5			
3⁄4—10	105	14.5	142.3	270	37.3	366.0	280	38.7	379.6
—16	115	15.9	155.9	295	40.8	400.0			
7⁄8— 9	160	22.1	216.9	395	54.6	535.5	440	60.9	596.5
—14	175	24.2	237.2	435	60.1	589.7			
1— 8	236	32.5	318.6	590	81.6	799.9	660	91.3	894.8
—14	250	34.6	338.9	660	91.3	849.8			

METRIC BOLTS

NOTE: *Metric bolts are marked with a number indicating the relative strength of the bolt. These numbers have nothing to do with size.*

Description	Torque ft-lbs (Nm)			
Thread size x pitch (mm)	Head mark—4		Head mark—7	
6 x 1.0	2.2–2.9	(3.0–3.9)	3.6–5.8	(4.9–7.8)
8 x 1.25	5.8–8.7	(7.9–12)	9.4–14	(13–19)
10 x 1.25	12–17	(16–23)	20–29	(27–39)
12 x 1.25	21–32	(29–43)	35–53	(47–72)
14 x 1.5	35–52	(48–70)	57–85	(77–110)
16 x 1.5	51–77	(67–100)	90–120	(130–160)
18 x 1.5	74–110	(100–150)	130–170	(180–230)
20 x 1.5	110–140	(150–190)	190–240	(160–320)
22 x 1.5	150–190	(200–260)	250–320	(340–430)
24 x 1.5	190–240	(260–320)	310–410	(420–550)

NOTE: *This engine rebuilding section is a guide to accepted rebuilding procedures. Typical examples of standard rebuilding procedures are illustrated. Use these procedures along with the detailed instructions earlier in this chapter, concerning your particular engine.*

Cylinder Head Reconditioning

Procedure	Method
Remove the cylinder head:	See the engine service procedures earlier in this chapter for details concerning specific engines.
Identify the valves:	Invert the cylinder head, and number the valve faces front to rear, using a permanent felt-tip marker.
Remove the rocker arms:	Remove the rocker arms with shaft(s) or balls and nuts. Wire the sets of rockers, balls and nuts together, and identify according to the corresponding valve.
Remove the valves and springs:	Using an appropriate valve spring compressor (depending on the configuration of the cylinder head), compress the valve springs. Lift out the keepers with needlenose pliers, release the compressor, and remove the valve, spring, and spring retainer. See the engine service procedures earlier in this chapter for details concerning specific engines.
Check the valve stem-to-guide clearance: Check the valve stem-to-guide clearance	Clean the valve stem with lacquer thinner or a similar solvent to remove all gum and varnish. Clean the valve guides using solvent and an expanding wire-type valve guide cleaner. Mount a dial indicator so that the stem is at 90° to the valve stem, as close to the valve guide as possible. Move the valve off its seat, and measure the valve guide-to-stem clearance by rocking the stem back and forth to actuate the dial indicator. Measure the valve stems using a micrometer, and compare to specifications, to determine whether stem or guide wear is responsible for excessive clearance. NOTE: *Consult the Specifications tables earlier in this chapter.*

Cylinder Head Reconditioning

Procedure	Method
De-carbon the cylinder head and valves: 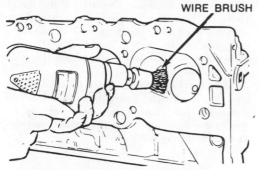 **Remove the carbon from the cylinder head with a wire brush and electric drill**	Chip carbon away from the valve heads, combustion chambers, and ports, using a chisel made of hardwood. Remove the remaining deposits with a stiff wire brush. NOTE: *Be sure that the deposits are actually removed, rather than burnished.*
Hot-tank the cylinder head (cast iron heads only): CAUTION: *Do not hot-tank aluminum parts.*	Have the cylinder head hot-tanked to remove grease, corrosion, and scale from the water passages. NOTE: *In the case of overhead cam cylinder heads, consult the operator to determine whether the camshaft bearings will be damaged by the caustic solution.*
Degrease the remaining cylinder head parts:	Clean the remaining cylinder head parts in an engine cleaning solvent. Do not remove the protective coating from the springs.
Check the cylinder head for warpage: 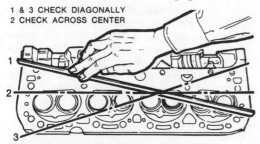 **Check the cylinder head for warpage**	Place a straight-edge across the gasket surface of the cylinder head. Using feeler gauges, determine the clearance at the center of the straight-edge. If warpage exceeds .003″ in a 6″ span, or .006″ over the total length, the cylinder head must be resurfaced. NOTE: *If warpage exceeds the manufacturer's maximum tolerance for material removal, the cylinder head must be replaced.* When milling the cylinder heads of V-type engines, the intake manifold mounting position is altered, and must be corrected by milling the manifold flange a proportionate amount.
*Knurl the valve guides: 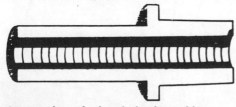 **Cut-away view of a knurled valve guide**	*Valve guides which are not excessively worn or distorted may, in some cases, be knurled rather than replaced. Knurling is a process in which metal is displaced and raised, thereby reducing clearance. Knurling also provides excellent oil control. The possibility of knurling rather than replacing valve guides should be discussed with a machinist.
Replace the valve guides: NOTE: *Valve guides should only be replaced if damaged or if an oversize valve stem is not available.*	See the engine service procedures earlier in this chapter for details concerning specific engines. Depending on the type of cylinder head, valve guides may be pressed, hammered, or shrunk in. In cases where the guides are shrunk into the head, replacement should be left to an equipped machine shop. In other

In the warpage illustration:
1 & 3 CHECK DIAGONALLY
2 CHECK ACROSS CENTER

In the de-carbon illustration: WIRE BRUSH

Cylinder Head Reconditioning

Procedure	Method

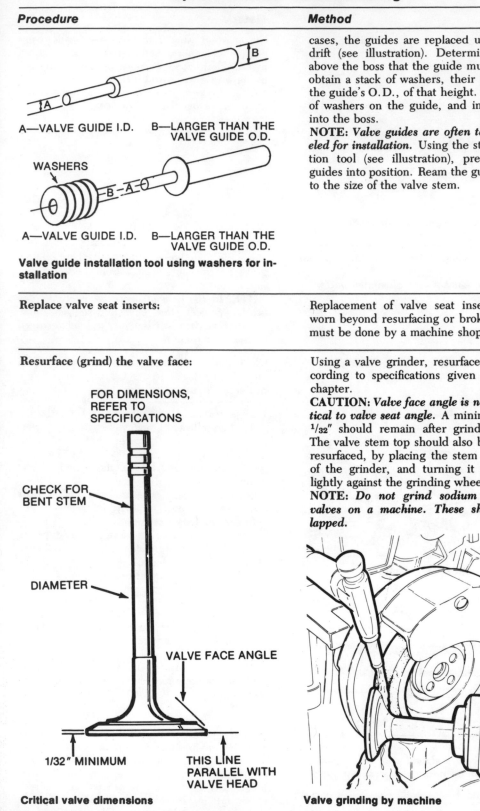

A—VALVE GUIDE I.D.   B—LARGER THAN THE VALVE GUIDE O.D.

WASHERS

A—VALVE GUIDE I.D.   B—LARGER THAN THE VALVE GUIDE O.D.

Valve guide installation tool using washers for installation

cases, the guides are replaced using a stepped drift (see illustration). Determine the height above the boss that the guide must extend, and obtain a stack of washers, their I.D. similar to the guide's O.D., of that height. Place the stack of washers on the guide, and insert the guide into the boss.

NOTE: *Valve guides are often tapered or beveled for installation.* Using the stepped installation tool (see illustration), press or tap the guides into position. Ream the guides according to the size of the valve stem.

Replace valve seat inserts:

Replacement of valve seat inserts which are worn beyond resurfacing or broken, if feasible, must be done by a machine shop.

Resurface (grind) the valve face:

FOR DIMENSIONS, REFER TO SPECIFICATIONS

CHECK FOR BENT STEM

DIAMETER

VALVE FACE ANGLE

1/32" MINIMUM

THIS LINE PARALLEL WITH VALVE HEAD

Critical valve dimensions

Using a valve grinder, resurface the valves according to specifications given earlier in this chapter.

CAUTION: *Valve face angle is not always identical to valve seat angle.* A minimum margin of $1/32''$ should remain after grinding the valve. The valve stem top should also be squared and resurfaced, by placing the stem in the V-block of the grinder, and turning it while pressing lightly against the grinding wheel.

NOTE: *Do not grind sodium filled exhaust valves on a machine. These should be hand lapped.*

Valve grinding by machine

Cylinder Head Reconditioning

Procedure	Method
Resurface the valve seats using reamers of grinder: 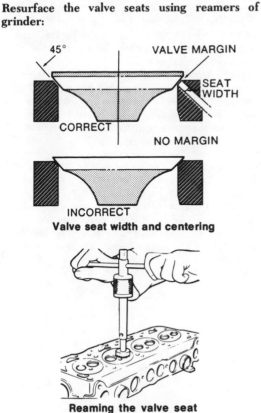 **Valve seat width and centering**	Select a reamer of the correct seat angle, slightly larger than the diameter of the valve seat, and assemble it with a pilot of the correct size. Install the pilot into the valve guide, and using steady pressure, turn the reamer clockwise. **CAUTION:** *Do not turn the reamer counterclockwise.* Remove only as much material as necessary to clean the seat. Check the concentricity of the seat (following). If the dye method is not used, coat the valve face with Prussian blue dye, install and rotate it on the valve seat. Using the dye marked area as a centering guide, center and narrow the valve seat to specifications with correction cutters. **NOTE:** *When no specifications are available, minimum seat width for exhaust valves should be $5/64''$, intake valves $1/16''$.* After making correction cuts, check the position of the valve seat on the valve face using Prussian blue dye.
Reaming the valve seat with a hand reamer	To resurface the seat with a power grinder, select a pilot of the correct size and coarse stone of the proper angle. Lubricate the pilot and move the stone on and off the valve seat at 2 cycles per second, until all flaws are gone. Finish the seat with a fine stone. If necessary the seat can be corrected or narrowed using correction stones.
Check the valve seat concentricity:  **Check the valve seat concentricity with a dial gauge**	Coat the valve face with Prussian blue dye, install the valve, and rotate it on the valve seat. If the entire seat becomes coated, and the valve is known to be concentric, the seat is concentric. *Install the dial gauge pilot into the guide, and rest of the arm on the valve seat. Zero the gauge, and rotate the arm around the seat. Run-out should not exceed .002".

Cylinder Head Reconditioning

Procedure	Method

*Lap the valves:
NOTE: *Valve lapping is done to ensure efficient sealing of resurfaced valves and seats.*

Invert the cylinder head, lightly lubricate the valve stems, and install the valves in the head as numbered. Coat valve seats with fine grinding compound, and attach the lapping tool suction cup to a valve head.
NOTE: *Moisten the suction cup.* Rotate the tool between the palms, changing position and lifting the tool often to prevent grooving. Lap the valve until a smooth, polished seat is evident. Remove the valve and tool, and rinse away all traces of grinding compound.

** Fasten a suction cup to a piece of drill rod, and mount the rod in a hand drill. Proceed as above, using the hand drill as a lapping tool.
CAUTION: *Due to the higher speeds involved when using the hand drill, care must be exercised to avoid grooving the seat.* Lift the tool and change direction of rotation often.

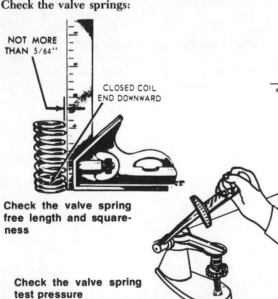

Lapping the valves by hand

HAND DRILL

ROD

SUCTION CUP

Home-made valve lapping tool

Check the valve springs:

NOT MORE THAN 5/64"

CLOSED COIL END DOWNWARD

Check the valve spring free length and squareness

Check the valve spring test pressure

Place the spring on a flat surface next to a square. Measure the height of the spring, and rotate it against the edge of the square to measure distortion. If spring height varies (by comparison) by more than $1/16''$ or if distortion exceeds $1/16''$, replace the spring.

** In addition to evaluating the spring as above, test the spring pressure at the installed and compressed (installed height minus valve lift) height using a valve spring tester. Springs used on small displacement engines (up to 3 liters) should be ∓ 1 lb of all other springs in either position. A tolerance of ∓ 5 lbs is permissible on larger engines.

Cylinder Head Reconditioning

Procedure	Method

*Install valve stem seals:

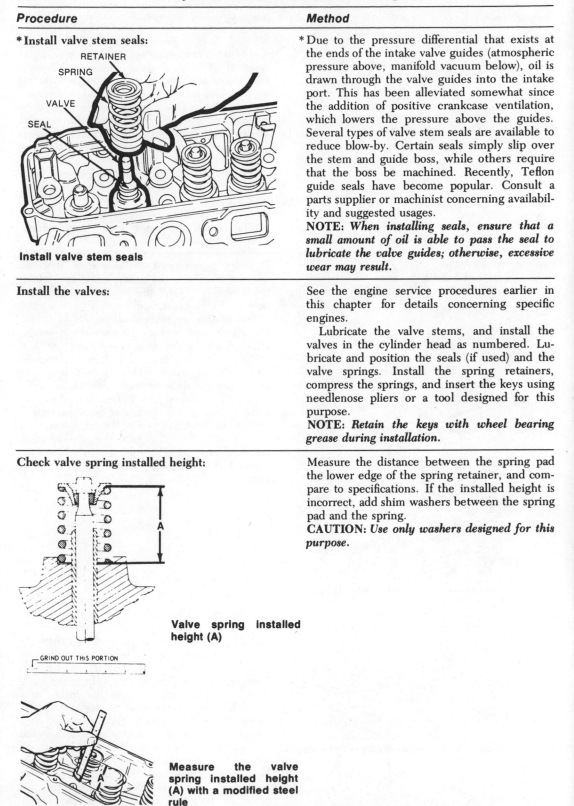

RETAINER

SPRING

VALVE

SEAL

Install valve stem seals

* Due to the pressure differential that exists at the ends of the intake valve guides (atmospheric pressure above, manifold vacuum below), oil is drawn through the valve guides into the intake port. This has been alleviated somewhat since the addition of positive crankcase ventilation, which lowers the pressure above the guides. Several types of valve stem seals are available to reduce blow-by. Certain seals simply slip over the stem and guide boss, while others require that the boss be machined. Recently, Teflon guide seals have become popular. Consult a parts supplier or machinist concerning availability and suggested usages.

NOTE: *When installing seals, ensure that a small amount of oil is able to pass the seal to lubricate the valve guides; otherwise, excessive wear may result.*

Install the valves:

See the engine service procedures earlier in this chapter for details concerning specific engines.

Lubricate the valve stems, and install the valves in the cylinder head as numbered. Lubricate and position the seals (if used) and the valve springs. Install the spring retainers, compress the springs, and insert the keys using needlenose pliers or a tool designed for this purpose.

NOTE: *Retain the keys with wheel bearing grease during installation.*

Check valve spring installed height:

A

Valve spring installed height (A)

GRIND OUT THIS PORTION

Measure the valve spring installed height (A) with a modified steel rule

Measure the distance between the spring pad the lower edge of the spring retainer, and compare to specifications. If the installed height is incorrect, add shim washers between the spring pad and the spring.

CAUTION: *Use only washers designed for this purpose.*

Cylinder Head Reconditioning

Procedure	Method
Inspect the rocker arms, balls, studs, and nuts: **Stress cracks in the rocker nuts**	Visually inspect the rocker arms, balls, studs, and nuts for cracks, galling, burning, scoring, or wear. If all parts are intact, liberally lubricate the rocker arms and balls, and install them on the cylinder head. If wear is noted on a rocker arm at the point of valve contact, grind it smooth and square, removing as little material as possible. Replace the rocker arm if excessively worn. If a rocker stud shows signs of wear, it must be replaced (see below). If a rocker nut shows stress cracks, replace it. If an exhaust ball is galled or burned, substitute the intake ball from the same cylinder (if it is intact), and install a new intake ball. **NOTE:** *Avoid using new rocker balls on exhaust valves.*
Replace rocker studs: **Extracting a pressed-in rocker stud** **Ream the stud bore for oversize rocker studs**	In order to remove a threaded stud, lock two nuts on the stud, and unscrew the stud using the lower nut. Coat the lower threads of the new stud with Loctite, and install. Two alternative methods are available for replacing pressed in studs. Remove the damaged stud using a stack of washers and a nut (see illustration). In the first, the boss is reamed .005–.006″ oversize, and an oversize stud pressed in. Control the stud extension over the boss using washers, in the same manner as valve guides. Before installing the stud, coat it with white lead and grease. To retain the stud more positively drill a hole through the stud and boss, and install a roll pin. In the second method, the boss is tapped, and a threaded stud installed.
Inspect the rocker shaft(s) and rocker arms: **Check the rocker arm-to-rocker shaft contact area**	Remove the rocker arms, springs and washers from rocker shaft. **NOTE:** *Lay out parts in the order as they are removed.* Inspect rocker arms for pitting or wear on the ,valve contact point, or excessive bushing wear. Bushings need only be replaced if wear is excessive, because the rocker arm normally contacts the shaft at one point only. Grind the valve contact point of rocker arm smooth if necessary, removing as little material as possible. If excessive material must be removed to smooth and square the arm, it should be replaced. Clean out all oil holes and passages in rocker shaft. If shaft is grooved or worn, replace it. Lubricate and assemble the rocker shaft.

Cylinder Head Reconditioning

Procedure	Method
Inspect the pushrods:	Remove the pushrods, and, if hollow, clean out the oil passages using fine wire. Roll each pushrod over a piece of clean glass. If a distinct clicking sound is heard as the pushrod rolls, the rod is bent, and must be replaced.
	*The length of all pushrods must be equal. Measure the length of the pushrods, compare to specifications, and replace as necessary.
*Inspect the valve lifters: CHECK FOR CONCAVE WEAR ON FACE OF TAPPET USING TAPPET FOR STRAIGHT EDGE **Check the lifter face for squareness**	Remove lifters from their bores, and remove gum and varnish, using solvent. Clean walls of lifter bores. Check lifters for concave wear as illustrated. If face is worn concave, replace lifter, and carefully inspect the camshaft. Lightly lubricate lifter and insert it into its bore. If play is excessive, an oversize lifter must be installed (where possible). Consult a machinist concerning feasibility. If play is satisfactory, remove, lubricate, and reinstall the lifter.
*Testing hydraulic lifter leak down:	Submerge lifter in a container of kerosene. Chuck a used pushrod or its equivalent into a drill press. Position container of kerosene so pushrod acts on the lifter plunger. Pump lifter with the drill press, until resistance increases. Pump several more times to bleed any air out of lifter. Apply very firm, constant pressure to the lifter, and observe rate at which fluid bleeds out of lifter. If the fluid bleeds very quickly (less than 15 seconds), lifter is defective. If the time exceeds 60 seconds, lifter is sticking. In either case, recondition or replace lifter. If lifter is operating properly (leak down time 15–60 seconds), lubricate and install it.

Cylinder Block Reconditioning

Procedure	Method
Checking the main bearing clearance: PLASTIGAGE® **Plastigage® installed on the lower bearing shell**	Invert engine, and remove cap from the bearing to be checked. Using a clean, dry rag, thoroughly clean all oil from crankshaft journal and bearing insert. NOTE: *Plastigage® is soluble in oil; therefore, oil on the journal or bearing could result in erroneous readings.* Place a piece of Plastigage along the full length of journal, reinstall cap, and torque to specifications. NOTE: Specifications are given in the engine specifications earlier in this chapter. Remove bearing cap, and determine bearing clearance by comparing width of Plastigage to the scale on Plastigage envelope. Journal taper is determined by comparing width of the Plas-

Cylinder Block Reconditioning

Procedure	Method

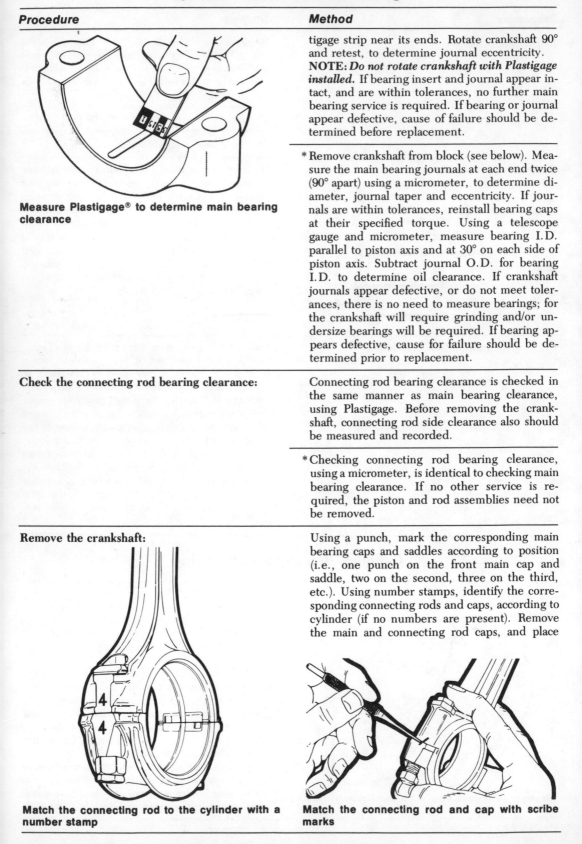

tigage strip near its ends. Rotate crankshaft 90° and retest, to determine journal eccentricity. **NOTE:** *Do not rotate crankshaft with Plastigage installed.* If bearing insert and journal appear intact, and are within tolerances, no further main bearing service is required. If bearing or journal appear defective, cause of failure should be determined before replacement.

Measure Plastigage® to determine main bearing clearance

* Remove crankshaft from block (see below). Measure the main bearing journals at each end twice (90° apart) using a micrometer, to determine diameter, journal taper and eccentricity. If journals are within tolerances, reinstall bearing caps at their specified torque. Using a telescope gauge and micrometer, measure bearing I.D. parallel to piston axis and at 30° on each side of piston axis. Subtract journal O.D. for bearing I.D. to determine oil clearance. If crankshaft journals appear defective, or do not meet tolerances, there is no need to measure bearings; for the crankshaft will require grinding and/or undersize bearings will be required. If bearing appears defective, cause for failure should be determined prior to replacement.

Check the connecting rod bearing clearance:

Connecting rod bearing clearance is checked in the same manner as main bearing clearance, using Plastigage. Before removing the crankshaft, connecting rod side clearance also should be measured and recorded.

* Checking connecting rod bearing clearance, using a micrometer, is identical to checking main bearing clearance. If no other service is required, the piston and rod assemblies need not be removed.

Remove the crankshaft:

Using a punch, mark the corresponding main bearing caps and saddles according to position (i.e., one punch on the front main cap and saddle, two on the second, three on the third, etc.). Using number stamps, identify the corresponding connecting rods and caps, according to cylinder (if no numbers are present). Remove the main and connecting rod caps, and place

Match the connecting rod to the cylinder with a number stamp

Match the connecting rod and cap with scribe marks

Cylinder Block Reconditioning

Procedure	Method
	sleeves of plastic tubing or vacuum hose over the connecting rod bolts, to protect the journals as the crankshaft is removed. Lift the crankshaft out of the block.
Remove the ridge from the top of the cylinder: 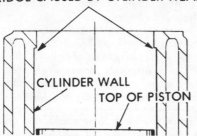 RIDGE CAUSED BY CYLINDER WEAR CYLINDER WALL TOP OF PISTON **Cylinder bore ridge**	In order to facilitate removal of the piston and connecting rod, the ridge at the top of the cylinder (unworn area; see illustration) must be removed. Place the piston at the bottom of the bore, and cover it with a rag. Cut the ridge away using a ridge reamer, exercising extreme care to avoid cutting too deeply. Remove the rag, and remove cuttings that remain on the piston. **CAUTION:** *If the ridge is not removed, and new rings are installed, damage to rings will result.*
Remove the piston and connecting rod: 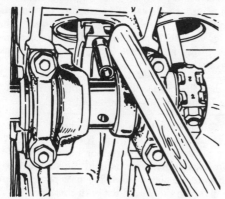 **Push the piston out with a hammer handle**	Invert the engine, and push the pistons and connecting rods out of the cylinders. If necessary, tap the connecting rod boss with a wooden hammer handle, to force the piston out. **CAUTION:** *Do not attempt to force the piston past the cylinder ridge* (see above).
Service the crankshaft:	Ensure that all oil holes and passages in the crankshaft are open and free of sludge. If necessary, have the crankshaft ground to the largest possible undersize.
	** Have the crankshaft Magnafluxed, to locate stress cracks. Consult a machinist concerning additional service procedures, such as surface hardening (e.g., nitriding, Tuftriding) to improve wear characteristics, cross drilling and chamfering the oil holes to improve lubrication, and balancing.
Removing freeze plugs:	Drill a small hole in the middle of the freeze plugs. Thread a large sheet metal screw into the hole and remove the plug with a slide hammer.
Remove the oil gallery plugs:	Threaded plugs should be removed using an appropriate (usually square) wrench. To remove soft, pressed in plugs, drill a hole in the plug, and thread in a sheet metal screw. Pull the plug out by the screw using pliers.

Cylinder Block Reconditioning

Procedure	Method
Hot-tank the block: NOTE: *Do not hot-tank aluminum parts.*	Have the block hot-tanked to remove grease, corrosion, and scale from the water jackets. NOTE: *Consult the operator to determine whether the camshaft bearings will be damaged during the hot-tank process.*
Check the block for cracks:	Visually inspect the block for cracks or chips. The most common locations are as follows: Adjacent to freeze plugs. Between the cylinders and water jackets. Adjacent to the main bearing saddles. At the extreme bottom of the cylinders. Check only suspected cracks using spot check dye (see introduction). If a crack is located, consult a machinist concerning possible repairs.
	** Magnaflux the block to locate hidden cracks. If cracks are located, consult a machinist about feasibility of repair.
Install the oil gallery plugs and freeze plugs:	Coat freeze plugs with sealer and tap into position using a piece of pipe, slightly smaller than the plug, as a driver. To ensure retention, stake the edges of the plugs. Coat threaded oil gallery plugs with sealer and install. Drive replacement soft plugs into block using a large drift as a driver.
	* Rather than reinstalling lead plugs, drill and tap the holes, and install threaded plugs.
Check the bore diameter and surface:	Visually inspect the cylinder bores for roughness, scoring, or scuffing. If evident, the cylinder bore must be bored or honed oversize to eliminate imperfections, and the smallest possible oversize piston used. The new pistons should be given to the machinist with the block, so that the cylinders can be bored or honed exactly to the piston size (plus clearance). If no flaws are evident, measure the bore diameter using a telescope gauge and micrometer, or dial gauge, parallel and perpendicular to the engine centerline, at the top (below the ridge) and bottom of the bore. Subtract the bottom measurements from the top to determine taper, and the parallel to

Measure the cylinder bore with a dial gauge

A—AT RIGHT ANGLE TO CENTERLINE OF ENGINE
B—PARALLEL TO CENTERLINE OF ENGINE

Cylinder bore measuring points

TELESCOPE GAUGE 90° FROM PISTON PIN

Measure the cylinder bore with a telescope gauge

TELESCOPE GAUGE

MICROMETER

Measure the telescope gauge with a micrometer to determine the cylinder bore

Cylinder Block Reconditioning

Procedure	Method
	the centerline measurements from the perpendicular measurements to determine eccentricity. If the measurements are not within specifications, the cylinder must be bored or honed, and an oversize piston installed. If the measurements are within specifications the cylinder may be used as is, with only finish honing (see below). NOTE: *Prior to submitting the block for boring, perform the following operation(s).*
Check the cylinder block bearing alignment: **Check the main bearing saddle alignment**	Remove the upper bearing inserts. Place a straightedge in the bearing saddles along the centerline of the crankshaft. If clearance exists between the straightedge and the center saddle, the block must be alignbored.
*Check the deck height:	The deck height is the distance from the crankshaft centerline to the block deck. To measure, invert the engine, and install the crankshaft, retaining it with the center main cap. Measure the distance from the crankshaft journal to the block deck, parallel to the cylinder centerline. Measure the diameter of the end (front and rear) main journals, parallel to the centerline of the cylinders, divide the diameter in half, and subtract it from the previous measurement. The results of the front and rear measurements should be identical. If the difference exceeds .005″, the deck height should be corrected. NOTE: *Block deck height and warpage should be corrected at the same time.*
Check the block deck for warpage:	Using a straightedge and feeler gauges, check the block deck for warpage in the same manner that the cylinder head is checked (see Cylinder Head Reconditioning). If warpage exceeds specifications, have the deck resurfaced. NOTE: *In certain cases a specification for total material removal (cylinder head and block deck) is provided. This specification must not be exceeded.*
Clean and inspect the pistons and connecting rods: RING EXPANDER **Remove the piston rings**	Using a ring expander, remove the rings from the piston. Remove the retaining rings (if so equipped) and remove piston pin. NOTE: *If the piston pin must be pressed out, determine the proper method and use the proper tools; otherwise the piston will distort.* Clean the ring grooves using an appropriate tool, exercising care to avoid cutting too deeply. Thoroughly clean all carbon and varnish from the piston with solvent. CAUTION: *Do not use a wire brush or caustic solvent on pistons.* Inspect the pistons for scuffing, scoring, cracks, pitting, or excessive ring

Cylinder Block Reconditioning

Procedure	Method

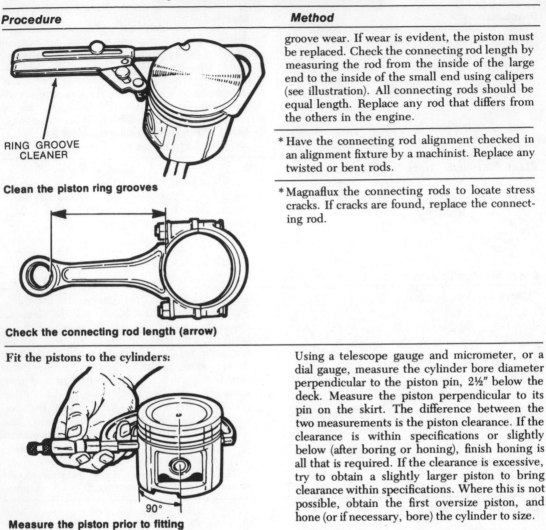

RING GROOVE
CLEANER

Clean the piston ring grooves

Check the connecting rod length (arrow)

groove wear. If wear is evident, the piston must be replaced. Check the connecting rod length by measuring the rod from the inside of the large end to the inside of the small end using calipers (see illustration). All connecting rods should be equal length. Replace any rod that differs from the others in the engine.

* Have the connecting rod alignment checked in an alignment fixture by a machinist. Replace any twisted or bent rods.

* Magnaflux the connecting rods to locate stress cracks. If cracks are found, replace the connecting rod.

Fit the pistons to the cylinders:

90°

Measure the piston prior to fitting

Using a telescope gauge and micrometer, or a dial gauge, measure the cylinder bore diameter perpendicular to the piston pin, 2½" below the deck. Measure the piston perpendicular to its pin on the skirt. The difference between the two measurements is the piston clearance. If the clearance is within specifications or slightly below (after boring or honing), finish honing is all that is required. If the clearance is excessive, try to obtain a slightly larger piston to bring clearance within specifications. Where this is not possible, obtain the first oversize piston, and hone (or if necessary, bore) the cylinder to size.

Assemble the pistons and connecting rods:

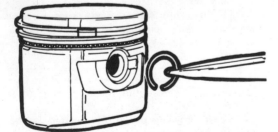

Install the piston pin lock-rings (if used)

Inspect piston pin, connecting rod small end bushing, and piston bore for galling, scoring, or excessive wear. If evident, replace defective part(s). Measure the I.D. of the piston boss and connecting rod small end, and the O.D. of the piston pin. If within specifications, assemble piston pin and rod.
CAUTION: *If piston pin must be pressed in, determine the proper method and use the proper tools; otherwise the piston will distort.*
    Install the lock rings; ensure that they seat properly. If the parts are not within specifications, determine the service method for the type of engine. In some cases, piston and pin are serviced as an assembly when either is defective. Others specify reaming the piston and connecting rods for an oversize pin. If the connecting rod bushing is worn, it may in many cases be replaced. Reaming the piston and replacing the rod bushing are machine shop operations.

Cylinder Block Reconditioning

Procedure	Method

Clean and inspect the camshaft:

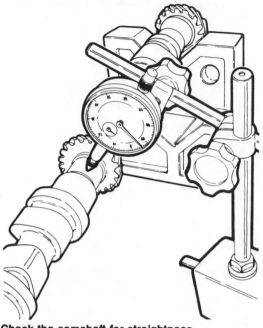

Check the camshaft for straightness

Degrease the camshaft, using solvent, and clean out all oil holes. Visually inspect cam lobes and bearing journals for excessive wear. If a lobe is questionable, check all lobes as indicated below. If a journal or lobe is worn, the camshaft must be regrounded or replaced.
NOTE: *If a journal is worn, there is a good chance that the bushings are worn.* If lobes and journals appear intact, place the front and rear journals in V-blocks, and rest a dial indicator on the center journal. Rotate the camshaft to check straightness. If deviation exceeds .001″, replace the camshaft.

*Check the camshaft lobes with a micrometer, by measuring the lobes from the nose to base and again at 90° (see illustration). The lift is determined by subtracting the second measurement from the first. If all exhaust lobes and all intake lobes are not identical, the camshaft must be reground or replaced.

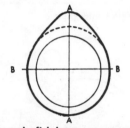

Camshaft lobe measurement

Replace the camshaft bearings:

EXPANDING COLLET
THRUST BEARING   EXPANDING MANDREL   BACK-UP NUT
PULLING NUT
PULLER SCREW
PULLING PLATE   PULLER SCREW   CAMSHAFT BEARING
EXTENSION   (LOOSE)

Camshaft bearing removal and installation tool (OHV engines only)

If excessive wear is indicated, or if the engine is being completely rebuilt, camshaft bearings should be replaced as follows: Drive the camshaft rear plug from the block. Assemble the removal puller with its shoulder on the bearing to be removed. Gradually tighten the puller nut until bearing is removed. Remove remaining bearings, leaving the front and rear for last. To remove front and rear bearings, reverse position of the tool, so as to pull the bearings in toward the center of the block. Leave the tool in this position, pilot the new front and rear bearings on the installer, and pull them into position: Return the tool to its original position and pull remaining bearings into position.
NOTE: *Ensure that oil holes align when installing bearings.* Replace camshaft rear plug, and stake it into position to aid retention.

Finish hone the cylinders:

Chuck a flexible drive hone into a power drill, and insert it into the cylinder. Start the hone, and remove it up and down in the cylinder at a rate which will produce approximately a 60° cross-hatch pattern.
NOTE: *Do not extend the hone below the cylinder bore.* After developing the pattern, remove

Cylinder Block Reconditioning

Procedure	Method

CROSS HATCH PATTERN

50°-60°

Cylinder bore after honing

the hone and recheck piston fit. Wash the cylinders with a detergent and water solution to remove abrasive dust, dry, and wipe several times with a rag soaked in engine oil.

Check piston ring end-gap:

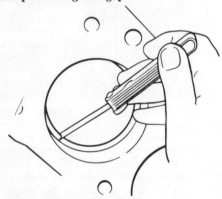

Check the piston ring end gap

Compress the piston rings to be used in a cylinder, one at a time, into that cylinder, and press them approximately 1″ below the deck with an inverted piston. Using feeler gauges, measure the ring end-gap, and compare to specifications. Pull the ring out of the cylinder and file the ends with a fine file to obtain proper clearance.
CAUTION: *If inadequate ring end-gap is utilized, ring breakage will result.*

Install the piston rings:

PISTON RING

FEELER GAUGE

RING GROOVE

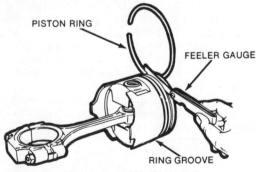

Check the piston ring side clearance

Inspect the ring grooves in the piston for excessive wear or taper. If necessary, recut the groove(s) for use with an overwidth ring or a standard ring and spacer. If the groove is worn uniformly, overwidth rings, or standard rings and spacers may be installed without recutting. Roll the outside of the ring around the groove to check for burrs or deposits. If any are found, remove with a fine file. Hold the ring in the groove, and measure side clearance. If necessary, correct as indicated above.
NOTE: *Always install any additional spacers above the piston ring.*
The ring groove must be deep enough to allow the ring to seat below the lands (see illustration). In many cases, a "go-no-go" depth gauge will be provided with the piston rings. Shallow grooves may be corrected by recutting, while deep grooves require some type of filler or expander

Cylinder Block Reconditioning

Procedure	Method
	behind the piston. Consult the piston ring supplier concerning the suggested method. Install the rings on the piston, lowest ring first, using a ring expander. NOTE: *Position the rings as specified by the manufacturer.* Consult the engine service procedures earlier in this chapter for details concerning specific engines.
Install the camshaft:	Liberally lubricate the camshaft lobes and journals, and install the camshaft. CAUTION: *Exercise extreme care to avoid damaging the bearings when inserting the camshaft.* Install and tighten the camshaft thrust plate retaining bolts.
	See the engine service procedures earlier in this chapter for details concerning specific engines.
Check camshaft end-play (OHV engines only): **Check the camshaft end-play with a feeler gauge** DIAL INDICATOR CAMSHAFT **Check the camshaft end-play with a dial indicator**	Using feeler gauges, determine whether the clearance between the camshaft boss (or gear) and backing plate is within specifications. Install shims behind the thrust plate, or reposition the camshaft gear and retest endplay. In some cases, adjustment is by replacing the thrust plate. See the engine service procedures earlier in this chapter for details concerning specific engines. *Mount a dial indicator stand so that the stem of the dial indicator rests on the nose of the camshaft, parallel to the camshaft axis. Push the camshaft as far in as possible and zero the gauge. Move the camshaft outward to determine the amount of camshaft endplay. If the endplay is not within tolerance, install shims behind the thrust plate, or reposition the camshaft gear and retest. See the engine service procedures earlier in this chapter for details concerning specific engines.
Install the rear main seal:	See the engine service procedures earlier in this chapter for details concerning specific engines.
Install the crankshaft: INSTALLING BEARING SHELL REMOVING BEARING SHELL **Remove or install the upper bearing insert using a roll-out pin**	Thoroughly clean the main bearing saddles and caps. Place the upper halves of the bearing inserts on the saddles and press into position. NOTE: *Ensure that the oil holes align.* Press the corresponding bearing inserts into the main bearing caps. Lubricate the upper main bearings, and lay the crankshaft in position. Place a strip of Plastigage on each of the crankshaft journals, install the main caps, and torque to specifications. Remove the main caps, and compare the Plastigage to the scale on the Plastigage envelope. If clearances are within tolerances, remove the Plastigage, turn the crankshaft 90°, wipe off all oil and retest. If all clearances are correct,

Cylinder Block Reconditioning

Procedure	Method

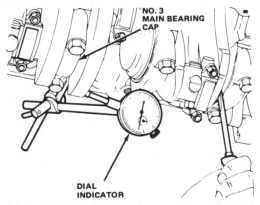

Home-made bearing roll-out pin

remove all Plastigage, thoroughly lubricate the main caps and bearing journals, and install the main caps. If clearances are not within tolerance, the upper bearing inserts may be removed, without removing the crankshaft, using a bearing roll out pin (see illustration). Roll in a bearing that will provide proper clearance, and retest. Torque all main caps, excluding the thrust bearing cap, to specifications. Tighten the thrust bearing cap finger tight. To properly align the thrust bearing, pry the crankshaft the extent of its axial travel several times, the last movement held toward the front of the engine, and torque the thrust bearing cap to specifications. Determine the crankshaft end-play (see below), and bring within tolerance with thrust washers.

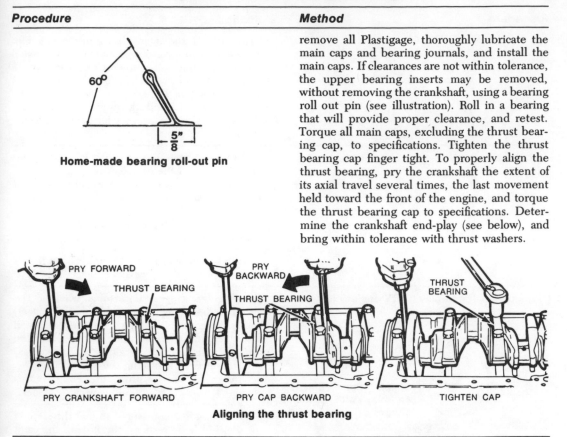

Aligning the thrust bearing

Measure crankshaft end-play:

Mount a dial indicator stand on the front of the block, with the dial indicator stem resting on the nose of the crankshaft, parallel to the crankshaft axis. Pry the crankshaft the extent of its travel rearward, and zero the indicator. Pry the crankshaft forward and record crankshaft end-play.
NOTE: *Crankshaft end-play also may be measured at the thrust bearing, using feeler gauges (see illustration).*

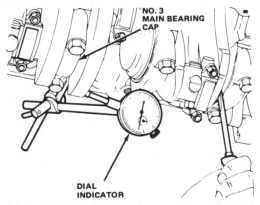

Check the crankshaft end-play with a dial indicator

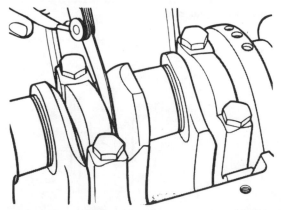

Check the crankshaft end-play with a feeler gauge

Cylinder Block Reconditioning

Procedure	Method
Install the pistons:	Press the upper connecting rod bearing halves into the connecting rods, and the lower halves into the connecting rod caps. Position the piston ring gaps according to specifications (see car section), and lubricate the pistons. Install a ring compresser on a piston, and press two long (8″) pieces of plastic tubing over the rod bolts. Using the tubes as a guide, press the pistons into the bores and onto the crankshaft with a wooden hammer handle. After seating the rod on the crankshaft journal, remove the tubes and install the cap finger tight. Install the remaining pistons in the same manner. Invert the engine and check the bearing clearance at two points (90° apart) on each journal with Plastigage.

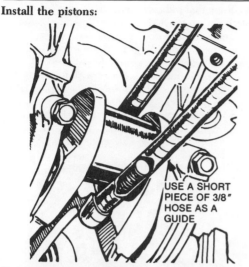

USE A SHORT PIECE OF 3/8″ HOSE AS A GUIDE

Use lengths of vacuum hose or rubber tubing to protect the crankshaft journals and cylinder walls during piston installation

NOTE: *Do not turn the crankshaft with Plastigage installed.* If clearance is within tolerances, remove *all* Plastigage, thoroughly lubricate the journals, and torque the rod caps to specifications. If clearance is not within specifications, install different thickness bearing inserts and recheck.

CAUTION: *Never shim or file the connecting rods or caps.* Always install plastic tube sleeves over the rod bolts when the caps are not installed, to protect the crankshaft journals.

RING COMPRESSOR

Install the piston using a ring compressor

| Check connecting rod side clearance: | Determine the clearance between the sides of the connecting rods and the crankshaft using feeler gauges. If clearance is below the minimum tolerance, the rod may be machined to provide adequate clearance. If clearance is excessive, substitute an unworn rod, and recheck. If clearance is still outside specifications, the crankshaft must be welded and reground, or replaced. |

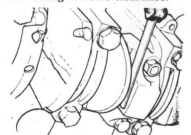

Check the connecting rod side clearance with a feeler gauge

| Inspect the timing chain (or belt): | Visually inspect the timing chain for broken or loose links, and replace the chain if any are found. If the chain will flex sideways, it must be replaced. Install the timing chain as specified. Be sure the timing belt is not stretched, frayed or broken.
NOTE: *If the original timing chain is to be reused, install it in its original position.* |

Cylinder Block Reconditioning

Procedure	*Method*
Check timing gear backlash and runout (OHV engines):	Mount a dial indicator with its stem resting on a tooth of the camshaft gear (as illustrated). Rotate the gear until all slack is removed, and zero the indicator. Rotate the gear in the opposite direction until slack is removed, and record gear backlash. Mount the indicator with its stem resting on the edge of the camshaft gear, parallel to the axis of the camshaft. Zero the indicator, and turn the camshaft gear one full turn, recording the runout. If either backlash or runout exceed specifications, replace the worn gear(s).

Check the camshaft gear backlash

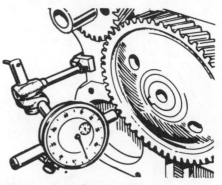

Check the camshaft gear run-out

Completing the Rebuilding Process

Follow the above procedures, complete the rebuilding process as follows:

Fill the oil pump with oil, to prevent cavitating (sucking air) on initial engine start up. Install the oil pump and the pickup tube on the engine. Coat the oil pan gasket as necessary, and install the gasket and the oil pan. Mount the flywheel and the crankshaft vibration damper or pulley on the crankshaft. NOTE: *Always use new bolts when installing the flywheel.* Inspect the clutch shaft pilot bushing in the crankshaft. If the bushing is excessively worn, remove it with an expanding puller and a slide hammer, and tap a new bushing into place.

Position the engine, cylinder head side up. Lubricate the lifters, and install them into their bores. Install the cylinder head, and torque it as specified. Insert the pushrods and install the rocker shaft(s) or position the rocker arms on the pushrods. Adjust the valves.

Install the intake and exhaust manifolds, the carburetor(s), the distributor and spark plugs. Adjust the point gap and the static ignition timing. Mount all accessories and install the engine in the car. Fill the radiator with coolant, and the crankcase with high quality engine oil.

Break-in Procedure

Start the engine, and allow it to run at low speed for a few minutes, while checking for leaks. Stop the engine, check the oil level, and fill as necessary. Restart the engine, and fill the cooling system to capacity. Check the point dwell angle and adjust the ignition timing and the valves. Run the engine at low to medium speed (800–2500 rpm) for approximately ½ hour, and retorque the cylinder head bolts. Road test the car, and check again for leaks.

Follow the manufacturer's recommended engine break-in procedure and maintenance schedule for new engines.

4

Emission Controls and Fuel System

EMISSION CONTROLS

There are three sources of automotive pollutants: crankcase fumes, exhaust gases, and gasoline evaporation. The pollutants formed from these substances fall into three categories: unburnt hydrocarbons (HC), carbon monoxide (CO), and oxides of nitrogen (NO_x). The equipment that is used to limit these pollutants is commonly called emission control equipment.

Crankcase Emission Controls

POSITIVE CRANKCASE VENTILATION SYSTEM

All X-Body cars are equipped with a positive crankcase ventilation (PCV) system to control crankcase blow-by vapors. The system functions as follows:

When the engine is running, a small portion of the gases which are formed in the combustion chamber leak by the piston rings and enter the crankcase. Since these gases are under pressure, they tend to escape from the crankcase and enter the atmosphere. If these gases are allowed to remain in the crankcase for any period of time, they contaminate the engine oil and cause sludge to build up in the crankcase. If the gases are allowed to escape into the atmosphere, they pollute the air with unburned hydrocarbons. The job of the crankcase emission control equipment is to recycle these gases back into the engine combustion chamber where they are reburned.

The crankcase (blow-by) gases are recycled in the following way: as the engine is running, clean, filtered air is drawn through the air filter and into the crankcase. As the air passes through the crankcase, it picks up the combustion gases and carries them out of the crankcase, through the oil separator, through the PCV valve, and into the induction system. As they enter the intake manifold, they are drawn into the combustion chamber where they are reburned.

The most critical component in the system is the PCV valve. This valve controls the amount of gases which are recycled into the combustion chamber. At low engine speeds, the valve is partially closed, limiting the flow of the gases into the intake manifold. As engine speed increases, the valve opens to admit greater quantities of the gases into the intake manifold. If the valve should become blocked or plugged, the gases will be prevented from escaping from the crankcase by the normal route. Since these gases are under pressure, they will find their own way out of the crankcase. This alternate route is usually a weak oil seal or gasket in the

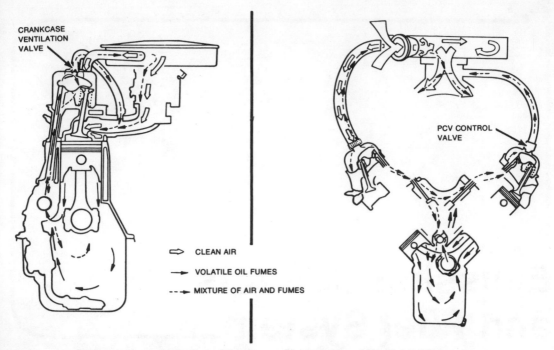

CRANKCASE
VENTILATION
VALVE

PCV CONTROL
VALVE

⇨ CLEAN AIR

→ VOLATILE OIL FUMES

--→ MIXTURE OF AIR AND FUMES

Cross-section schematics of the four cylinder (left) and V6 (right) PCV systems

engine. As the gas escapes by the gasket, it also creates an oil leak. Besides causing oil leaks, a clogged PCV valve also allows these gases to remain in the crankcase for an extended period of time, promoting the formation of sludge in the engine.

Service

Inspect the PCV system hose and connections at each tune-up and replace any deteriorated hoses. Check the PCV valve at every tune-up and replace it at 30,000 mile intervals. Replacement procedures are in Chapter One.

PCV FILTER REMOVAL AND INSTALLATION—FOUR CYLINDER ONLY

1. Slide the rubber coupling that joins the tube coming from the valve cover to the filter off from the filter nipple. Remove the air cleaner case lid. Slide the spring clamp off the filter, and remove the filter.

2. Inspect the rubber grommet in the valve cover and the rubber coupling for brittleness or cracking. Replace parts as necessary.

3. Insert the new PCV filter through the hole in the air cleaner case, with the open portion of the filter upward. Make sure the square portion of the filter behind the nipple

fits into the square hole in the air cleaner case.

4. Install a new spring clamp onto the nipple. Make sure that the clamp goes under the ridge on the filter nipple all the way around. Reconnect the rubber coupling and install the cover.

Evaporative Emission Control

This system, standard on all X-Body cars, reduces the amount of gasoline vapors escaping into the atmosphere. Float bowl emissions are controlled by internal carburetor modifications. Redesigned bowl vents, reduced bowl capacity, heat shields, and improved intake manifold-to-carburetor insulation reduce vapor loss. The venting of fuel tank vapors into the air has been stopped. Fuel vapors are directed through lines to a canister (located in the engine compartment) containing an activated charcoal filter. Unburned vapors are trapped here until the engine is started. When the engine is running, the canister is purged by air drawn in by manifold vacuum. The air and fuel vapors are directed into the engine to be burned.

Service

The only service required is the periodic replacement of the canister filter. This proce-

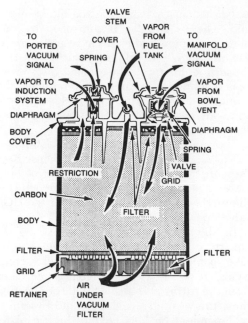

TO PORTED VACUUM SIGNAL

VALVE STEM

COVER

SPRING

VAPOR FROM FUEL TANK

TO MANIFOLD VACUUM SIGNAL

VAPOR TO INDUCTION SYSTEM

DIAPHRAGM

BODY COVER

VAPOR FROM BOWL VENT

DIAPHRAGM

SPRING

RESTRICTION

VALVE GRID

CARBON

FILTER

BODY

FILTER

FILTER

GRID

RETAINER

AIR UNDER VACUUM FILTER

Cross-sectional diagram of the charcoal canister

dure is covered in Chapter One. If the fuel tank cap on your X-car requires replacement, it must be of the same type as the original.

Exhaust Emission Control

Exhaust emission control systems constitute the largest body of emission control devices installed on your X-car. Included in this category are: Catalytic Converter, Early Fuel Evaporation system (EFE), Exhaust Gas Recirculation system (EGR), Thermostatic Air Cleaner (Theramac), Pulse Air Injection (Pulsair), Deceleration Valve, and the Computer Controlled Catalytic Converter system (C-4) used only on X-Body cars sold in California. A brief description of each system and applicable service procedures follows.

CATALYTIC CONVERTER

The catalytic converter, installed in all X-Body cars, is a muffler-shaped device installed in the exhaust system. The converter is a chamber containing beads of material (or, in the C-4 system, a honeycomb monolithic substrate) coated with either platinum and palladium (in the conventional system) or platinum and rhodium (in the C-4 system) which, through catalytic action, oxidize HC and CO into H_2O and CO_2. (In the C-4 system, the chemical reaction is actually an oxidation-reduction process, oxidizing HC and CO as described, and reducing NO_x to N_2 and O_2.)

There are no service procedures required for the catalytic converter, although the converter body should be inspected occasionally for damage.

Some X-Body cars with the V6 engine require a catalyst change at 30,000 mile intervals. The first such replacement is covered under an extended emissions warranty by General Motors, and is performed at no charge by your dealer. Subsequent bead replacement is the responsibility of the owner.

There are a few precautions to be observed in connection with the converter. When working under the car, be very careful not to touch the converter body if the engine is warm. Internal converter temperatures reach 1700° F; external temperatures can reach 1000° F when the exhaust system is hot.

Secondly, the converter requires the use of unleaded fuel. The use of leaded fuel in a catalyst-equipped car will quickly render the converter useless. The lead will also slowly plug the converter, increasing exhaust back pressure and reducing fuel economy. Eventually, the converter will become so blocked that the engine will not be able to run. Con-

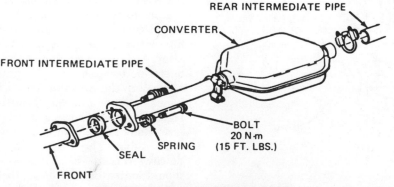

REAR INTERMEDIATE PIPE

CONVERTER

FRONT INTERMEDIATE PIPE

BOLT 20 N·m (15 FT. LBS.)

SPRING

SEAL

FRONT

Catalytic converter installation details

taminating the converter with leaded fuel also raises the emission content of the exhaust to illegal and environmentally unacceptable levels. If you are thinking of running your X-car on leaded fuel in order to take advantage of its relatively cheaper price, don't succumb to the temptation.

EARLY FUEL EVAPORATION

All V6 engines have this system to reduce engine warm-up time, improve driveability, and reduce emissions. On start-up, a vacuum motor acts to close a heat valve in the exhaust manifold which causes exhaust gases to enter the intake manifold heat riser passages. The incoming fuel mixture is thus heated, resulting in more complete fuel evaporation. When the engine warms up, the valve opens. Vacuum to the EFE valve is controlled by a thermal vacuum switch (TVS) installed in the intake manifold, which monitors engine coolant temperatures and permits or restricts manifold vacuum to the valve accordingly.

Service procedures for this system are covered in Chapter One.

EXHAUST GAS RECIRCULATION

All engines are equipped with this system, which consists of a metering valve, a vacuum line to the carburetor or intake manifold, and

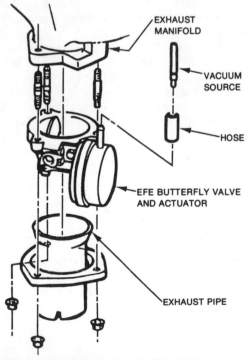

EXHAUST MANIFOLD

VACUUM SOURCE

HOSE

EFE BUTTERFLY VALVE AND ACTUATOR

EXHAUST PIPE

EFE valve installation detail (V6 only)

cast-in exhaust passages in the intake manifold. The EGR valve is controlled by vacuum, and opens and closes in response to the vacuum signals to admit exhaust gases into the air/fuel mixture. The exhaust gases lower peak combustion temperatures, reducing the formation of NO_x. The valve is closed at idle and wide open throttle, but is open between the two extreme positions.

There are actually two types of EGR systems: Vacuum Modulated and Exhaust Back Pressure Modulated. The principle of both systems is the same; the only difference is in the method used to control how far the EGR valve opens.

In the Vacuum Modulated system, the amount of exhaust gas admitted into the intake manifold depends on a ported vacuum signal. A ported vacuum signal is one taken from the carburetor above the throttle plates; thus, the vacuum signal (amount of vacuum) is dependent on how far the throttle plates are opened. When the throttle is closed (idle or deceleration) there is no vacuum signal. Thus, the EGR valve is closed, and no exhaust gas enters the intake manifold. As the throttle is opened, a vacuum is produced, which opens the EGR valve, admitting exhaust gas into the intake manifold.

In the Exhaust Back Pressure Modulated system, a transducer is installed in the EGR valve body. The vacuum is still ported vacuum, but the transducer uses exhaust gas pressure to control an air bleed within the valve to modify this vacuum signal.

System Checks

1. Check to see if the EGR valve diaphragm moves freely. Use your finger to reach up under the valve and push on the diaphragm. If it doesn't move freely, the valve should be replaced. The use of a mirror will aid the inspection process.

CAUTION: *If the engine is hot, wear a glove to protect your hand.*

2. Install a vacuum gauge into the vacuum line between the EGR valve and the carburetor. Start the engine and allow it to reach operating temperature.

3. With the car in either Park or Neutral, increase the engine speed until at least 5 in. Hg. is showing on the gauge.

4. Remove the vacuum hose from the EGR valve. The diaphragm should move downward (valve closed). The engine speed should increase.

5. Install the vacuum hose and watch for

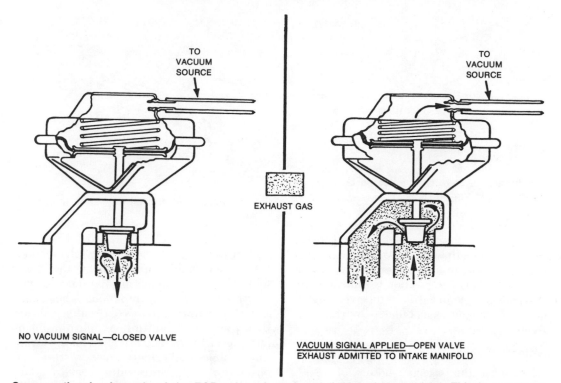

TO VACUUM SOURCE

TO VACUUM SOURCE

EXHAUST GAS

NO VACUUM SIGNAL—CLOSED VALVE

VACUUM SIGNAL APPLIED—OPEN VALVE
EXHAUST ADMITTED TO INTAKE MANIFOLD

Cross-sectional schematic of the EGR valve when closed (left) and open (right). This is a vacuum-modulated valve; exhaust gas-modulated valves have more complicated innards, but the operating principle is the same

the EGR valve to open (diaphragm moving upward). The engine speed should decrease to its former level, indicating exhaust recirculation.

If the diaphragm doesn't move:

1. Check engine vacuum; it should be at least 5 in. Hg. with the throttle open and engine running.

2. Check to see that the engine is at normal operating temperature.

3. Check for vacuum at the EGR hose. If no vacuum is present, check the hose for leaks, breaks, kinks, improper connections, etc., and replace as necessary.

If the diaphragm moves, but the engine speed doesn't change, check the EGR passages in the intake manifold for blockage.

EGR Valve Replacement

1. Disconnect the vacuum hose.

2. Remove the bolts or nuts holding the EGR valve to the engine.

3. Remove the valve.

4. Clean the mounting surfaces before replacing the valve. Install the valve onto the manifold, using a new gasket. Be sure to install the spacer, if used. Connect the vacuum hose and check the valve operation.

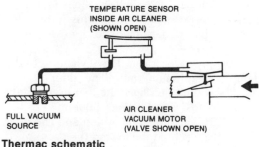

TEMPERATURE SENSOR
INSIDE AIR CLEANER
(SHOWN OPEN)

FULL VACUUM
SOURCE

AIR CLEANER
VACUUM MOTOR
(VALVE SHOWN OPEN)

Thermac schematic

THERMOSTATIC AIR CLEANER

All engines use the Thermac system. This system is designed to warm the air entering the carburetor when underhood temperatures are low, and to maintain a controlled air temperature into the carburetor at all times. By allowing preheated air to enter the carburetor, the amount of time the choke is on is reduced, resulting in better fuel economy and lower emissions. Engine warm-up time is also reduced.

The Thermac system is composed of the air cleaner body, a filter, sensor unit, vacuum diaphragm, damper door, and associated hoses and connections. Heat radiating from the exhaust manifold is trapped by a heat stove and is ducted to the air cleaner to

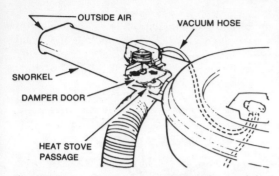

The thermac system can be tested by applying vacuum to the unit when cold

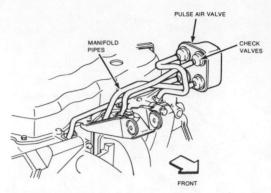

Pulsair installed on the four cylinder engine; V6 similar

supply heated air to the carburetor. A movable door in the air cleaner case snorkel allows air to be drawn in from the heat stove (cold operation) or from underhood air (warm operation). The door position is controlled by the vacuum motor, which receives intake manifold vacuum as modulated by the temperature sensor.

System Checks

1. Check the vacuum hoses for leaks, kinks, breaks, or improper connections and correct any defects.

2. With the engine off, check the position of the damper door within the snorkel. A mirror can be used to make this job easier. The damper door should be open to admit outside air.

3. Apply at least 7 in. Hg of vacuum to the damper diaphragm unit. The door should close. If it doesn't, check the diaphragm linkage for binding and correct hookup.

4. With vacuum still applied and the door closed, clamp the tube to trap the vacuum. If the door doesn't remain closed, there is a leak in the diaphragm assembly.

PULSE AIR INJECTION

All engines use the Pulsair air injection system, which uses exhaust system air pulses to siphon fresh air into the exhaust manifold. The injected air supports continued combustion of the hot exhaust gases in the exhaust manifold, reducing exhaust emissions. A secondary purpose of the Pulsair system is to introduce more oxygen into the exhaust system upstream of the catalytic converter, to supply the converter with the oxygen required for the oxidation reaction.

Air is drawn into the Pulsair valve through a hose connected to the air cleaner. The air passes through a check valve (there is one check valve for each cylinder; all check valves

are installed in the Pulsair valve), then through a manifold pipe to the exhaust manifold. All manifold pipes are the same length, to prevent uneven pulsation. The check valves open during pulses of negative exhaust back pressure, admitting air into the manifold pipe and the exhaust manifold. During pulses of positive exhaust back pressure, the check valves close, preventing backfiring into the Pulsair valve and air cleaner.

The Pulsair check valves, hoses and pipes should be checked occasionally for leaks, cracks, or breaks.

Removal and Installation

1. Remove the air cleaner case. Disconnect the rubber hose(s) from the Pulsair valve(s).

2. Disconnect the support bracket, if present. Some V6 engines have a Pulsair solenoid and bracket, which must be removed.

3. Unscrew the attaching nuts and remove the Pulsair tubes from the exhaust manifold(s).

4. To install, first apply a light coat of clean oil to the ends of the Pulsair tubes.

5. Install the tubes to the exhaust manifold(s), tightening the nuts to 10–13 ft lbs (10 Nm.). Connect the support bracket and solenoid and bracket, if used. Connect the rubber hose(s) and intall the air cleaner.

DECELERATION VALVE

All engines have a deceleration valve to prevent backfiring in the exhaust system during engine deceleration. The valve is normally closed. When the throttle is suddenly closed, vacuum increases in the signal line (hose) to the valve. This opens the valve, which bleeds

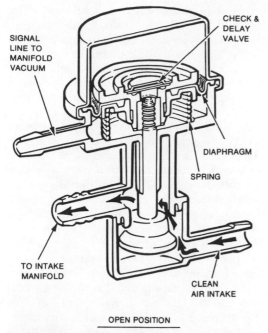

Cross-section of the deceleration valve in the open position

air into the intake manifold, leaning out the rich deceleration mixture.

Air trapped in a chamber above the vacuum diaphragm bleeds at a predetermined rate through the delay valve portion of a check and delay valve, located centrally in the diaphragm. The air bleed reduces vacuum acting on the diaphragm. When vacuum above the diaphragm falls below the level necessary to counteract diaphragm-closing spring pressure, the delay valve closes, shutting off intake air bleed.

The check valve portion of the check and delay valve balances vacuum chamber pressure when vacuum is caused by acceleration, rather than deceleration.

COMPUTER CONTROLLED CATALYTIC CONVERTER SYSTEM

The C-4 System, installed on all X-Body cars sold in California, is an electronically controlled exhaust emissions system. The purpose of the system is to maintain the ideal air/fuel ratio at which the catalytic converter is most effective.

Major components of the system include an Electronic Control Module (ECM), an oxygen sensor, an electronically controlled carburetor, and a three-way oxidation-reduction catalytic converter. The system also includes a maintenance reminder flag connected to the odometer which becomes visible in the instrument cluster at regular intervals, signaling the need for oxygen sensor replacement.

The oxygen sensor, installed in the exhaust manifold, generates a voltage which varies with exhaust gas oxygen content. Lean mixtures (more oxygen) reduce voltage; rich mix-

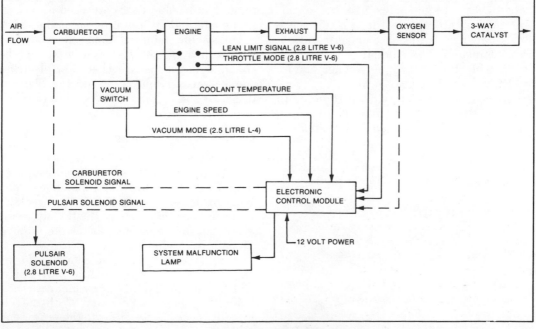

C-4 system schematic

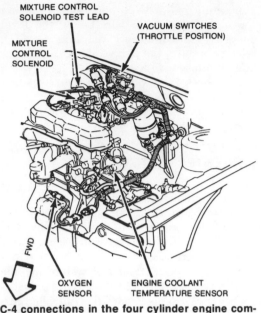

C-4 connections in the four cylinder engine compartment

tures (less oxygen) increase voltage. Voltage output is sent to the ECM.

An engine temperature sensor installed in the engine coolant outlet monitors engine coolant temperatures. Vacuum control switches and throttle position sensors also monitor engine conditions and supply signals to the ECM.

The Electronic Control Module receives input signals from all sensors. It processes these signals and generates a control signal sent to the carburetor. The control signal cycles between on (lean command) and off (rich command). The amount of on and off time is a function of the input voltage sent to the ECM by the oxygen sensor.

A Rochester Dualjet E2SE carburetor is used with the C-4 System. Basically, an electrically operated mixture control solenoid is

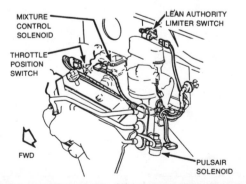

C-4 connections in the V6 engine compartment

installed in the carburetor float bowl. The solenoid controls the air/fuel mixture metered to the idle and main metering systems. Air metering to the idle system is controlled by an idle air bleed valve. It follows the movement of the mixture solenoid to control the amount of air bled into the idle system, enrichening or leaning out the mixture as appropriate. Air/fuel mixture enrichment occurs when the fuel valve is open and the air bleed valve is closed. All cycling of this system, which occurs ten times per second, is controlled by the ECM. A throttle position switch informs the ECM of open or closed throttle operation. A number of different switches are used, varying with application. The 1980 Citation, Omega, Phoenix and Skylark use two vacuum switches on the four cylinder engine, and a throttle position sensor on the V6. When the ECM receives a signal from the throttle switch, indicating a change of position, it immediately searches its memory for the last set of operating conditions that resulted in an ideal air/fuel ratio, and shifts to that set of conditions. The memory is continually updated during normal operation.

A "Check-Engine" light is included in the C-4 System installation. When a fault develops, the light comes on, and a trouble code is set into the ECM memory. However, if the fault is intermittent, the light will go out, but the trouble code will remain in the ECM memory as long as the engine is running. The trouble codes are used as a diagnostic aid, and are pre-programmed.

Unless the required tools are available, troubleshooting the C-4 System should be confined to mechanical checks of electrical connectors, vacuum hoses and the like. All diagnosis and repair should be performed by a qualified mechanic.

Oxygen Sensor Replacement

The oxygen sensor must be replaced every 30,000 miles (48,000 km.). The sensor may be difficult to remove when the engine temperature is below 120° F (48° C). Excessive removal force may damage the threads in the exhaust manifold or pipe; follow the removal procedure carefully.

1. On the four cylinder, remove the air cleaner and the Thermac heat stove pipe, which is attached to the air cleaner case snorkel with a sheet metal screw. With the V6, raise the car to make access to the sensor easier.

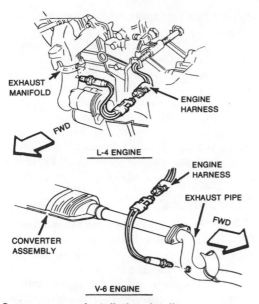

Oxygen sensor installation details

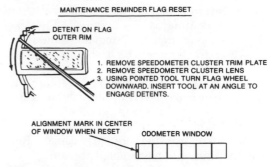

Mileage counter reset details

2. Disconnect the electrical connector from the oxygen sensor.

3. Spray a commercial heat riser solvent onto the sensor threads and allow it to soak in for at least five minutes.

4. Carefully unscrew and remove the sensor.

5. To install, first coat the new sensor's threads with G.M. anti-seize compound no. 5613695 or the equivalent. This is *not* a conventional anti-seize paste. The use of a regular compound may electrically insulate the sensor, rendering it inoperative. You must coat the threads with an electrically conductive anti-seize compound.

6. Installation torque is 30 ft lbs (42 Nm.). Do not overtighten.

7. Reconnect the electrical connector. Be careful not to damage the electrical pigtail. Check the sensor boot for proper fit and installation. Install the air cleaner, if removed.

Mileage Counter Reset

NOTE: *The mileage counter must only be reset after the oxygen sensor has been replaced. If the sensor is not changed at regular intervals, it will cease to monitor the exhaust gas content, resulting in incorrect interpretation of its signal by the ECM. The result will be an overly rich fuel mixture, causing stumbling, stalling, and poor fuel economy.*

At 30,000 mile intervals, the word "Sensor" will appear in the speedometer face, indicating the need for oxygen sensor replacement. After the sensor has been replaced, the mileage counter may be reset as follows:

1. Remove the instrument cluster bezel. This procedure is covered in Chapter Five.

2. Remove the instrument cluster lens.

3. Using an awl, punch, or other pointed tool, apply a light downward force on the detent on the outer rim of the reminder flag, until it "clicks" into place.

4. Install the lens and bezel.

Do *not* reset the reminder flag until the sensor has been replaced. See the note at the beginning of this procedure.

FUEL SYSTEM

Fuel Pump

Mechanical fuel pumps are used on both the four cylinder and V6 engines. The V6 engine pump has a vapor return line for both emission control purposes and to reduce the likelihood of vapor lock.

TESTING THE FUEL PUMP

To determine if the pump is in good condition, tests for both volume and pressure should be performed. The tests are made with the pump installed, and the engine at normal operating temperature and idle speed. Never replace a fuel pump without first performing these simple tests.

Be sure that the fuel filter has been changed at the specified interval. If in doubt, install a new filter first.

Pressure Test

1. Disconnect the fuel line at the carburetor and connect a fuel pump pressure gauge. Fill the carburetor float bowl with gasoline.

2. Start the engine and check the pressure with the engine at idle. If the pump has a

vapor return hose, squeeze it off so that an accurate reading can be obtained. Pressure for the four cylinder engine should be 6.5–8.0 psi; for the V6, it should measure 6.0–7.5 psi.

3. If the pressure is incorrect, replace the pump. If it is ok, go on to the volume test.

Volume Test

4. Disconnect the pressure gauge. Run the fuel line into a graduated container.

5. Run the engine at idle until one pint of gasoline has been pumped. One pint should be delivered in 30 seconds or less. There is normally enough fuel in the carburetor float bowl to perform this test, but refill it if necessary.

6. If the delivery rate is below the minimum, check the lines for restrictions or leaks, then replace the pump.

REMOVAL AND INSTALLATION

All Models

The fuel pump is located at the center rear of the four cylinder engine, and at the right front of the V6.

1. Disconnect the negative cable at the battery. Raise and support the car.

2. On X-Bodies with the V6 engine, remove the pump shields and the oil filter.

3. Disconnect the inlet hose from the pump. Disconnect the vapor return hose, if equipped.

4. Loosen the fuel line at the carburetor, then disconnect the outlet pipe from the pump.

5. Remove the two mounting bolts and remove the pump from the engine.

6. To install, place a new gasket on the pump and install the pump on the engine.

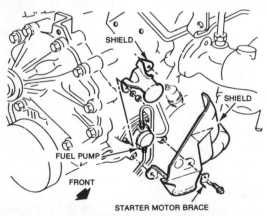

SHIELD

SHIELD

FUEL PUMP

FRONT

STARTER MOTOR BRACE

V6 fuel pump installation; four cylinder similar

Tighten the two mounting bolts alternately and evenly.

7. Install the pump outlet pipe. This is easier if the pipe is disconnected from the carburetor. Tighten the fitting while backing up the pump nut with another wrench. Install the pipe at the carburetor.

8. Install the inlet and vapor hoses. Install the shields and oil filter on the V6 engine. Lower the car, connect the negative battery cable, start the engine, and check for leaks.

Carburetors

The Rochester 2SE and E2SE Varajet II carburetors are two barrel, two stage downdraft units. Most carburetor components are aluminum, although a zinc choke housing is used on the four cylinder engine installations. The E2SE is used both in conventional installations and in the Computer Controlled Catalytic Converter System. In that installation, the E2SE is equipped with an electrically operated mixture control solenoid, controlled by the Electronic Control Module.

REMOVAL AND INSTALLATION

1. Remove the air cleaner and gasket.

2. Disconnect the fuel line. Disconnect and label the vapor hoses and electrical connectors from the carburetor.

3. Disconnect the accelerator linkage.

4. Remove the mounting bolts and remove the carburetor and gasket.

5. Before installing the carburetor, fill the float bowl with gasoline to reduce battery strain and the possibility of backfiring when the engine is started.

6. Check the mating surfaces on the carburetor and intake manifold for cleanliness. Install a new gasket.

7. Place the carburetor on the gasket and loosely install the attaching bolts.

8. Install the vacuum lines and loosely install the fuel line.

9. Tighten the carburetor mounting nuts evenly to 145 in. lbs (16 Nm.).

10. Tighten the fuel line. Connect the accelerator linkage and electrical connectors.

11. Adjust the idle speed and install the air cleaner.

FLOAT ADJUSTMENT

1. Remove the air horn from the throttle body.

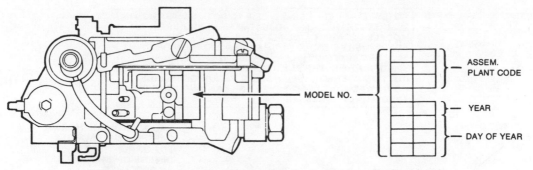

MODEL NO.

ASSEM. PLANT CODE

YEAR

DAY OF YEAR

The carburetor identification number is stamped on the float bowl

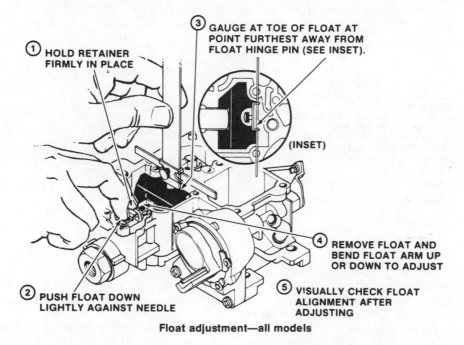

① HOLD RETAINER FIRMLY IN PLACE

③ GAUGE AT TOE OF FLOAT AT POINT FURTHEST AWAY FROM FLOAT HINGE PIN (SEE INSET).

(INSET)

④ REMOVE FLOAT AND BEND FLOAT ARM UP OR DOWN TO ADJUST

② PUSH FLOAT DOWN LIGHTLY AGAINST NEEDLE

⑤ VISUALLY CHECK FLOAT ALIGNMENT AFTER ADJUSTING

Float adjustment—all models

2. Use your fingers to hold the retainer in place, and to push the float down into light contact with the needle.

3. Measure the distance from the toe of the float (furthest from the hinge) to the top of the carburetor (gasket removed).

4. To adjust, remove the float and gently bend the arm to specification. After adjustment, check the float alignment in the chamber.

PUMP ADJUSTMENT

1. With the throttle closed and the fast idle screw off the steps of the fast idle cam, measure the distance from the air horn casting to the top of the pump stem.

2. To adjust, remove the retaining screw and washer and remove the pump lever. Bend the end of the lever to correct the stem height. Do not twist the lever or bend it sideways.

3. Install the lever, washer and screw and check the adjustment. When correct, open and close the throttle a few times to check the linkage movement and alignment.

FAST IDLE ADJUSTMENT

1. Set the ignition timing and curb idle speed, and disconnect and plug hoses as directed on the emission control decal.

2. Place the fast idle screw on the highest step of the cam.

3. Start the engine and adjust the engine speed to specification with the fast idle screw.

CHOKE COIL LEVER ADJUSTMENT

1. Remove the three retaining screws and remove the choke cover and coil. On models

NOTE: ON MODELS USING A CLIP TO RETAIN PUMP ROD IN PUMP LEVER, NO PUMP ADJUSTMENT IS REQUIRED. ON MODELS USING THE "CLIPLESS" PUMP ROD, THE PUMP ADJUSTMENT SHOULD NOT BE CHANGED FROM ORIGINAL FACTORY SETTING UNLESS GAUGING SHOWS OUT OF SPECIFICATION. THE PUMP LEVER IS MADE FROM HEAVY DUTY, HARDENED STEEL MAKING BENDING DIFFICULT. DO NOT REMOVE PUMP LEVER FOR BENDING UNLESS ABSOLUTELY NECESSARY.

② GAUGE FROM AIR HORN CASTING SURFACE TO TOP OF PUMP STEM. DIMENSION SHOULD BE AS SPECIFIED.

① THROTTLE VALVES COMPLETELY CLOSED. MAKE SURE FAST IDLE SCREW IS OFF STEPS OF FAST IDLE CAM.

③ IF NECESSARY TO ADJUST, REMOVE PUMP LEVER RETAINING SCREW AND WASHER AND REMOVE PUMP LEVER BY ROTATING LEVER TO REMOVE FROM PUMP ROD. PLACE LEVER IN A VISE, PROTECTING LEVER FROM DAMAGE, AND BEND END OF LEVER (NEAREST NECKED DOWN SECTION).

⑤ OPEN AND CLOSE THROTTLE VALVES CHECKING LINKAGE FOR FREEDOM OF MOVEMENT AND OBSERVING PUMP LEVER ALIGNMENT.

④ REINSTALL PUMP LEVER, WASHER AND RETAINING SCREW. RECHECK PUMP ADJUSTMENT ① AND ②. TIGHTEN RETAINING SCREW SECURELY AFTER THE PUMP ADJUSTMENT IS CORRECT.

NOTE: DO NOT BEND LEVER IN A SIDEWAYS OR TWISTING MOTION.

Pump adjustment—all models

with a riveted choke cover, drill out the three rivets and remove the cover and choke coil.

NOTE: *A choke stat cover retainer kit is required for reassembly.*

2. Place the fast idle screw on the high step of the cam.

3. Close the choke by pushing in on the intermediate choke lever. On V6 models, the intermediate choke lever is behind the choke vacuum diaphragm.

4. Insert a drill or gauge of the specified size into the hole in the choke housing. The choke lever in the housing should be up against the side of the gauge.

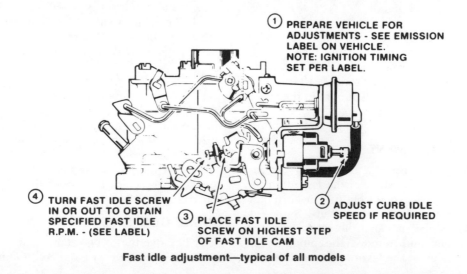

① PREPARE VEHICLE FOR ADJUSTMENTS - SEE EMISSION LABEL ON VEHICLE. NOTE: IGNITION TIMING SET PER LABEL.

④ TURN FAST IDLE SCREW IN OR OUT TO OBTAIN SPECIFIED FAST IDLE R.P.M. - (SEE LABEL)

③ PLACE FAST IDLE SCREW ON HIGHEST STEP OF FAST IDLE CAM

② ADJUST CURB IDLE SPEED IF REQUIRED

Fast idle adjustment—typical of all models

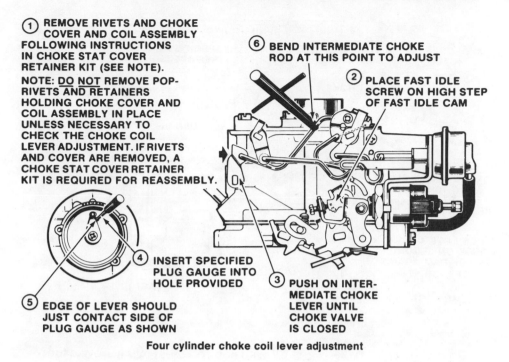

(1) REMOVE RIVETS AND CHOKE COVER AND COIL ASSEMBLY FOLLOWING INSTRUCTIONS IN CHOKE STAT COVER RETAINER KIT (SEE NOTE).
NOTE: DO NOT REMOVE POP-RIVETS AND RETAINERS HOLDING CHOKE COVER AND COIL ASSEMBLY IN PLACE UNLESS NECESSARY TO CHECK THE CHOKE COIL LEVER ADJUSTMENT. IF RIVETS AND COVER ARE REMOVED, A CHOKE STAT COVER RETAINER KIT IS REQUIRED FOR REASSEMBLY.

(6) BEND INTERMEDIATE CHOKE ROD AT THIS POINT TO ADJUST

(2) PLACE FAST IDLE SCREW ON HIGH STEP OF FAST IDLE CAM

(4) INSERT SPECIFIED PLUG GAUGE INTO HOLE PROVIDED

(3) PUSH ON INTER-MEDIATE CHOKE LEVER UNTIL CHOKE VALVE IS CLOSED

(5) EDGE OF LEVER SHOULD JUST CONTACT SIDE OF PLUG GAUGE AS SHOWN

Four cylinder choke coil lever adjustment

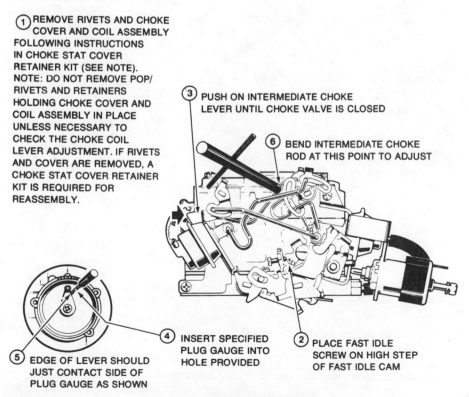

(1) REMOVE RIVETS AND CHOKE COVER AND COIL ASSEMBLY FOLLOWING INSTRUCTIONS IN CHOKE STAT COVER RETAINER KIT (SEE NOTE).
NOTE: DO NOT REMOVE POP/RIVETS AND RETAINERS HOLDING CHOKE COVER AND COIL ASSEMBLY IN PLACE UNLESS NECESSARY TO CHECK THE CHOKE COIL LEVER ADJUSTMENT. IF RIVETS AND COVER ARE REMOVED, A CHOKE STAT COVER RETAINER KIT IS REQUIRED FOR REASSEMBLY.

(3) PUSH ON INTERMEDIATE CHOKE LEVER UNTIL CHOKE VALVE IS CLOSED

(6) BEND INTERMEDIATE CHOKE ROD AT THIS POINT TO ADJUST

(4) INSERT SPECIFIED PLUG GAUGE INTO HOLE PROVIDED

(2) PLACE FAST IDLE SCREW ON HIGH STEP OF FAST IDLE CAM

(5) EDGE OF LEVER SHOULD JUST CONTACT SIDE OF PLUG GAUGE AS SHOWN

V6 choke coil lever adjustment

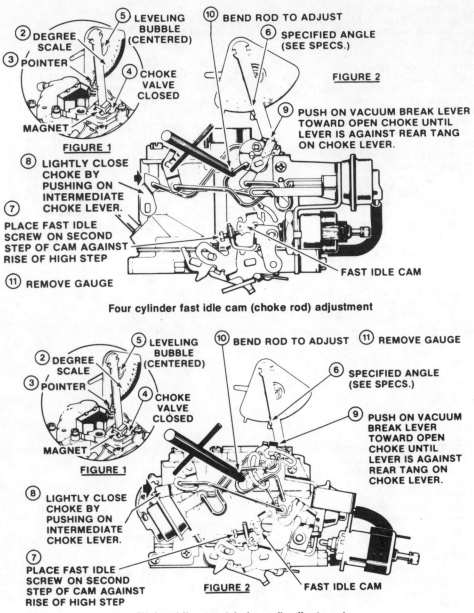

Four cylinder fast idle cam (choke rod) adjustment

V6 fast idle cam (choke rod) adjustment

5. If the lever does not just touch the gauge, bend the intermediate choke rod to adjust.

FAST IDLE CAM (CHOKE ROD) ADJUSTMENT

NOTE: *A special angle gauge should be used. If it is not available, an inch measurement can be made.*

1. Adjust the choke coil lever and fast idle first.

2. Rotate the degree scale until it is zeroed.

3. Close the choke and install the degree scale onto the choke plate. Center the leveling bubble.

4. Rotate the scale so that the specified degree is opposite the scale pointer.

5. Place the fast idle screw on the second step of the cam (against the high step). Close the choke by pushing in the intermediate lever.

6. Push on the vacuum break lever in the direction of opening choke until the lever is against the rear tang on the choke lever.

7. Bend the fast idle cam rod at the U to adjust angle to specifications.

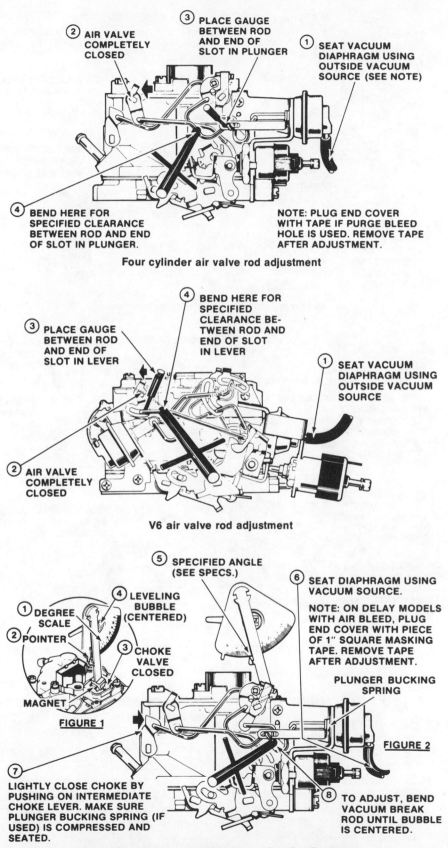

Four cylinder air valve rod adjustment

V6 air valve rod adjustment

Four cylinder primary side vacuum break adjustment

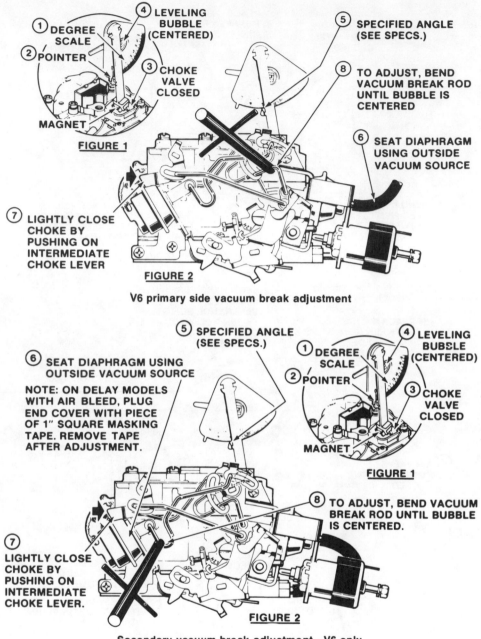

V6 primary side vacuum break adjustment

Secondary vacuum break adjustment—V6 only

AIR VALVE ROD ADJUSTMENT

1. Seat the vacuum diaphragm with an outside vacuum source. Tape over the purge bleed hole if present.

2. Close the air valve.

3. Insert the specified gauge between the rod and the end of the slot in the plunger on fours, or between the rod and the end of the slot in the air valve on V6s.

4. Bend the rod to adjust the clearance.

PRIMARY SIDE VACUUM BREAK ADJUSTMENT

1. Follow Steps 1–4 of the Fast Idle Cam Adjustment.

2. Seat the choke vacuum diaphragm with an outside vacuum source.

3. Push in on the intermediate choke lever to close the choke valve, and hold closed during adjustment.

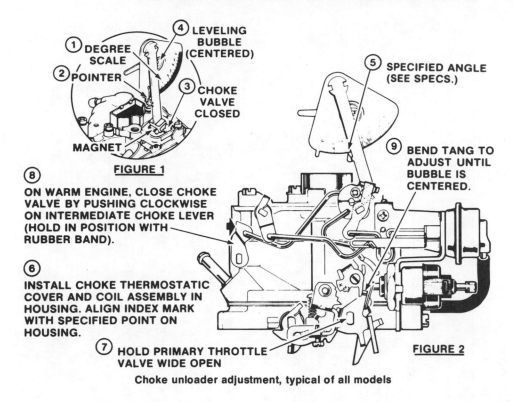

① DEGREE SCALE

② POINTER

④ LEVELING BUBBLE (CENTERED)

③ CHOKE VALVE CLOSED

MAGNET

FIGURE 1

⑤ SPECIFIED ANGLE (SEE SPECS.)

⑨ BEND TANG TO ADJUST UNTIL BUBBLE IS CENTERED.

⑧ ON WARM ENGINE, CLOSE CHOKE VALVE BY PUSHING CLOCKWISE ON INTERMEDIATE CHOKE LEVER (HOLD IN POSITION WITH RUBBER BAND).

⑥ INSTALL CHOKE THERMOSTATIC COVER AND COIL ASSEMBLY IN HOUSING. ALIGN INDEX MARK WITH SPECIFIED POINT ON HOUSING.

⑦ HOLD PRIMARY THROTTLE VALVE WIDE OPEN

FIGURE 2

Choke unloader adjustment, typical of all models

4. Adjust by bending the vacuum break rod until the bubble is centered.

ELECTRIC CHOKE SETTING

This procedure is only for those carburetors with choke covers retained by screws. Riveted choke covers are preset and nonadjustable.

1. Loosen the three retaining screws.
2. Place the fast idle screw on the high step of the cam.
3. Rotate the choke cover to align the cover mark with the specified housing mark.

SECONDARY VACUUM BREAK ADJUSTMENT

This procedure is for V6 installations only.
1. Follow Steps 1–4 of the Fast Idle Cam Adjustment.
2. Seat the choke vacuum diaphragm with an outside vacuum source.
3. Push in on the intermediate choke lever to close the choke valve, and hold closed during adjustment. Make sure the plunger spring is compressed and seated, if present.
4. Bend the vacuum break rod at the U next to the diaphragm until the bubble is centered.

CHOKE UNLOADER ADJUSTMENT

1. Follow Steps 1–4 of the Fast Idle Cam Adjustment.
2. Install the choke cover and coil, if removed, aligning the marks on the housing and cover as specified.
3. Hold the primary throttle wide open.
4. If the engine is warm, close the choke valve by pushing in on the intermediate choke lever.
5. Bend the unloader tang until the bubble is centered.

SECONDARY LOCKOUT ADJUSTMENT

1. Pull the choke wide open by pushing out on the intermediate choke lever.
2. Open the throttle until the end of the secondary actuating lever is opposite the toe of the lockout lever.
3. Gauge clearance between the lockout lever and secondary lever should be as specified.
4. To adjust, bend the lockout lever where it contacts the fast idle cam.

OVERHAUL

Efficient carburetion depends greatly on careful cleaning and inspection during over-

Carburetor Specifications
Citation, Omega, Phoenix, Skylark

Year	Carburetor Identification	Float Level (in.)	Pump Rod (in.)	Fast Idle (rpm)	Choke Coil Lever (in.)	Fast Idle Cam (deg./in.)	Air Valve Rod (in.)	Primary Vacuum Break (deg./in.)	Choke Setting (notches)	Secondary Vacuum Break (deg./in.)	Choke Unloader (deg./in.)	Secondary Lockout (in.)
1980	17059614	3/16	1/2	2600	.085	18/.096	.025	17/.090	Fixed	—	36/.227	.120
	17059615	3/16	5/32	2600	.085	18/.096	.025	19/.103	Fixed	—	36/.227	.120
	17059616	3/16	1/2	2600	.085	18/.096	.025	17/.090	Fixed	—	36/.227	.120
	17059617	3/16	5/32	2600	.085	18/.096	.025	19/.103	Fixed	—	36/.227	.120
	17059650	3/16	3/32	2000	.085	27/.157	.025	30/.179	Fixed	38/.243	30/.179	.120
	17059651	3/16	3/32	1900	.085	27/.157	.025	22/.123	Fixed	23/.120	30/.179	.120
	17059652	3/16	3/32	2000	.085	27/.157	.025	30/.179	Fixed	38/.243	30/.179	.120
	17059653	3/16	3/32	1900	.085	27/.157	.025	22/.123	Fixed	23/.120	30/.179	.120
	17059714	11/16	5/32	2600	.085	18/.096	.025	23/.129	Fixed	—	32/.195	.120
	17059715	11/16	3/32	2200	.085	18/.096	.025	25/.142	Fixed	—	32/.195	.120
	17059716	11/16	5/32	2600	.085	18/.096	.025	23/.129	Fixed	—	32/.195	.120
	17059717	11/16	3/32	2200	.085	18/.096	.025	25/.142	Fixed	—	32/.195	.120

17059760	1/8	5/64	2000	.085	17.5/.093	.025	20/.110	Fixed	33/.203	35/.220	.120
17059762	1/8	5/64	2000	.085	17.5/.093	.025	20/.110	Fixed	33/.203	35/.220	.120
17059763	1/8	5/64	2000	.085	17.5/.093	.025	20/.110	Fixed	33/.203	35/.220	.120
17059618	3/16	1/2	2600	.085	18/.096	.025	17/.090	Fixed	—	36/.227	.120
17059619	3/16	5/32	2600	.085	18/.096	.025	19/.103	Fixed	—	36/.227	.120
17059620	3/16	1/2	2600	.085	18/.096	.025	17/.090	Fixed	—	36/.227	.120
17059621	3/16	5/32	2600	.085	18/.096	.025	19/.103	Fixed	—	36/.227	.120

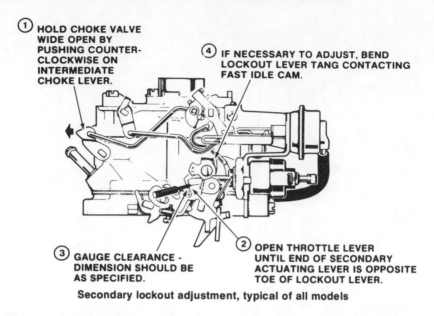

① HOLD CHOKE VALVE WIDE OPEN BY PUSHING COUNTER-CLOCKWISE ON INTERMEDIATE CHOKE LEVER.

④ IF NECESSARY TO ADJUST, BEND LOCKOUT LEVER TANG CONTACTING FAST IDLE CAM.

③ GAUGE CLEARANCE - DIMENSION SHOULD BE AS SPECIFIED.

② OPEN THROTTLE LEVER UNTIL END OF SECONDARY ACTUATING LEVER IS OPPOSITE TOE OF LOCKOUT LEVER.

Secondary lockout adjustment, typical of all models

haul, since dirt, gum, water, or varnish in or on the carburetor parts are often responsible for poor performance.

Overhaul your carburetor in a clean, dust-free area. Carefully disassemble the carburetor, referring often to the exploded view supplied in the rebuilding kit. Keep all similar and look-alike parts segregated during disassembly and cleaning to avoid accidental interchange during assembly. Make a note of all jet sizes.

When the carburetor is disassembled, wash all parts (except diaphragms, electric choke units, pump plunger, and any other plastic, leather, fiber, or rubber parts) in clean carburetor solvent. Do not leave parts in the solvent any longer than is necessary to sufficiently loosen the deposits. Excessive cleaning may remove the special finish from the float bowl and choke valve bodies, leaving these parts unfit for service. Rinse all parts in clean solvent and blow them dry with compressed air or allow them to air dry. Wipe clean all cork, plastic, leather, and fiber parts with a clean, lint-free cloth.

Blow out all passages and jets with compressed air and be sure that there are no restrictions or blockages. Never use wire or similar tools to clean jets, fuel passages, or air bleeds. Clean all jets and valves separately to avoid accidental interchange.

Check all parts for wear or damage. If wear or damage is found, replace the defective parts. Especially check the following:

1. Check the float needle and seat for wear. If wear is found, replace the complete assembly.

2. Check the float hinge pin for wear and the float(s) for dents or distortion. Replace the float if fuel has leaked into it.

3. Check the throttle and choke shaft bores for wear or an out-of-round condition. Damage or wear to the throttle arm, shaft, or shaft bore will often require replacement of the throttle body. These parts require a close tolerance of fit; wear may allow air leakage, which could affect starting and idling.

NOTE: *Throttle shafts and bushings are not included in overhaul kits. They can be purchased separately.*

4. Inspect the idle mixture adjusting needles for burrs or grooves. Any such condition requires replacement of the needle, since you will not be able to obtain a satisfactory idle.

5. Test the accelerator pump check valves. They should pass air one way but not the other. Test for proper seating by blowing and sucking on the valve. Replace the valve if necessary. If the valve is satisfactory, wash the valve again to remove breath moisture.

6. Check the bowl cover for warped surfaces with a straightedge.

7. Closely inspect the valves and seats for wear and damage, replacing as necessary.

8. After the carburetor is assembled, check the choke valve for freedom of operation.

Carburetor overhaul kits are recommended for each overhaul. These kits contain

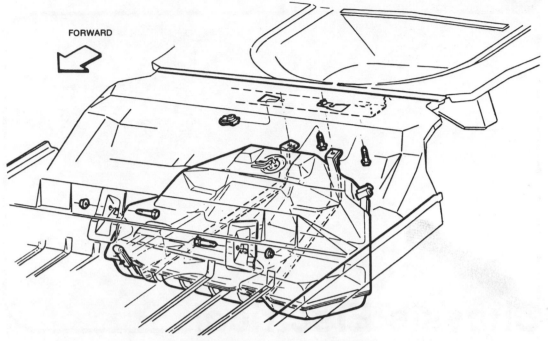

FORWARD

Fuel tank installation details—all models

all gaskets and new parts to replace those which deteriorate most rapidly. Failure to replace all parts supplied with the kit (especially gaskets) can result in poor performance later.

Some carburetor manufacturers supply overhaul kits of three basic types: minor repair; major repair; and gasket kits.

After cleaning and checking all components, reassemble the carburetor, using new parts and referring to the exploded view. When reassembling, make sure that all screws and jets are tight in their seats, but do not overtighten as the tips will be distorted. Tighten all screws gradually, in rotation. Do not tighten needle valves into their seats; uneven jetting will result. Always use new gaskets. Be sure to adjust the float level when reassembling.

Fuel Tank
REMOVAL AND INSTALLATION

1. Disconnect the negative cable at the battery. Raise and support the car.

2. Drain the tank. There is no drain plug; remaining fuel in the tank must be siphoned through the fuel feed line (the line to the fuel pump), because of the restrictor in the filler neck.

3. Disconnect the hose and the vapor return hose from the level sending unit fittings.

4. Remove the ground wire screw.

5. Unplug the level sending unit electrical connector.

6. Disconnect the vent hose.

7. Unbolt the support straps, and lower and remove the tank. Installation is the reverse.

5

Chassis Electrical

UNDERSTANDING AND TROUBLESHOOTING ELECTRICAL SYSTEMS

For any electrical system to operate, it must make a complete circuit. This simply means that the power flow from the battery must make a complete circle. When an electrical component is operating, power flows from the battery to the component, passes through the component causing it to perform its function and then returns to the battery through the ground of the circuit. This ground is usually (but not always) the metal part of the car on which the electrical component is mounted.

Perhaps the easiest way to visualize this is to think of connecting a light bulb with two wires attached to it to your car's battery. The battery has two posts (negative and positive). If one of the two wires attached to the light bulb was attached to the negative post of the battery and the other wire was attached to the positive post of the battery, you would have a complete circuit. Current from the battery would flow out one post, through the wire attached to it and then to the light bulb, where it would pass through causing it to light. It would then leave the light bulb, travel through the other wire, and return to the other post of the battery.

The normal automotive circuit differs from this simple example in two ways. First, instead of having a return wire from the bulb to the battery, the light bulb returns the current to the battery through the chassis of the vehicle. Since the negative battery cable is attached to the chassis and the chassis is made of electrically conductive metal, the chassis of the vehicle can serve as a ground wire to complete the circuit. Secondly, most automotive circuits contain switches to turn components on and off as required.

There are many types of switches, but the most common simply serves to prevent the passage of current when it is turned off. Since the switch is a part of the circle necessary for a complete circuit, it operates to leave an opening in the circuit, and thus an incomplete or open circuit, when it is turned off.

Some electrical components which require a large amount of current to operate also have a relay in their circuit. Since these circuits carry a large amount of current, the thickness of the wire in the circuit (gauge size) is also greater. If this large wire were connected from the component to the control switch on the instrument panel, and then back to the component, a voltage drop would occur in the circuit. To prevent this potential drop in voltage, an electromagnetic switch (relay) is used. The large wires in the circuit are connected from the battery to one side of the relay, and from the opposite side of the relay to the component. The relay is normally open, preventing current from passing through the circuit. An additional, smaller, wire is connected from the relay to the control switch for the circuit. When the control switch is turned on, it grounds the smaller wire from the relay and completes the circuit. This closes the relay and allows current to flow from the battery to the component. The horn, headlight, and starter circuits are three which use relays.

Have you ever noticed how the instrument panel lights get slightly brighter when the engine speed rises above idle? This happens because the alternator (which supplies current to the battery) puts out more current at speeds above idle. This is normal. However, it is possible for larger surges of current to pass through the electrical system. If this surge of current were to reach an electrical component, it could burn it out. To prevent this from happening, fuses are connected into the current supply wires of most of the major electrical systems. The fuse serves to head off the surge at the pass. When an electrical current of excessive power passes through the component's fuse, the fuse blows out and breaks the circuit, saving it from destruction.

The fuse also protects the component from damage if the power supply wire to the component is grounded before the current reaches the component.

Let us here interject another rule to the complete circle circuit. *Every complete circuit from a power source must include a component which is using the power from the power source.* If you were to disconnect the light bulb (from the previous example of a lightbulb being connected to the battery by two wires) from the wires and touch the two wires together (please take my word for this; don't try it), the result would be a shower of sparks. A similar thing happens (on a smaller scale) when the power supply wire to a component or the electrical component itself becomes grounded before the normal ground connection for the circuit. To prevent damage to the system, the fuse for the circuit blows to interrupt the circuit—protecting the components from damage. Because grounding a wire from a power source makes a complete circuit—less the required component to use the power—this is called a short circuit. The most common causes of short circuits are either the rubber insulation on a wire breaking or rubbing through to expose the current carrying core of the wire to a metal part of the car, or a short circuited switch.

Some electrical systems are protected by a circuit breaker which is, basically, a self-repairing fuse. When either of the above-described events takes place in a system which is protected by a circuit breaker, the circuit breaker opens the circuit the same way a fuse does. However, when either the short is removed from the circuit or the surge subsides, the circuit breaker resets itself and does not have to be replaced as a fuse does.

The final protective device in the chassis electrical system is a fuse (or fusible) link. A fuse link is a wire that acts as a fuse. It is under the hood next to the battery, and protects all the chassis electrical components. It is the probable cause of trouble when none of the electrical components function, unless the battery is disconnected or dead.

Electrical problems generally fall into one of three areas:

1. The component that is not functioning is not receiving current.

2. The component itself is not functioning.

3. The component is not properly grounded.

Problems that fall into the first category are by far the most complicated. It is the current supply system to the component which contains all the switches, relays, fuses, etc.

The electrical system can be checked with a test light and a jumper wire. A test light is a device that looks like a pointed screwdriver with a wire attached to it. It has a light bulb in its handle. A jumper wire is a piece of insulated wire with an alligator clip attached to each end. To check the system (an inoperative light bulb in the following example) you must follow a systematic plan to determine which of the three causes is the villain:

1. Turn on the switch that controls the inoperable bulb.

2. Disconnect the power supply wire from the bulb.

3. Attach the ground wire on the test light to a good metal ground.

4. Touch the probe end of the test light to the end of the power supply wire that was disconnected from the bulb. If the bulb is receiving current, the test light will go on.

NOTE: *If the bulb is one which works only when the ignition key is turned on make sure the key is turned on.*

If the test light does not go on, then the problem is in the circuit between the battery and the bulb. As mentioned before, this includes all the switches, fuses, and relays in the system. Follow the wire that runs back to the battery. If the fuse is blown and, when replaced, immediately blows again, there is a short circuit in the system which must be located and repaired. If there is a switch in the system, bypass it with a jumper wire. This is done by connecting one end of the jumper wire to the power supply wire into the switch and the other end of the jumper

wire to the wire coming out of the switch. If the test light lights with the jumper wire installed, the switch or whatever was bypassed is defective.

NOTE: *Never substitute the jumper wire for the bulb, as the bulb is the component required to use the power from the power source.*

5. If the bulb in the test light goes on, then the current is getting to the bulb that is not working. This eliminates the first of the three possible causes. Connect the power supply wire and connect a jumper wire from

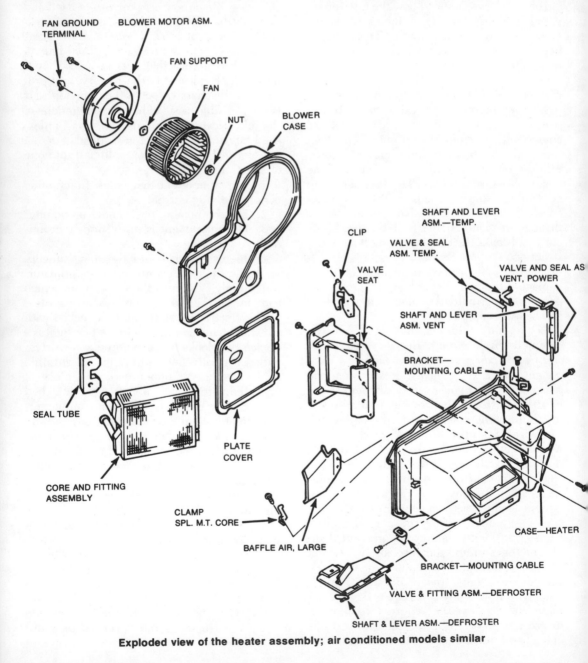

Exploded view of the heater assembly; air conditioned models similar

the bulb to a good metal ground. Do this with the switch which controls the bulb turned on, and also the ignition switch turned on if it is required for the light to work. If the bulb works with the jumper wire installed, then it has a bad ground. This is usually caused by the metal area on which the bulb mounts being coated with some type of foreign matter.

6. If neither test located the source of the trouble, then the light bulb itself is defective.

The above test procedure can be applied to any of the components of the chassis electrical system by substituting the component that is not working for the light bulb. Remember that for any electrical system to work, all connections must be clean and tight.

HEATER

Blower

REMOVAL AND INSTALLATION

This procedure is for all cars, with or without air conditioning.

1. Disconnect the negative cable at the battery.

2. Working inside the engine compartment, disconnect the blower motor electrical leads.

3. Remove the motor retaining screws, and remove the blower motor.

4. Reverse to install.

The blower is accessible through the engine compartment

The heater inlet and outlet hoses connect to the core tubes at the firewall, below the windshield wiper motor

Heater Core

REMOVAL AND INSTALLATION

Cars Without Air Conditioning

1. Drain the cooling system.

2. Remove the heater inlet and outlet hoses at the firewall, inside the engine compartment.

3. Remove the radio noise suppression strap.

4. Remove the heater core cover retaining screws. Remove the cover.

5. Remove the core. Reverse to install.

Cars With Air Conditioning

1. Drain the cooling system.

2. Remove the heater hoses from the core tubes at the firewall.

3. Remove the heater duct and heater case side cover from under the instrument panel.

4. Remove the core retaining clamps. Remove the inlet and outlet tube support clamps.

5. Remove the core. Reverse to install.

RADIO

REMOVAL AND INSTALLATION

NOTE: *Do not operate the radio with the speaker leads disconnected. Operating the radio without an electrical load will damage the output transistors.*

Citation

1. Disconnect the negative cable at the battery.

2. Remove the radio knobs (pull off), the radio shaft nuts, and the clock knob if your Citation has one.

3. Remove the instrument cluster trim bezel attaching screws and pull the bezel rearward.

4. Remove the headlamp switch and knob.

5. Disconnect the wiring and remove the bezel.

6. Remove the two screws attaching the radio bracket to the instrument panel.

7. Pull the radio rearward while, at the same time, twisting it slightly to the left, and disconnect the electrical connectors and antenna lead. Remove the lamp socket.

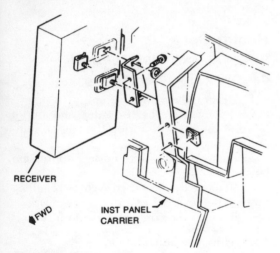

Citation radio removal

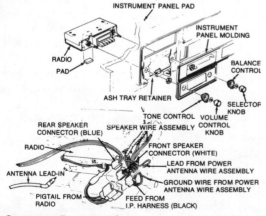

Omega radio removal

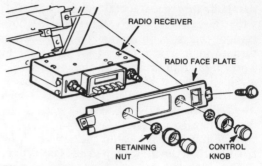

Phoenix radio removal

8. Remove the radio. Installation is the reverse.

Omega

1. Disconnect the negative cable at the battery.

2. Remove the instrument panel molding.

3. Remove the ash tray.

4. Remove the four screws attaching the ash tray retaining assembly to the instrument panel.

5. Remove the ash tray lamp bulb and socket assembly from the housing.

6. Pull the radio and ash tray retaining assembly out far enough to disconnect the radio wiring and antenna lead.

7. Remove the radio. Installation is the reverse.

Phoenix

1. Disconnect the negative cable at the battery.

2. Remove the trim plate from the center of the instrument panel.

3. Remove the two attaching screws, and pull the radio out far enough to disconnect the wiring and antenna lead.

4. Remove the radio knobs and separate the face plate from the radio. Installation is the reverse.

Skylark

1. Disconnect the negative cable at the battery.

2. Remove the instrument panel trim plate.

3. Remove the four radio mounting plate screws.

4. Pull the radio out far enough to disconnect the wiring and antenna cable.

5. Pull the radio out through the instrument panel carrier housing.

6. Installation is the reverse.

WINDSHIELD WIPERS

Blade replacement procedures are in Chapter One.

Arm

REMOVAL AND INSTALLATION

Removal of the wiper arms requires the use of a special tool, G.M. J-8966, or the equivalent. Versions of this tool are generally available in auto parts stores.

1. Insert the tool under the wiper arm and lever the arm off the shaft.

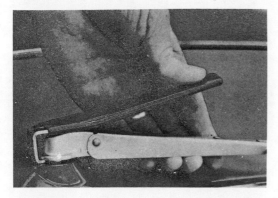

The wiper arms can be removed with the aid of this special tool

2. Detach the washer hose from the arm.

3. Remove the arm. Installation is the reverse. The proper park position for the arms is with the blades approximately 2 inches (50 mm) above the lower molding of the windshield. Be sure the motor is in the park position before installing the arms.

Motor

REMOVAL AND INSTALLATION

1. Remove the wiper arms.

2. Remove the lower windshield reveal molding, the front cowl panel and the cowl screen. Disconnect the washer hose under the screen.

3. Disconnect the motor electrical leads.

4. Loosen, but do not remove, the transmission drive link attaching nuts to the motor crank arm.

5. Disconnect the drive link from the motor crank arm.

6. Remove the three motor attaching bolts. On models with air conditioning, remove the bolts and while supporting the motor, remove the motor crank arm nut using lock-ring type pliers and a closed end wrench. The motor attaching bolts must be removed first to avoid damage to the nylon

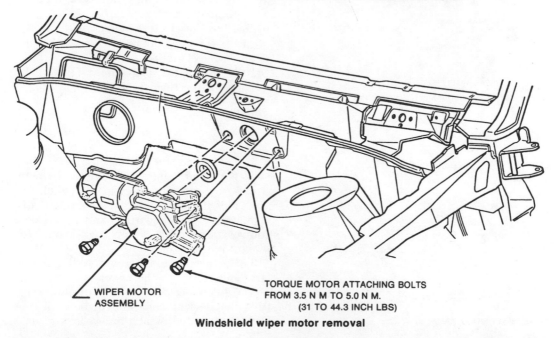

ON STYLES EQUIPPED WITH AIR CONDITIONING, REMOVE MOTOR ATTACHING BOLTS PRIOR TO REMOVING CRANK ARM ATTACHING NUT. CRANK ARM MUST BE REMOVED BEFORE MOTOR CAN BE LIFTED PAST A C EVAPORATOR UNIT.

WIPER MOTOR ASSEMBLY

TORQUE MOTOR ATTACHING BOLTS FROM 3.5 N M TO 5.0 N M. (31 TO 44.3 INCH LBS)

Windshield wiper motor removal

gear inside the motor. On all models, rotate the motor up and out to remove.

7. Reverse the procedure to install.

Linkage
REMOVAL AND INSTALLATION

1. Remove the lower windshield reveal molding, the wiper arms, and the cowl panel.

2. Loosen but do not remove the drive link to crank arm attaching nuts.

3. Remove the linkage to cowl panel attaching bolts.

4. Installation is the reverse. Tighten the attaching bolts to 27–36 in. lbs (3–4 Nm.).

INSTRUMENT CLUSTER

REMOVAL AND INSTALLATION
Citation

1. Disconnect the negative battery cable.

2. Remove the radio knobs (pull off), the shaft nuts, and the clock knob.

3. Remove the instrument cluster bezel (trim plate) attaching screws; there are three at the top and one each in the two lower corners. Pull the bezel slightly rearward.

4. Remove the headlamp shaft and knob.

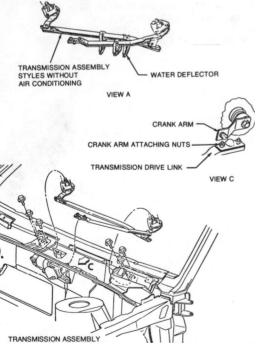

TRANSMISSION ASSEMBLY STYLES WITHOUT AIR CONDITIONING — WATER DEFLECTOR

VIEW A

CRANK ARM

CRANK ARM ATTACHING NUTS

TRANSMISSION DRIVE LINK

VIEW C

TRANSMISSION ASSEMBLY STYLE WITH AIR CONDITIONING VIEW B

Windshield wiper linkage

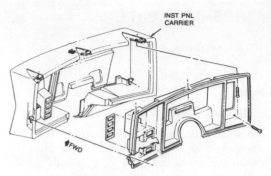

INST PNL CARRIER

FWD

Citation trim plate removal

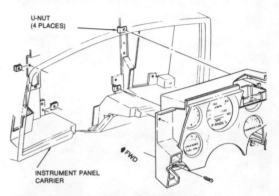

U-NUT (4 PLACES)

FWD

INSTRUMENT PANEL CARRIER

Citation instrument cluster removal

5. Disconnect the accessory switch wiring.

6. Remove the bezel.

7. Remove the four screws holding the instrument cluster to the instrument panel.

8. Disconnect the shift indicator cable from the steering column shift bowl on models with automatic transaxle.

9. Pull the cluster towards you and disconnect the speedometer cable and instrument electrical connections.

10. Remove the instrument cluster. Installation is the reverse.

Omega

1. Remove the steering column trim cover.

2. Lower the steering column.

3. Remove the four screws holding the instrument panel trim cover to the panel.

4. Pull the trim cover rearward and disconnect the switch wiring, and the remote control mirror cable if your car has one. Remove the trim panel.

5. Remove the four screws holding the instrument cluster to the panel.

6. Disconnect the shift indicator cable from the steering column shift bowl, if your Omega has an automatic transaxle.

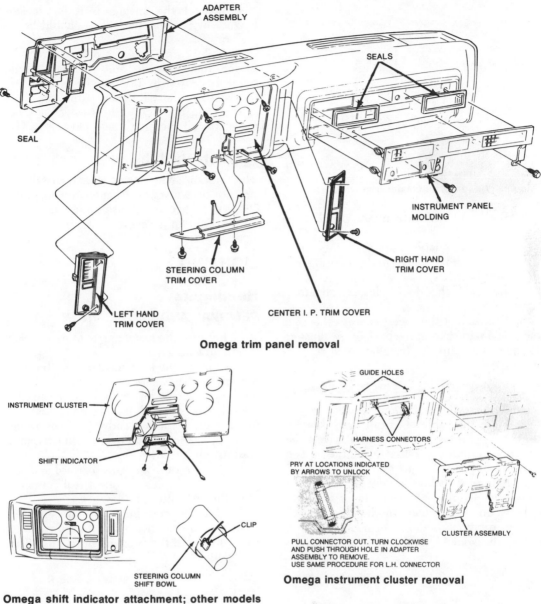

Omega trim panel removal

Omega shift indicator attachment; other models similar

Omega instrument cluster removal

7. Pull the cluster towards you and disconnect the speedometer cable and electrical wiring.

8. Remove the instrument cluster. Installation is the reverse.

Phoenix

1. Disconnect the negative battery cable.

2. Remove the speedometer cluster trim plate. There is one screw in each corner.

3. Remove the screws attaching the steering column trim cover to the instrument panel and remove the trim cover.

4. Remove the four cluster attaching screws.

5. With automatic transaxle, disconnect the shift indicator cable, marking the cable location on the steering column shift bowl prior to disconnecting.

6. Disconnect the speedometer cable and pull the cluster towards you. Disconnect the electrical wiring from the back of the cluster and remove the cluster. Installation is the reverse.

Skylark

1. Disconnect the negative battery cable.

2. Remove the radio and accessory switch knobs.

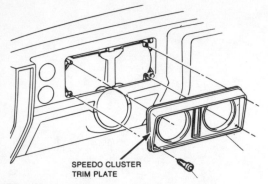

SPEEDO CLUSTER
TRIM PLATE

Phoenix speedometer cluster trim plate

3. Remove the instrument panel trim plate.

4. With automatic transaxle, disconnect the shift indicator cable from the steering column shift bowl.

5. Remove the four cluster attaching screws.

6. Disconnect the speedometer cable and electrical wiring from the back of the cluster. Remove the cluster. Installation is the reverse.

SPEEDOMETER CABLE REPLACEMENT

1. Remove the instrument cluster.

2. Slide the cable out from the casing. If the cable is broken, the casing will have to be unscrewed from the transaxle and the broken piece removed from that end.

3. Before installing a new cable, slip a piece of cable into the speedometer and spin it between your fingers in the direction of normal rotation. If the mechanism sticks or binds, the speedometer should be repaired or replaced.

4. Inspect the casing; if it is cracked, kinked, or broken, the casing should be replaced.

5. Slide a new cable into the casing, engaging the transaxle end securely. Sometimes it is easier to unscrew the casing at the transaxle end, install the cable into the transaxle fitting, and screw the casing back into place. Install the instrument cluster.

Ignition Switch

The ignition switch removal and installation procedure is given in Chapter Seven, under "Steering", because the steering wheel must be removed for access to the ignition switch.

LIGHTING

Headlights

REMOVAL AND INSTALLATION

1. Remove the headlamp trim panel (grille panel) attaching screws.

2. Remove the four headlamp bulb retaining screws. These are the screws which hold the retaining ring for the bulb to the front of the car. Do not touch the two headlamp aiming screws, at the top and side of the retaining ring, or the headlamp aim will have to be readjusted.

3. Pull the bulb and ring forward and separate them. Unplug the electrical connector from the rear of the bulb.

4. Plug the new bulb into the electrical connector. Install the bulb into the retaining ring and install the ring and bulb. Install the trim panel.

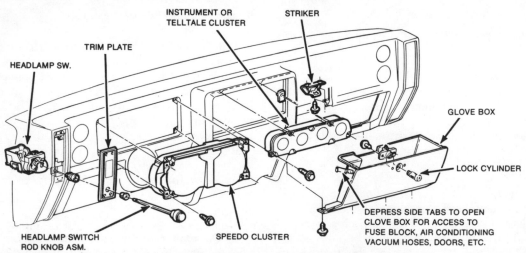

INSTRUMENT OR
TELLTALE CLUSTER

STRIKER

TRIM PLATE

HEADLAMP SW.

GLOVE BOX

LOCK CYLINDER

HEADLAMP SWITCH
ROD KNOB ASM.

SPEEDO CLUSTER

DEPRESS SIDE TABS TO OPEN
CLOVE BOX FOR ACCESS TO
FUSE BLOCK, AIR CONDITIONING
VACUUM HOSES, DOORS, ETC.

Phoenix instrument cluster removal

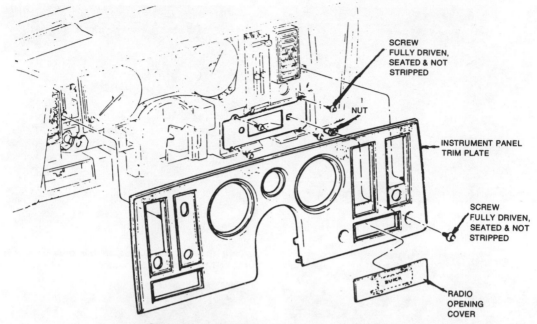

SCREW
FULLY DRIVEN,
SEATED & NOT
STRIPPED

NUT

INSTRUMENT PANEL
TRIM PLATE

SCREW
FULLY DRIVEN,
SEATED & NOT
STRIPPED

RADIO
OPENING
COVER

Skylark instrument panel trim plate removal

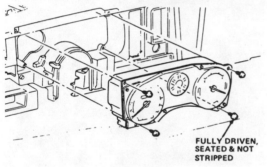

FULLY DRIVEN,
SEATED & NOT
STRIPPED

Skylark instrument cluster removal

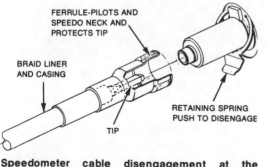

FERRULE-PILOTS AND
SPEEDO NECK AND
PROTECTS TIP

BRAID LINER
AND CASING

RETAINING SPRING
PUSH TO DISENGAGE

TIP

Speedometer cable disengagement at the speedometer

Taillights

REMOVAL AND INSTALLATION

1. Open the trunk or hatch lid.
2. Unscrew the four wingnuts on the taillight cover assembly and remove the cover.

3. Pull the taillight outward for access to the lamp sockets.
4. Remove the bulb socket(s). Remove the bulb(s) (press and turn). Installation is the reverse.

CIRCUIT PROTECTION

Fusible Links

A fusible link is a protective device used in an electrical circuit. When the current increases

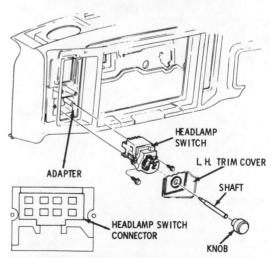

HEADLAMP
SWITCH

L. H. TRIM COVER

SHAFT

ADAPTER

HEADLAMP SWITCH
CONNECTOR

KNOB

The headlamp switch is removed on all models by pulling the knob out, depressing the retaining button on the switch assembly, removing the knob and shaft, and removing the switch

The arrows point to the headlight aiming screws; don't touch these when replacing the headlamp

Remove the trim panel attaching bolts

Remove the four retaining screws

Unplug the old bulb, plug in the new one, and reverse the removal process

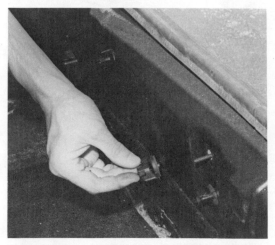

The taillight assemblies are retained by four wing-nuts

beyond a certain amperage, the fusible metal of the wire link melts, thus breaking the electrical circuit and preventing further damage to other components and wiring. Whenever a fusible link is melted because of a short circuit, correct the cause before installing a new one.

The X-Body cars have three fusible links.

Two of them are located at the front center of the engine, at the starter solenoid. One protects the lighting circuit and the other protects the starting and charging circuit. The third fusible link is in the wiring harness at the right hand side of the car, at the cowl; it protects the engine cooling fan.

To replace a fusible link, cut off the burned link beyond the original splice. Replace the link with a new one of the same rating. If the splice has two wires, two repair links are required, one for each wire. Connect the new fusible link to the wires, then crimp securely.

CAUTION: *Use only replacements of the same electrical capacity as the original, available from your dealer. Replacements of a different electrical value will not provide adequate system protection.*

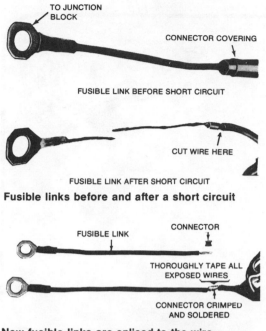

FUSIBLE LINK BEFORE SHORT CIRCUIT

FUSIBLE LINK AFTER SHORT CIRCUIT

Fusible links before and after a short circuit

New fusible links are spliced to the wire

Fuses

Fuses protect all the major electrical systems in the car. In case of an electrical overload, the fuse melts, breaking the circuit and stopping the flow of electricity.

If a fuse blows, the cause should be investigated and corrected before the installation of a new fuse. This, however, is easier to say than to do. Because each fuse protects a limited number of components, your job is narrowed down somewhat. Begin your investigation by looking for obvious fraying, loose connections, breaks in insulation, etc. Use the techniques outlined at the beginning of this chapter. Electrical problems are almost always a real headache to solve, but if you are patient and persistent, and approach the problem logically (that is, don't start replacing electrical components randomly), you will eventually find the solution.

The amperage of each fuse and the circuit it protects are marked on the fusebox, which is located under the left side (driver's side) of the instrument panel.

Circuit Breakers

The headlights are protected by a circuit breaker in the headlamp switch. If the circuit breaker trips, the headlights will either flash on and off, or stay off altogether. The circuit breaker resets automatically after the overload is removed.

The windshield wipers are also protected by a circuit breaker. If the motor overheats, the circuit breaker will trip, remaining off until the motor cools or the overload is removed. One common cause of overheating is operation of the wipers in heavy snow.

The circuit breakers for the power door locks and power windows are located in the wiring harness in the engine compartment, on the firewall.

Flashers

The hazard flasher is located at the top left corner of the fusebox. The turn signal flasher is installed in a clamp attached to the base of the steering column support inside the car. In both cases, replacement is made by unplugging the old flasher and plugging in a new one.

WIRING DIAGRAMS

Wiring diagrams have been omitted from this book. As cars have become more complex, wiring diagrams have grown in size and complexity as well. It has become impossible to provide a readable reproduction in a reasonable number of pages. Information on ordering wiring diagrams from the vehicle manufacturer can be found in the owner's manual.

6

Clutch and Transaxle

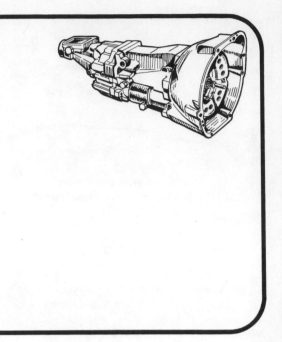

MANUAL TRANSAXLE

"Transaxle" is the term used to identify a unit which combines the transmission and drive axle into one component. The X-Body cars use a model MT-125 manual transaxle as standard equipment. This is an all-new design, sharing no parts with any other G.M. transmission or differential. All forward gears in this design are in constant mesh. Final drive from the transmission is taken from the output gear, which is an integral part of the output shaft; the output gear transfers power to the differential ring gear and differential assembly. The differential is of conventional design.

Because of the complexity of the transaxle, no overhaul procedures are given in this book. However, removal and installation, adjustment, and halfshaft removal, installation and overhaul are covered.

TRANSAXLE REMOVAL AND INSTALLATION

1. Disconnect the negative battery cable from the transaxle case.
2. Remove the two transaxle strut bracket bolts on the left side of the engine compartment, if equipped.
3. Remove the top four engine-to-transaxle bolts, and the one at the rear near the firewall. The one at the rear is installed from the engine side.
4. Loosen the engine-to-transaxle bolt near the starter, but do not remove.
5. Disconnect the speedometer cable at the transaxle, or at the speed control transducer on cars so equipped.
6. Remove the retaining clip and washer from the shift linkage at the transaxle. Remove the clips holding the cables to the mounting bosses on the case.
7. Support the engine with a lifting chain.
8. Unlock the steering column and raise

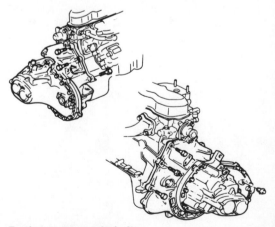

Engine-to-transaxle bolts

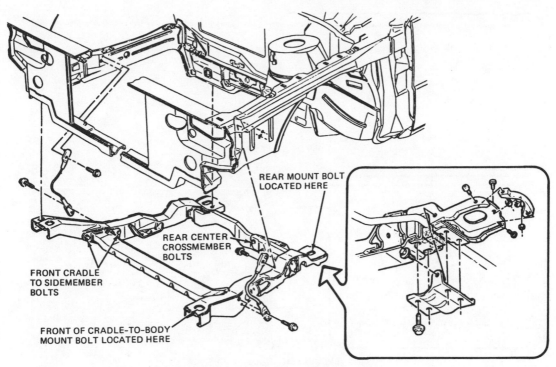

REAR MOUNT BOLT LOCATED HERE

REAR CENTER CROSSMEMBER BOLTS

FRONT CRADLE TO SIDEMEMBER BOLTS

FRONT OF CRADLE-TO-BODY MOUNT BOLT LOCATED HERE

Transaxle and engine cradle assembly

and support the car. Drain the transaxle. Remove the two nuts attaching the stabilizer bar to the left lower control arm. Remove the four bolts which attach the left retaining plate to the engine cradle. The retaining plate covers and holds the stabilizer bar.

9. Loosen the four bolts holding the right stabilizer bracket.

10. Disconnect and remove the exhaust pipe if necessary.

11. Pull the stabilizer bar down on the left side.

12. Remove the four nuts and disconnect the front and rear transaxle mounts from the engine cradle. Remove the two rear center crossmember bolts.

13. Remove the three right side front cradle attaching bolts. They are accessible under the splash shield.

14. Remove the top bolt from the lower front transaxle shock absorber if equipped.

15. Remove the left front wheel. Remove the front cradle-to-body bolts on the left side, and the rear cradle-to-body bolts.

16. Pull the left side drive shaft from the transaxle using G.M. special tool J-28468 or the equivalent. The right side axle shaft will simply disconnect from the case. When the transaxle is removed, the right shaft can be swung out of the way. A boot protector

should be used when disconnecting the driveshafts.

17. Swing the cradle to the left side. Secure out of the way, outboard of the fender well.

18. Remove the flywheel and starter shield bolts, and remove the shields.

19. Remove the two transaxle extension bolts from the engine-to-transaxle bracket, if equipped.

20. Place a jack under the transaxle case. Remove the last engine-to-transaxle bolt. Pull the transaxle to the left, away from the engine, then down and out from under the car.

Installation is the reverse.

1. Position the right axle shaft into its bore as the transaxle is being installed.

2. When the transaxle is bolted to the engine, swing the cradle into position and install the cradle-to-body bolts immediately. Be sure to guide the left axle shaft into place as the cradle is moved back into position.

SHIFT LINKAGE ADJUSTMENT

Shift linkage in the X-Body cars is via a push-pull two cable affair. One cable is called the "trans-selector" cable, and the other is called the "trans-shifter" cable. The range provided for shift linkage adjustments is fairly narrow,

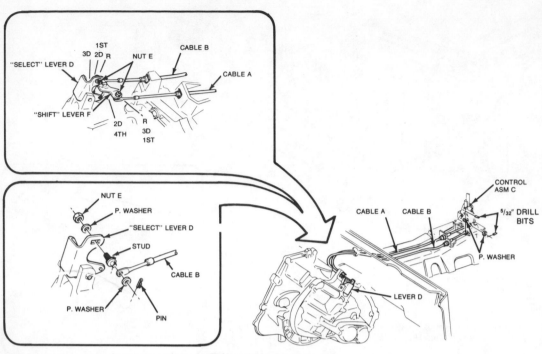

Shift cable adjustments

and it may be necessary to fine tune the adjustment after the factory-recommended procedure is completed.

1. Remove the shifter boot and retainer inside the car. Shift into first gear.

2. Install two No. 22 drill bits, or two ⁵/₃₂ in. rods, into the two alignment holes in the shifter assembly to hold it in first gear.

3. Place the transaxle into first gear by pushing the rail selector shaft down just to the point of feeling the resistance of the inhibitor spring. Then rotate the shift lever all the way counterclockwise.

4. Install the stud, with the cable attached, into the slotted area of the shift lever.

5. Install the stud, with the cable attached, into the slotted area of the select lever, while gently pulling on the lever to remove all lash.

Remove the two drill bits or pins from the shifter.

Check the shifter for proper operation. It may be necessary to fine tune the adjustment after road testing.

Halfshafts

The X-Body cars use unequal-length halfshafts, with specific applications for automatic and manual transaxle use. All halfshafts except the left hand inboard joint of the automatic transaxle incorporate a male spline; the shafts interlock with the transaxle gears through the use of barrel-type snap rings. The left hand inboard shaft on the automatic transaxle uses a female spline which installs over a stub shaft protruding from the transaxle. Four constant velocity joints are used, two on each shaft. The inner joints are of the double offset design; the outer joints are Rzeppa-type.

REMOVAL AND INSTALLATION

1. Remove the hub nut.

2. Raise the front of the car. Remove the wheel and tire.

3. Install an axle shaft boot seal protector, G.M. special tool no. J-28712 or the equivalent, onto the seal.

4. Disconnect the brake hose clip from the MacPherson strut, but do not disconnect the hose from the caliper. Remove the brake caliper from the spindle, and hang the caliper out of the way by a length of wire. Do not allow the caliper to hang by the brake hose.

5. Mark the camber alignment cam bolt for reassembly. Remove the cam bolt and the upper attaching bolt from the strut and spindle.

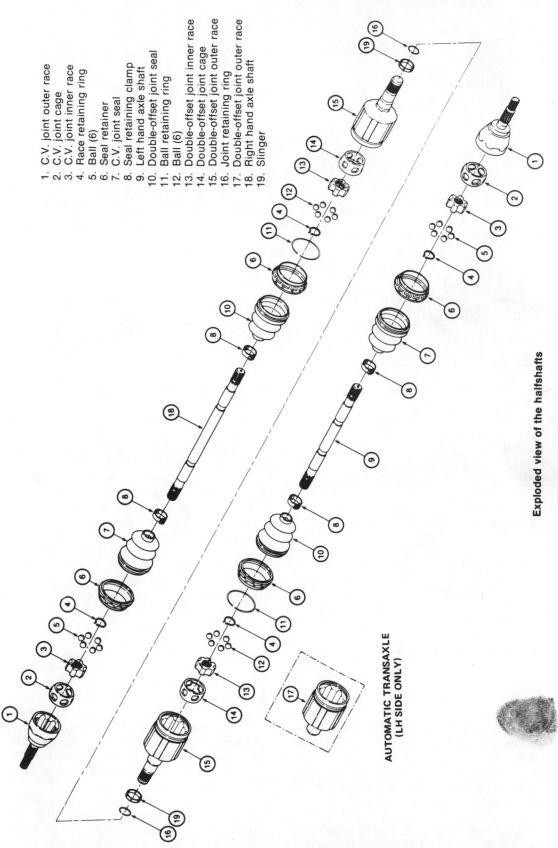

1. C.V. joint outer race
2. C.V. joint cage
3. C.V. joint inner race
4. Race retaining ring
5. Ball (6)
6. Seal retainer
7. C.V. joint seal
8. Seal retaining clamp
9. Left hand axle shaft
10. Double-offset joint seal
11. Ball retaining ring
12. Ball (6)
13. Double-offset joint inner race
14. Double-offset joint cage
15. Double-offset joint outer race
16. Joint retaining ring
17. Double-offset joint outer race
18. Right hand axle shaft
19. Slinger

Exploded view of the halfshafts

AUTOMATIC TRANSAXLE
(LH SIDE ONLY)

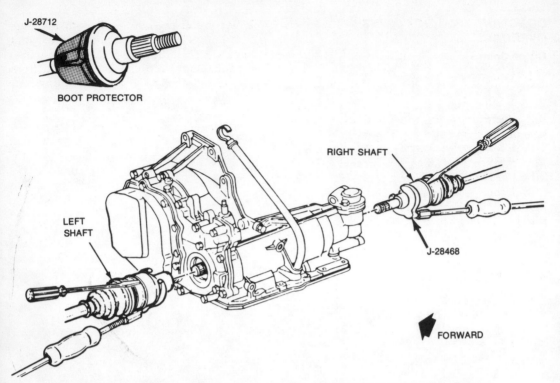

J-28712

BOOT PROTECTOR

RIGHT SHAFT

LEFT SHAFT

J-28468

FORWARD

Halfshaft removal; the special tools are attached to slide hammers in this diagram

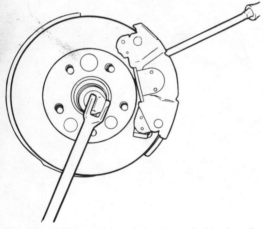

Insert a drift into the caliper when tightening the hub nut

6. Pull the steering knuckle assembly from the strut bracket.

7. Using G.M. special tool J-28468 or the equivalent, remove the axle shaft from the transaxle.

8. Using G.M. special tool J-28733 or the equivalent spindle remover, remove the axle shaft from the hub and bearing assembly.

To install:

1. If a new drive axle is to be installed, a new knuckle seal should be installed first.

2. Loosely install the drive axle into the transaxle and steering knuckle.

3. Loosely attach the steering knuckle to the suspension strut.

4. Install the brake caliper. Tighten the bolts to 30 ft lbs (40 Nm.).

5. The drive axle is an interference fit in the steering knuckle. Press the axle into place, then install the hub nut. When the shaft begins to turn with the hub, insert a drift through the caliper into one of the cooling slots in the rotor to keep it from turning. Tighten the hub nut to 70 ft lbs (100 Nm.) to completely seat the shaft.

6. Load the hub assembly by lowering it onto a jackstand. Align the camber cam bolt marks made during removal, install the bolt and tighten to 140 ft lbs (190 Nm.). Tighten the upper nut to the same value.

7. Install the axle shaft all the way into the transaxle using a screwdriver inserted into the groove provided on the inner retainer. Tap the screwdriver until the shaft seats in the transaxle.

8. Connect the brake hose clip to the strut. Install the tire and wheel, lower the car, and tighten the hub nut to 225 ft lbs (305 Nm.).

CONSTANT VELOCITY JOINT OVERHAUL

Outer Joint

1. Remove the axle shaft.

2. Cut off the seal retaining clamp. Using a brass drift and a hammer, lightly tap the seal retainer from the outside toward the inside of the shaft to remove from the joint.

3. Use a pair of snap ring pliers to spread the retaining ring apart. Pull the axle shaft from the joint.

4. Using a brass drift and a hammer, lightly tap on the inner race cage until it has tilted sufficiently to remove one of the balls. Remove the other balls in the same manner.

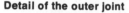

Detail of the outer joint

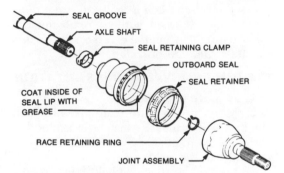

Use a brass drift to pivot the cage

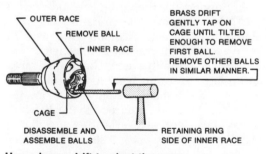

The inner race and cage can be removed from the outer race when pivoted 90°

5. Pivot the cage 90° and, with the cage ball windows aligned with the outer joint windows, lift out the cage and the inner race.

6. The inner race can be removed from the cage by pivoting it 90° and lifting out. Clean all parts thoroughly and inspect for wear.

7. To install, put a light coat of the grease provided in the rebuilding kit onto the ball grooves of the inner race and outer joint. Install the parts in the reverse order of removal. To install the seal retainer, install the axle shaft assembly into an arbor press. Support the seal retainer on blocks, and press the axle shaft down until the seal retainer seats on the outer joint. When assembling, apply half the grease provided in the rebuilding kit to the joint; fill the seal (boot) with the rest of the grease.

Inner Joint

1. The joint seal is removed in the same manner as the outer joint seal. Follow Steps 1–3 of the outer joint procedure.

2. To disassemble the inner joint, remove the ball retaining ring from the joint. Pull the cage and inner race from the joint. The balls will come out with the race.

3. Center the inner race lobes in the cage windows, pivot the race 90°, and lift the race from the cage.

4. Assembly of the joint is the reverse.

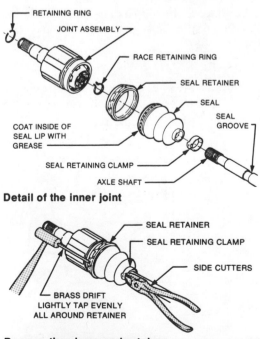

Detail of the inner joint

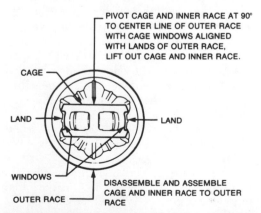

Remove the clamp and retainer

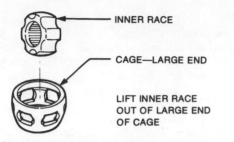

INNER RACE

CAGE—LARGE END

LIFT INNER RACE
OUT OF LARGE END
OF CAGE

The inner race exits from the large end of the cage

SMALL END OF CAGE

RETAINING RING ON INNER RACE FACES
SMALL END OF CAGE BEFORE
INSTALLING ANY BALLS

Inner race installed in the cage

The inner joint seal retainer must be pressed onto the joint. See Step 7 of the outer joint procedure.

CLUTCH

ADJUSTMENT

The X-Body cars have a self-adjusting clutch mechanism located on the clutch pedal, eliminating the need for periodic free play adjustments. The self-adjusting mechanism should be inspected periodically as follows:

1. Depress the clutch pedal and look for the pawl on the self-adjusting mechanism to firmly engage the teeth on the ratchet.

2. Release the clutch. The pawl should be lifted off of the teeth by the metal stop on the bracket.

NEUTRAL START SWITCH

A neutral start switch is located on the clutch pedal assembly; the switch prevents the

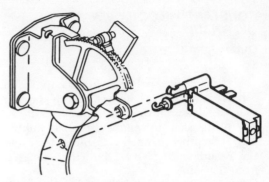

The neutral start switch is attached to the clutch pedal

engine from starting unless the clutch is depressed. If the switch is faulty, it can be unbolted and replaced without removing the pedal assembly from the car. No adjustments for the switch are provided.

CLUTCH REMOVAL AND INSTALLATION

1. Remove the transaxle.

2. Mark the pressure plate assembly and the flywheel so that they can be assembled in the same position. They were balanced as an assembly at the factory.

3. Loosen the attaching bolts one turn at a time until spring tension is relieved.

4. Support the pressure plate and remove the bolts. Remove the pressure plate and clutch disc. Do not disassemble the pressure plate assembly; replace it if defective.

5. Inspect the flywheel, clutch disc, pressure plate, throwout bearing and the clutch fork and pivot shaft assembly for wear. Replace the parts as required. If the flywheel shows any signs of overheating, or if it is badly grooved or scored, it should be refaced or replaced.

6. Clean the pressure plate and flywheel mating surfaces thoroughly. Position the clutch disc and pressure plate into the installed position, and support with a dummy shaft or clutch aligning tool. The clutch plate is assembled with the damper springs offset toward the transaxle. One side of the factory-supplied clutch disc is stamped "Flywheel side."

7. Install the pressure plate-to-flywheel bolts. Tighten them gradually in a criss-cross pattern.

8. Lubricate the outside groove and the inside recess of the release bearing with high temperature grease. Wipe off any excess. Install the release bearing.

9. Install the transaxle.

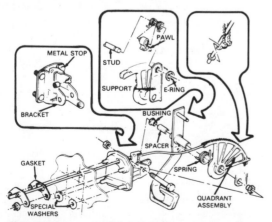

METAL STOP

PAWL

STUD

SUPPORT

E-RING

BRACKET

BUSHING

SPACER

GASKET

SPRING

SPECIAL
WASHERS

QUADRANT
ASSEMBLY

Clutch pedal installation details

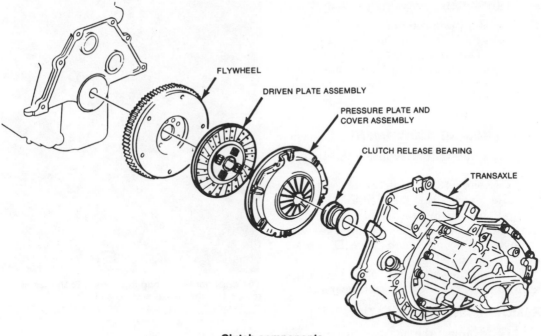

Clutch components

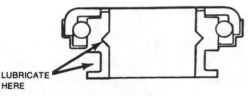

LUBRICATE
HERE

Release bearing lubrication

CLUTCH CABLE REPLACEMENT

1. Disconnect the end of the cable from the clutch release lever at the transaxle. Do not allow the cable to snap rapidly toward the rear of the car; doing so will damage the quadrant in the self-adjusting mechanism.

2. Disconnect the clutch cable from the self-adjusting quadrant. Lift the locking pawl away from the quadrant, then slide the cable out to the right.

3. Unbolt the two nuts holding the cable retainer to the upper studs on the engine side of the firewall. Disconnect the cable from the retaining bracket bolted to the transaxle. Remove the cable.

4. To install a new cable, place the gasket in position on the two upper studs on the firewall. Place a new cable into position with the retaining flange against the bracket.

5. Attach the end of the cable to the self-adjusting mechanism quadrant. Be sure to route the cable underneath the pawl.

6. Install the two nuts to the firewall cable retainer. Tighten to 30 ft lbs (38 Nm.).

7. Attach the cable to the transaxle bracket.

8. Attach the end of the cable to the clutch release lever. Don't yank too hard on the cable, which will damage the stop on the quadrant.

AUTOMATIC TRANSAXLE

All of the X-Body cars use the Turbo Hydra-Matic 125 automatic transaxle as optional equipment. This is a fully automatic unit of conventional design, incorporating a three element hydraulic torque converter, a compound planetary gear set, and a dual sprocket and drive link assembly. The sprockets and drive link (Hy-Vo® chain) connect the torque converter assembly to the transmission gears. The transaxle also incorporates the differential assembly, which is of conventional design. Power is transmitted from the transmission to the final drive and differential assembly through helical cut gears.

No overhaul procedures are given in this book because of the complexity of the transaxle. Transaxle removal and installation, adjustment, and halfshaft removal, installation, and overhaul procedures are covered.

Adjustments

The only adjustment required on the TH-M 125 transaxle is the shift linkage (cable) adjustment. The neutral start switch and throttle valve are self-adjusting. The transaxle has only one band, with no provision for periodic adjustment. Pan removal, fluid and filter changes are covered in Chapter One.

SHIFT LINKAGE ADJUSTMENT

1. Place the shift lever inside the car into Neutral.
2. Disconnect the shift cable from the transaxle lever. Place the transaxle lever in Neutral, by moving the lever clockwise to the Low (L) detent, then counterclockwise through the Second (S) and Drive (D) detents to the Neutral detent.
3. Attach the shift cable to the pin on the transaxle lever. Check the shift operation.

REMOVAL AND INSTALLATION

1. Disconnect the negative battery cable from the transaxle. Tape the wire to the upper radiator hose to keep it out of the way.
2. Slide the detent cable in the opposite direction of the cable to remove it from the carburetor.
3. Unbolt the detent cable attaching bracket at the transaxle.
4. Pull up on the detent cable cover at the transaxle until the cable is exposed. Disconnect the cable from the rod.
5. Remove the two transaxle strut bracket bolts at the transaxle, if equipped.
6. Remove all the engine-to-transaxle bolts except the one near the starter. The one nearest the firewall is installed from the

The speedometer coupling is next to the left strut tower and the brake master cylinder

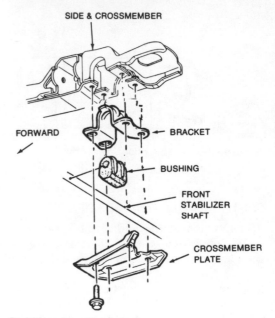

Stabilizer bar attachment

engine side; you will need a short handled box wrench or ratchet to reach it.

7. Loosen but do not remove the engine-to-transaxle bolt near the starter.
8. Disconnect the speedometer cable at the upper and lower coupling. On cars with cruise control, remove the speedometer cable at the transducer.
9. Remove the retaining clip and washer from the shift linkage at the transaxle. Remove the two shift linkage bracket bolts.
10. Disconnect and plug the two fluid

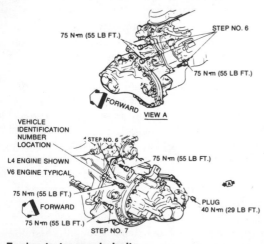

Engine-to-transaxle bolts

cooler lines at the transaxle. These are inch-size fittings (½ and ¹¹/₁₆); use a back-up wrench to avoid twisting the lines.

11. Install an engine holding chain or hoist. Raise the engine enough to take its weight off the mounts.

12. Unlock the steering column and raise the car.

13. Remove the two nuts holding the anti-sway (stabilizer) bar to the left lower control arm (driver's side).

14. Remove the four bolts attaching the covering plate over the stabilizer bar to the engine cradle on the left side (driver's side).

15. Loosen but do not remove the four bolts holding the stabilizer bar bracket to the right side (passenger's side) of the engine cradle. Pull the bar down on the driver's side.

16. Disconnect the front and rear transaxle mounts at the engine cradle.

17. Remove the two rear center crossmember bolts.

18. Remove the three right (passenger) side front engine cradle attaching bolts. The nuts are accessible under the splash shield next to the frame rail.

19. Remove the top bolt from the lower front transaxle shock absorber, if equipped (V6 engine only).

20. Remove the left (driver) side front and rear cradle-to-body bolts.

21. Remove the left front wheel. Attach an

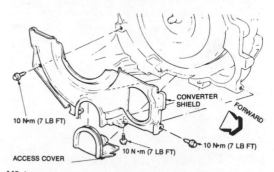

V6 torque converter and starter shields

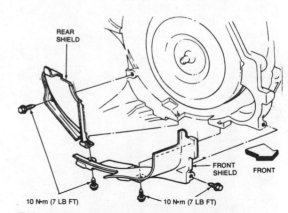

Four cylinder torque converter and starter shields

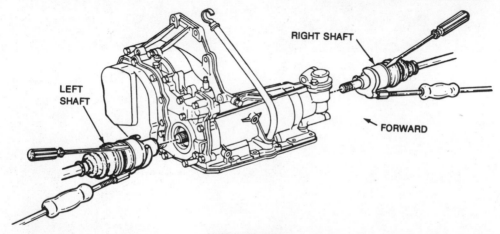

V6 transaxle shock absorber

Halfshaft removal

axle shaft removing tool (G.M. part no. J-28468 or the equivalent) to a slide hammer. Place the tool behind the axle shaft cones and pull the cones out away from the transaxle. Remove the right shaft in the same manner. Set the shafts out of the way. Plug the openings in the transaxle to prevent fluid leakage and the entry of dirt.

22. Swing the partial engine cradle to the left (driver) side and wire it out of the way outboard of the fender well.

23. Remove the four torque converter and starter shield bolts. Remove the two transaxle extension bolts from the engine-to-transaxle bracket.

24. Attach a transaxle jack to the case.

25. Use a felt pen to matchmark the torque converter and flywheel. Remove the three torque converter-to-flywheel bolts.

26. Remove the transaxle-to-engine bolt near the starter. Remove the transaxle by sliding it to the left, away from the engine.

Installation is the reverse. As the transaxle is installed, slide the right axle shaft into the case. Install the cradle-to-body bolts before the stabilizer bar is installed. To aid in stabilizer bar installation, a pry hole has been provided in the engine cradle.

HALFSHAFT REMOVAL, INSTALLATION AND OVERHAUL

The procedures for the automatic transaxle halfshafts are the same as those outlined earlier for the manual transaxle.

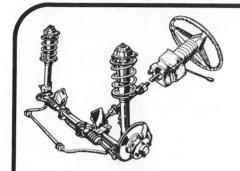

7

Suspension
and Steering

FRONT SUSPENSION

The Citation, Omega, Phoenix and Skylark use a MacPherson strut front suspension design. This is an all-new design, not shared with any other G.M. car. A MacPherson strut combines the functions of a shock absorber and an upper suspension member (upper arm) into one unit. The strut is surrounded by a coil spring, which provides normal front suspension functions.

The strut bolts to the body shell at its upper end, and to the steering knuckle at the lower end. The strut pivots with the steering knuckle by means of a sealed mounting assembly at the upper end which contains a preloaded, non-adjustable bearing.

The steering knuckle is connected to the chassis at the lower end by a conventional lower arm, and pivots in the arm in a preloaded ball joint of standard design. The knuckle clamps to the ball joint stud.

Advantages of the MacPherson strut design, aside from its relative simplicity, include reduced weight and friction, minimal intrusion into the engine and passenger compartments, and ease of service.

MacPherson Strut Removal and Installation

The MacPherson strut is a combination coil spring and shock absorber (damper) unit. The strut is removed as an assembly from the car. A special strut compressor must be used to disassemble the strut and coil spring.

REMOVAL

1. Loosen the wheel nuts, raise the car, and remove the wheel and tire.
2. Remove the brake hose clip-to-strut bolt. Do not disconnect the hose from the caliper.
3. Mark the camber cam eccentric adjuster for assembly.
4. Remove the two lower strut-to-steering knuckle bolts and the three upper strut-to-body nuts. Remove the strut.

DISASSEMBLY

A MacPherson strut compressor tool, G.M. part J-26584 or the equivalent must be used.
1. Clamp the strut compressor in a vise.
2. Install the strut in the compressor. Install the compressor adapters, if used.

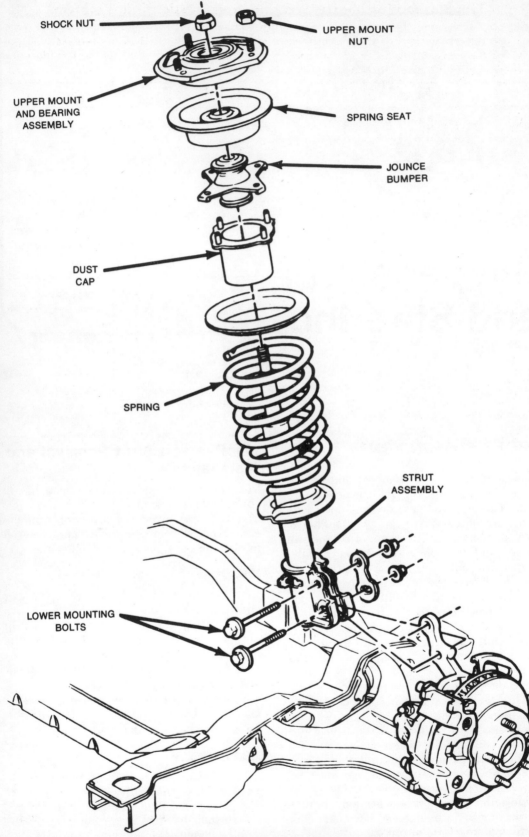

SHOCK NUT

UPPER MOUNT NUT

UPPER MOUNT AND BEARING ASSEMBLY

SPRING SEAT

JOUNCE BUMPER

DUST CAP

SPRING

STRUT ASSEMBLY

LOWER MOUNTING BOLTS

An exploded view of the MacPherson strut

Troubleshooting Basic Steering and Suspension Problems

Most problems in the front end and steering are caused by improperly maintained tires which you can correct yourself, or by incorrect wheel alignment, which requires the services of a professional mechanic. Get in the habit of checking tires frequently; this is usually the first place that problems in the front end or steering will show up.

The Condition	Is Caused By	What to Do
Hard Steering (steering wheel is hard to turn)	• Low or uneven tire pressure • Loose power steering pump drive belt • Low or incorrect power steering fluid • Incorrect front end alignment • Defective power steering pump • Bent or poorly lubricated front end parts	• Inflate tires to correct pressure • Adjust belt • Add fluid as necessary • Have front end alignment checked/adjusted • Have pump checked/repaired • Lubricate and/or have defective parts replaced
Loose Steering (too much play in the steering wheel)	• Loose wheel bearings • Loose or worn steering linkage • Faulty shocks • Worn ball joints	• Adjust wheel bearings • Have worn parts serviced • Replace shocks • Have ball joints checked/serviced
Car Veers or Wanders (car pulls to one side with hands off the steering wheel)	• Incorrect tire pressure • Improper front end alignment • Loose wheel bearings • Loose or bent front end components • Faulty shocks	• Inflate tires to correct pressure • Have front end alignment checked/adjusted • Adjust wheel bearings • Have worn components checked/serviced • Replace shocks
Wheel oscillation or vibration transmitted through steering wheel	• Improper tire pressures • Tires out of balance • Loose wheel bearings • Improper front end alignment • Worn or bent front end components	• Inflate tires to correct pressure • Have tires balanced • Adjust wheel bearings • Have front end alignment checked/adjusted • Have front end checked/serviced
Uneven tire wear	• Incorrect tire pressure • Front end out of alignment • Tires out of balance	• Inflate tires to correct pressure • Have front end alignment checked/adjusted • Have tires balanced

3. Compress the spring approximately ½ in. *Do not bottom the spring or the strut rod.*

4. Remove the strut shaft top nut and the top mount and bearing assembly from the strut.

5. Unscrew the compressor until all spring tension is relieved. Remove the spring.

ASSEMBLY

1. Place the strut into the compressor. Rotate the strut until the spindle mounting flange is facing out, away from the compressor.

2. Place the spring on the strut. Make

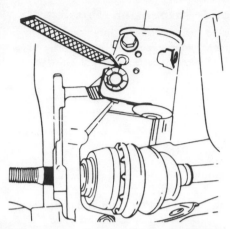

Mark the camber eccentric before removal

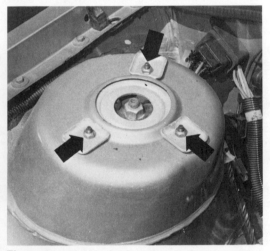

The upper strut-to-body nuts are in the engine compartment

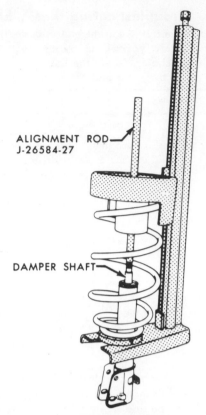

ASSEMBLE STRUT
Use an alignment rod when assembling the strut

sure it is properly seated on the strut bottom plate.

3. Install the strut spring assembly on the spring. Install the compressor adapters, if used.

4. Tighten the strut compressor until it just contacts the spring seat, or the adapters if a tool with adapters is being used.

5. Thread an alignment rod, G.M. tool J-26584-27 or the equivalent, onto the strut damper shaft, hand tight.

6. Compress the spring until approximately 1½ in. of the damper rod can be pulled up through the top spring seat. *Do not compress the spring until it bottoms.*

7. Remove the alignment rod and install the top mount and nut. Tighten the nut to 68 ft lbs (90 Nm.).

8. Unscrew the compressor and remove the strut.

INSTALLATION

1. Install the strut to the body. Tighten the upper nuts hand tight.

2. Place a jack under the lower arm. Raise the arm and install the lower strut-to-knuckle bolts. Align the camber eccentric cam with the marks made during removal. Tighten the strut-to-knuckle bolts to 140 ft lbs (190 Nm.), and the strut-to-body nuts to 18 ft lbs (24 Nm.).

3. Install the brake hose clip on the strut.

4. Install the wheel and lower the car.

NOTE: *If a new strut damper has been installed, the front end will have to be realigned.*

Ball Joints

INSPECTION

The ball joints have built-in wear indicators. As long as the wear indicator (part of the grease nipple) extends below the ball joint seat, the ball joint is OK. When the indicator recedes beneath the seat, replacement is necessary.

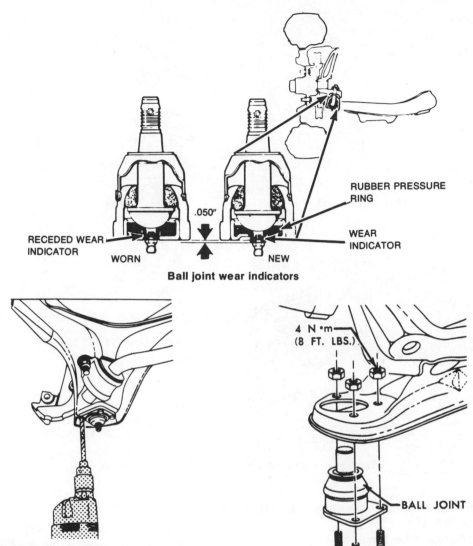

Ball joint wear indicators

RUBBER PRESSURE
RING

WEAR
INDICATOR

RECEDED WEAR
INDICATOR

WORN

.050"

NEW

Drill out the ball joint rivets

4 N•m
(8 FT. LBS.)

BALL JOINT

Ball joint installation

REPLACEMENT

Only one ball joint is used in each lower arm. The MacPherson strut design does not use an upper ball joint.

1. Loosen the wheel nuts, raise the car, and remove the wheel.
2. Use a ⅛ in. drill bit to drill a hole approximately ¼ in. deep in the center of each of the three ball joint rivets.
3. Use a ½ in. drill bit to drill off the rivet heads. Drill only enough to remove the rivet head.
4. Use a hammer and punch to remove the rivets. Drive them out from the bottom.
5. Loosen the ball joint pinch bolt in the steering knuckle.
6. Remove the ball joint.
7. Install the new ball joint in the control arm. Tighten the bolts supplied with the replacement joint to 8 ft lbs.
8. Install the ball stud into the knuckle pinch bolt fitting. It should go in easily; if not, check the stud alignment. Install the pinch bolt from the rear to the front. Tighten to 45 ft lbs (60 Nm.).
9. Install the wheel and lower the car.

Control Arm

REMOVAL AND INSTALLATION

1. Loosen the wheel nuts, raise the car, and remove the wheel.
2. Remove the stabilizer bar from the control arm.

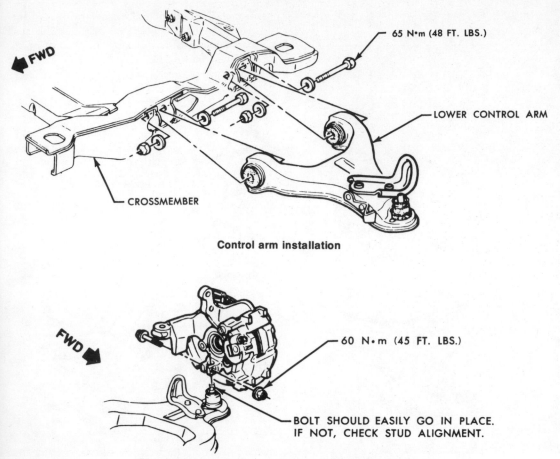

Control arm installation

The ball joint stud should slip into the knuckle fitting

3. Remove the ball joint pinch bolt in the steering knuckle.

4. Remove the control arm pivot bolts and the control arm.

5. To install, insert the control arm into its fittings. Install the pivot bolts from the rear to the front. Tighten the bolts to 48 ft lbs (68 Nm.).

6. Insert the ball stud into the knuckle pinch bolt fitting. It should go in easily; if not, check the ball joint stud alignment.

7. Install the pinch bolt from the rear to the front. Tighten to 45 ft lbs (60 Nm.).

8. Install the stabilizer bar clamp. Tighten to 35 ft lbs (45 Nm.).

9. Install the wheel and lower the car.

Wheel Bearings

The front wheel bearings are sealed, non-adjustable units which require no periodic attention. They are bolted to the steering knuckle by means of an integral flange.

REPLACEMENT

You will need a special tool to pull the bearing free of the halfshaft, G.M. tool no. J-28733 or the equivalent. You should also use a halfshaft boot protector, G.M. tool no. J-28712 or the equivalent to protect the parts from damage.

1. Remove the wheel cover, loosen the hub nut, and raise and support the car. Remove the front wheel.

2. Install the boot cover, G.M. part no. J-28712 or the equivalent.

3. Remove and discard the hub nut. Be sure to use a new one on assembly, not the old one.

4. Remove the brake caliper and rotor:

  a. Remove the allen head caliper mounting bolts;

  b. Remove the caliper from the knuckle and suspend from a length of wire. Do not allow the caliper to hang from the brake hose. Pull the rotor from the knuckle.

5. Remove the three hub and bearing at-

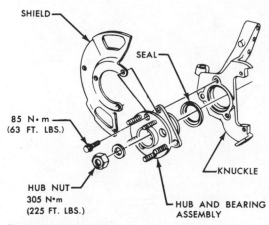

Exploded view of the hub and bearing attachment to the steering knuckle

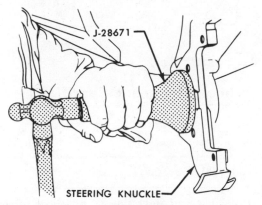

Use a seal driver when installing a new seal into the knuckle

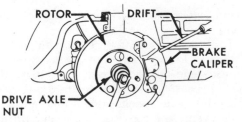

Insert a drift into the rotor when installing the hub nut

taching bolts. If the old bearing is to be re-used, match mark the bolts and holes for installation. The brake rotor splash shield will have to come off, too.

6. Attach a puller, G.M. part no. J-28733 or the equivalent, and remove the bearing. If corrosion is present, make sure the bearing is loose in the knuckle before using the puller.

7. Clean the mating surfaces of all dirt and corrosion. Check the knuckle bore and knuckle seal for damage. If a new bearing is to be installed, remove the old knuckle seal

and install a new one. Grease the lips of the new seal before installation; install with a seal driver made for the purpose, G.M. tool no. J-28671 or the equivalent.

8. Push the bearing onto the halfshaft. Install a new washer and hub nut.

9. Tighten the new hub nut on the half-shaft until the bearing is seated. If the rotor and hub start to rotate as the hub nut is tightened, insert a drift through the caliper and into the rotor cooling fins to prevent rotation. Do not apply full torque to the hub nut at this time—just seat the bearing.

10. Install the brake shield and the bearing retaining bolts. Tighten the bolts evenly to 63 ft lbs (85 Nm.).

11. Install the caliper and rotor. Be sure that the caliper hose isn't twisted. Install the caliper bolts and tighten to 21–35 ft lbs (28–47 Nm.).

12. Install the wheel. Lower the car. Tighten the hub nut to 225 ft lbs (305 Nm.).

Front End Alignment

Only camber and toe are adjustable on the X-cars; caster is preset and non-adjustable.

CAMBER

Camber is the inward or outward tilt from the vertical, measured in degrees, of the front wheels at the top. An outward tilt gives the wheel positive camber; an inward tilt is called negative camber. Proper camber is critical to assure even tire wear.

Camber angle is adjusted on the X-Bodies by loosening the cam and through bolts which attach the MacPherson strut to the steering knuckle and rotating the cam bolt to move the upper end of the knuckle in or out. The bolts must be tightened to 140 ft lbs (190 Nm.) afterwards. The cam bolt must be seated properly between the inner and outer guide surfaces on the strut flange. Measurement of the camber angle requires special alignment equipment; thus the adjustment of camber is not a do-it-yourself job, and not covered here.

TOE

Toe is the amount, measured in a fraction of a millimeter, that the wheels are closer together at one end than the other. Toe-in means that the front wheels are closer together at the front than the rear; toe-out means the rear of the front wheels are closer

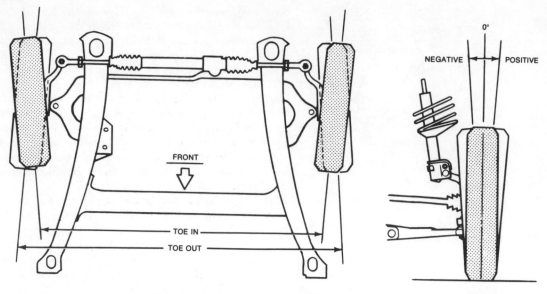

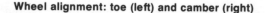

Wheel alignment: toe (left) and camber (right)

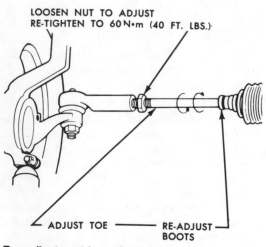

LOOSEN NUT TO ADJUST
RE-TIGHTEN TO 60 N•m (40 FT. LBS.)

ADJUST TOE — RE-ADJUST BOOTS

Toe adjustment is made at the tie rods

Wheel Alignment Specifications

Camber		Toe	
Range (degrees)	Preferred (degrees)	Range (mm)	Preferred (mm)
0.00–1.00	0.50①	0.0–5.0	2.5

① The left and right side to be equal within 0.50°

avoid errors caused by bent rims or wheel runout.

2. If the measurement is not within specifications, loosen the nuts at the steering knuckle end of the tie rod, and remove the tie rod boot clamps. Rotate the tie rods to align the toe to specifications. Rotate the tie rods evenly, or the steering wheel will be crooked when you're done.

3. When the adjustment is correct, tighten the nuts to 45 ft. lbs (60 Nm.). Adjust the boots and tighten the clamps.

REAR SUSPENSION

Rear suspension consists of a solid rear axle tube containing an integral, welded-in stabilizer bar, coil springs, shock absorbers, a lateral track bar, and trailing arms. The trailing arms (control arms) are welded to the axle, and pivot at the frame. Fore and aft movement is controlled by the trailing arms; lat-

together than the front. X-Body cars are designed to have a slight amount of toe-in.

Toe is adjusted by turning the tie rods. It must be checked after camber has been adjusted, but it can be adjusted without disturbing the camber setting. You can make this adjustment without special equipment if you make very careful measurements. The wheels must be straight ahead.

1. Toe can be determined by measuring the distance between the centers of the tire treads, at the front of the tire and at the rear. If the tread pattern makes this impossible, you can measure between the edges of the wheel rims, but make sure to move the car forward and measure in a couple of places to

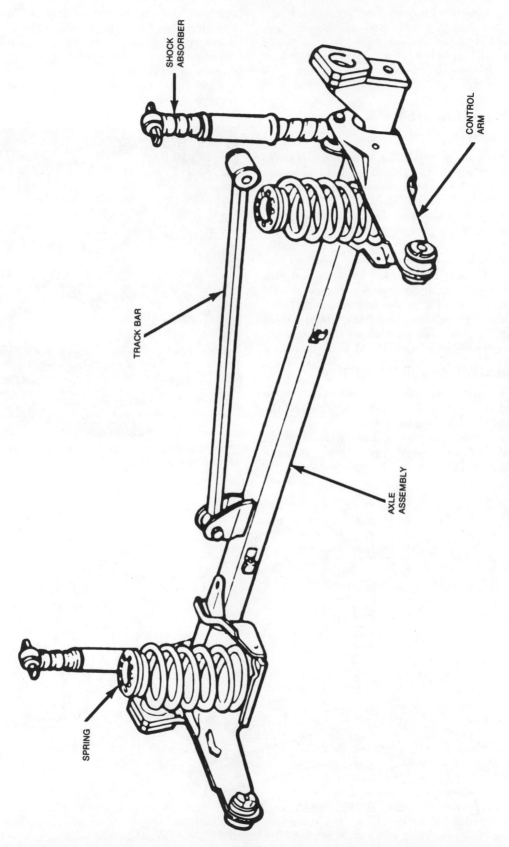

SHOCK ABSORBER

CONTROL ARM

TRACK BAR

AXLE ASSEMBLY

SPRING

Rear axle and suspension components

eral movement is controlled by the track bar. A permanently lubricated and sealed hub and bearing assembly is bolted to each end of the axle tube; it is a non-adjustable unit which must be replaced as an assembly if defective.

Shock Absorbers

TESTING

Visually inspect the shock absorber. If there is evidence of leakage and the shock absorber is covered with oil, the shock is defective and should be replaced.

If there is no sign of excessive leakage (a small amount of weeping is normal) bounce the car at one corner by pressing down on the fender or bumper and releasing. When you have the car bouncing as much as you can, release the fender or bumper. The car should stop bouncing after the first rebound. If the bouncing continues past the center point of the bounce more than once, the shock absorbers are worn and should be replaced.

REMOVAL AND INSTALLATION

1. Open the hatch or trunk lid, remove the trim cover if present, and remove the upper shock absorber nut.

2. Raise and support the car at a convenient working height if you desire. It is not necessary to remove the weight of the car from the shock absorbers, however, so you can leave the car on the ground if you prefer.

3. If the car is equipped with superlift shock absorbers, disconnect the air line.

4. Remove the lower attaching bolt and remove the shock.

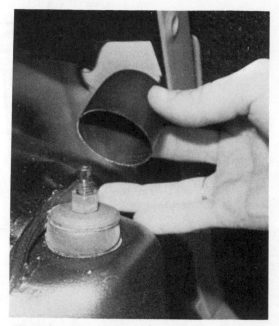

The upper shock absorber mounts are accessible in the trunk

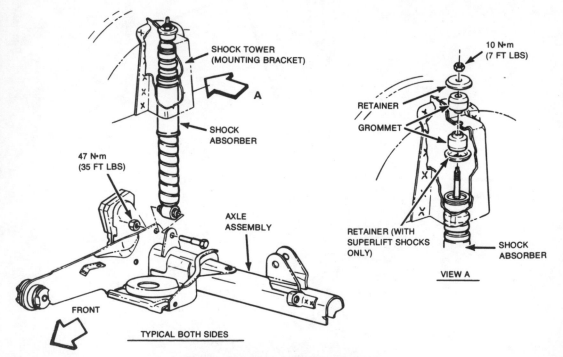

Shock absorber installation details

5. If new shock absorbers are being installed, repeatedly compress them while inverted and extend them in their normal upright position. This will purge them of air.

6. Install the shocks in the reverse order of removal. Tighten the lower mount nut and bolt to 35 ft lbs (47 Nm.), the upper to 7 ft lbs (10 Nm.).

Springs

REMOVAL AND INSTALLATION

CAUTION: *The coil springs are under a considerable amount of tension. Be very careful when removing or installing them; they can exert enough force to cause very serious injuries.*

1. Raise and support the car on a hoist. Do not use twin-post hoist. The swing arc of the axle may cause it to slip from the hoist when the bolts are removed. If a suitable hoist is not available, raise and support the car on jackstands, and use a jack under the axle.

2. Support the axle with a jack that can be raised and lowered.

3. Remove the brake hose attaching brackets (right and left), allowing the hoses to hang freely. Do not disconnect the hoses.

4. Remove the track bar attaching bolts from the rear axle.

5. Remove both shock absorber lower attaching bolts from the axle.

6. Lower the axle. Remove the coil spring retainer from the axle and remove the spring and insulator.

7. To install, position the spring and insulator on the axle. The leg on the upper coil of the spring must be parallel to the axle, facing the lefthand side of the car. Install the spring retainer.

Coil spring retainer at the axle

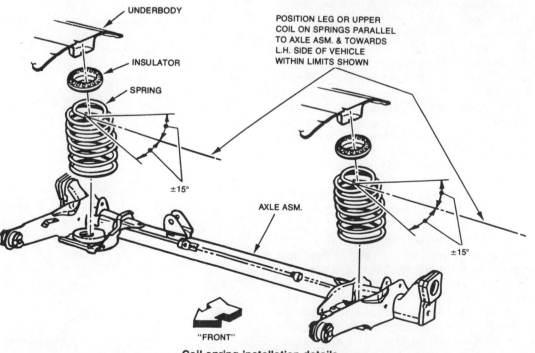

Coil spring installation details

8. Install the shock absorber bolts. Tighten to 34 ft lbs (47 Nm.). Install the track bar, tightening to 33 ft lbs (45 Nm.). Install the brake line brackets. Tighten to 8 ft lbs (11 Nm.).

Rear Hub and Bearing
REMOVAL AND INSTALLATION

1. Loosen the wheel lug nuts. Raise and support the car and remove the wheel.
2. Remove the brake drum. Removal procedures are covered in the next chapter, if needed.
NOTE: *Do not hammer on the brake drum to remove; damage to the bearing will result.*
3. Remove the four hub and bearing retaining bolts and remove the assembly from the axle.
4. Installation is the reverse. Hub and bearing bolt torque is 35 ft lbs (55 Nm.).

STEERING

The X-Body cars use an aluminum-housed Saginaw manual rack and pinion steering gear as standard equipment. The pinion is supported by and turns in a sealed ball bearing at the top and a pressed-in roller bearing at the bottom. The rack moves in bushings pressed into each end of the rack housing.

Wear compensation occurs through the action of an adjuster spring which forces the rack against the pinion teeth. This adjuster eliminates the need for periodic pinion preload adjustments. Preload is adjustable only at overhaul.

The inner tie rod assemblies are both threaded and staked to the rack. A special joint is used, allowing both rocking and rotating motion of the tie rods. The inner tie rod assemblies are lubricated for life and require no periodic attention.

Any service other than replacement of the outer tie rods or the boots requires removal of the unit from the car.

The optional power rack and pinion steering gear is an integral unit, and shares most features with the manual gear. A rotary control valve directs the hydraulic fluid to either side of the rack piston. The integral rack piston is attached to the rack and converts the hydraulic pressure into left or right linear motion. A vane-type constant displacement pump with integral reservoir provides hy-

draulic pressure. No in-car adjustments are necessary or possible on the system, except for periodic belt tension checks and adjustments for the pump. See Chapter One for belt tension adjustments.

Steering Wheel
REMOVAL AND INSTALLATION
Standard Wheel

1. Disconnect the negative cable at the battery.
2. Pull the pad from the wheel. The horn lead is attached to the pad at one end; the other end of the pad has a wire with a spade connector. The horn lead is disconnected by pushing and turning; the spade connector is simply unplugged.
3. Remove the retainer under the pad.
4. Remove the steering shaft nut.
5. There should be alignment marks already present on the wheel and shaft. If not, matchmark the parts.
6. Remove the wheel with a puller.
7. Install the wheel on the shaft, aligning the matchmarks. Install the shaft nut and tighten to 30 ft lbs (40 Nm.).
8. Install the retainer.
9. Plug in the spade connector, and push and turn the horn lead to connect. Install the pad. Connect the negative battery cable.

Sport Wheel

1. Disconnect the negative cable at the battery.
2. Pry the center cap from the wheel.
3. Remove the retainer.

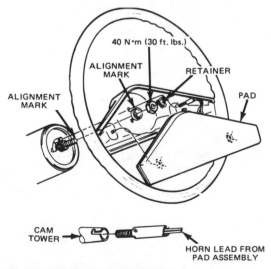

40 N·m (30 ft. lbs.)

ALIGNMENT MARK   RETAINER

ALIGNMENT MARK

PAD

CAM TOWER

HORN LEAD FROM PAD ASSEMBLY

Standard steering wheel removal

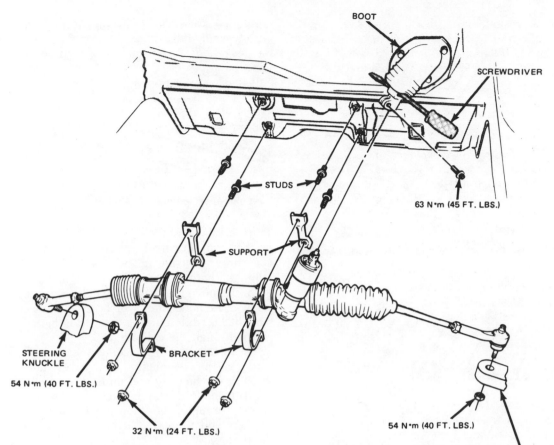

BOOT

SCREWDRIVER

STUDS

63 N·m (45 FT. LBS.)

SUPPORT

STEERING
KNUCKLE

54 N·m (40 FT. LBS.)

BRACKET

32 N·m (24 FT. LBS.)

54 N·m (40 FT. LBS.)

STEERING KNUCKLE

Manual steering gear installation details; power steering similar

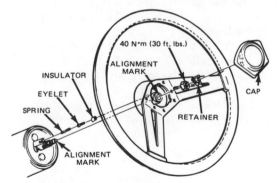

40 N·m (30 ft. lbs.)

ALIGNMENT
MARK

INSULATOR

EYELET

SPRING

CAP

RETAINER

ALIGNMENT
MARK

Sport steering wheel removal

4. Remove the shaft nut.

5. If the wheel and shaft do not have factory-installed alignment marks, matchmark the parts before removal of the wheel.

6. Install a puller and remove the wheel. A horn spring, eyelet and insulator are underneath; don't lose the parts.

7. Install the spring, eyelet and insulator into the tower on the column.

8. Align the matchmarks and install the wheel onto the shaft. Install the retaining nut and tighten to 30 ft lbs (40 Nm.).

9. Install the retainer. Install the center cap. Connect the negative battery cable.

Turn Signal Switch
REMOVAL AND INSTALLATION

1. Remove the steering wheel. Remove the trim cover.

2. Pry the cover from the steering column.

3. Position a U-shaped lockplate compressing tool on the end of the steering shaft and compress the lock plate by turning the shaft nut clockwise. Pry the wire snap-ring out of the shaft groove.

4. Remove the tool and lift the lockplate off the shaft.

5. Slip the cancelling cam, upper bearing preload spring, and thrust washer off the shaft.

6. Remove the turn signal lever. Remove

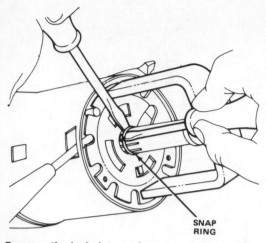

Depress the lockplate and remove the snap ring

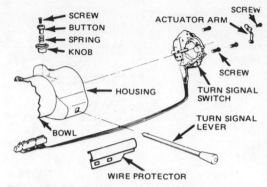

Turn signal switch installation details

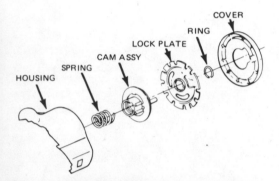

Remove these parts to get at the turn signal switch

the hazard flasher button retaining screw and remove the button, spring and knob.

7. Pull the switch connector out of the mast jacket and tape the upper part to facilitate switch removal. Attach a long piece of wire to the turn signal switch connector. When installing the turn signal switch, feed this wire through the column first, and then use this wire to pull the switch connector into

position. On tilt wheels, place the turn signal and shifter housing in low position and remove the harness cover.

8. Remove the three switch mounting screws. Remove the switch by pulling it straight up while guiding the wiring harness cover through the column.

9. Install the replacement switch by working the connector and cover down through the housing and under the bracket. On tilt models, the connector is worked down through the housing, under the bracket, and then the cover is installed on the harness.

10. Install the switch mounting screws and the connector on the mast jacket bracket. Install the column-to-dash trim plate.

11. Install the flasher knob and the turn signal lever.

12. With the turn signal lever in neutral and the flasher knob out, slide the thrust washer, upper bearing preload spring, and cancelling cam onto the shaft.

13. Position the lock plate on the shaft and press it down until a new snap-ring can be in-

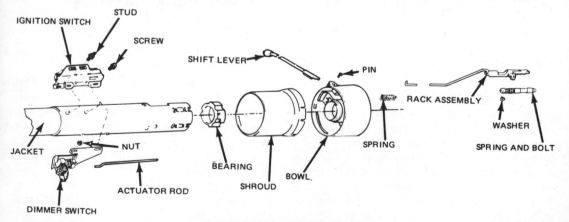

Ignition switch installation details

serted in the shaft groove. Always use a new snap-ring when assembling.

14. Install the cover and the steering wheel.

Ignition Switch
REMOVAL AND INSTALLATION

The switch is located inside the channel section of the brake pedal support and is completely inaccessible without first lowering the steering column. The switch is actuated by a rod and rack assembly. A gear on the end of the lock cylinder engages the toothed upper end of the rod.

1. Lower the steering column; be sure to properly support it.

2. Put the switch in the "Off-Unlocked" position. With the cylinder removed, the rod is in "Off-Unlocked" position when it is in the next to the uppermost detent.

3. Remove the two switch screws and remove the switch assembly.

4. Before installing, place the new switch in "Off-Unlocked" position and make sure the lock cylinder and actuating rod are in "Off-Unlocked" position (second detent from the top).

5. Install the activating rod into the switch and assemble the switch on the column. Tighten the mounting screws. Use only the specified screws, since overlength screws could impair the collapsibility of the column.

6. Reinstall the steering column.

Ignition Lock Cylinder
REMOVAL AND INSTALLATION

1. Remove the steering wheel.
2. Turn the lock to the Run position.
3. Remove the lock plate, turn signal switch, and the key warning buzzer switch.

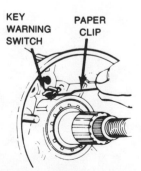

Remove the key warning buzzer switch with a paper clip

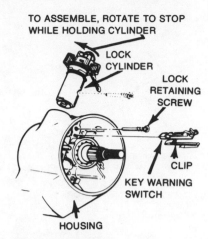

Lock cylinder installation

The warning buzzer switch can be fished out with a bent paper clip.

4. Remove the lock cylinder retaining screw and lock cylinder.

CAUTION: *If the screw is dropped on removal, it could fall into the column, requiring complete disassembly to retrieve the screw.*

5. Rotate the cylinder clockwise to align the cylinder key with the keyway in the housing.

6. Push the lock all the way in.

7. Install the screw. Tighten to 15 in. lbs.

8. The rest of installation is the reverse of removal. Turn the lock to Run to install the key warning buzzer switch, which is simply pushed down into place.

Tie-Rod Ends
REMOVAL AND INSTALLATION

1. Loosen the jam nut on the steering rack (inner tie-rod).

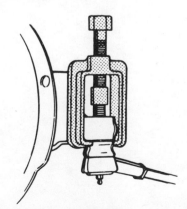

Separate the tie-rod end from the knuckle with a puller

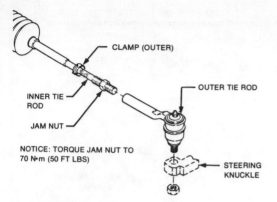

CLAMP (OUTER)

OUTER TIE ROD

INNER TIE ROD

JAM NUT

NOTICE: TORQUE JAM NUT TO 70 N•m (50 FT LBS)

STEERING KNUCKLE

Tie-rod end installation

2. Remove the tie-rod end nut. Separate the tie-rod end from the steering knuckle using a puller.

3. Unscrew the tie-rod end, counting the number of turns.

4. To install, screw the tie-rod end onto the steering rack (inner tie-rod) the same number of turns as counted for removal. This will give approximately correct toe.

5. Install the tie-rod end into the knuckle. Install the nut and tighten to 40 ft lbs (54 Nm.).

6. If the toe must be adjusted, use pliers to expand the boot clamp. Turn the inner tie-rod to adjust. Replace the clamp.

7. Tighten the jam nut to 50 ft lbs (70 Nm.).

Power Steering Pump
REMOVAL AND INSTALLATION

1. Remove the hoses at the pump and tape the openings shut to prevent contamination. Position the disconnected lines in a raised position to prevent leakage.

2. Remove the pump belt.

3. On the four cylinder, remove the radiator hose clamp bolt. On the V6, disconnect the negative battery cable, disconnect the electrical connector at the blower motor, drain the cooling system, and remove the heater hose at the water pump.

4. Loosen the retaining bolts and any braces, and remove the pump.

5. Install the pump on the engine with the retaining bolts handtight.

6. Connect and tighten the hose fittings.

7. Refill the pump with fluid and bleed by turning the pulley counterclockwise (viewed from the front). Stop the bleeding when air bubbles no longer appear.

8. Install the pump belt on the pulley and adjust the tension. Bleed the system.

9. Replace the four cylinder radiator hose clamp bolt. On the V6, install the heater hose. Install the blower and electrical connector. Refill the cooling system. Connect the negative battery cable.

BLEEDING THE POWER STEERING SYSTEM

1. Fill the reservoir.

2. Let the fluid stand undisturbed for two minutes, then crank the engine for about two seconds. Refill the reservoir if necessary.

3. Repeat Steps 1 and 2 until the fluid level remains constant after cranking the engine.

4. Raise the front of the car until the wheels are off the ground, then start the engine. Increase the engine speed to about 1,500 rpm.

5. Turn the wheels lightly against the stops to the left and right, checking the fluid level and refilling if necessary.

8

Brakes

UNDERSTANDING THE BRAKE SYSTEM

Hydraulic System

A hydraulic system is used to actuate the brakes. The system transports the power required to force the frictional surfaces of the braking system together from the pedal to the individual braking units at each wheel. A hydraulic system is used for three reasons. First, fluid under pressure can be carried to all parts of the automobile by small hoses—some of which are flexible—without taking up a significant amount of room or posing routing problems. Second, liquid is non-compressible; a hydraulic system can transport force without modifying or reducing that force. Third, a great mechanical advantage can be given to the brake pedal end of the system, and the foot pressure required to actuate the brakes can be reduced by making the surface area of the master cylinder pistons smaller than that of any of the pistons in the wheel cylinders or calipers.

The master cylinder consists of a fluid reservoir and a double cylinder and piston assembly. Double type master cylinders are designed to separate the front and rear braking systems hydraulically in case of a leak.

Steel lines carry the brake fluid to a point on the vehicle's frame near each of the vehicle's wheels. The fluid is then carried to the slave cylinders by flexible tubes in order to allow for suspension and steering movements.

In drum brake systems, the slave cylinders are called wheel cylinders. Each wheel cylinder contains two pistons, one at either end, which push outward in opposite directions. In disc brake systems, the slave cylinders are part of the calipers. One or four cylinders are used to force the brake pads against the disc, but all cylinders contain one piston only. All slave cylinder pistons employ some type of seal, usually made of rubber, to minimize the leakage of fluid around the piston. A rubber dust boot seals the outer end of the cylinder against dust and dirt. The boot fits around the outer end of the piston on disc brake calipers, and around the brake actuating rod on wheel cylinders.

The hydraulic system operates as follows: When at rest, the entire system, from the pistons in the master cylinder to those in the wheel cylinders or calipers, is full of brake fluid. Upon application of the brake pedal, fluid trapped in front of the master cylinder pistons is forced through the lines to the slave cylinders. Here, it forces the pistons outward, in the case of drum brakes, and inward toward the disc, in the case of disc brakes. The motion of the pistons is opposed by return springs mounted outside the cylinders in drum brakes, and by internal springs or spring seals in disc brakes.

Upon release of the brake pedal, a spring located inside the master cylinder immediately returns the master cylinder pistons to the normal position. The pistons contain check valves and the master cylinder has compensating ports drilled in it. These are uncovered as the pistons reach their normal position. The piston check valves allow fluid to flow toward the wheel cylinders or calipers as the pistons withdraw. Then, as the return springs force the brake pads or shoes into the released position, the excess fluid returns to the master cylinder fluid reservoir through the compensating ports. It is during the time the pedal is in the released position that any fluid that has leaked out of the system will be replaced through the compensating ports.

Dual circuit master cylinders employ two pistons, located one behind the other, in the same cylinder. The primary piston is actuated directly by mechanical linkage from the brake pedal. The secondary piston is actuated by fluid trapped between the two pistons. If a leak develops in front of the secondary piston, it moves forward until it bottoms against the front of the master cylinder, and the fluid trapped between the pistons will operate the rear brakes. If the rear brakes develop a leak, the primary piston will move forward until direct contact with the secondary piston takes place, and it will force the secondary piston to actuate the front brakes. In either case, the brake pedal moves farther when the brakes are applied, and less braking power is available.

All dual-circuit systems use a distributor switch to warn the driver when only half of the brake system is operational. This switch is located in a valve body which is mounted on the master cylinder. A hydraulic piston receives pressure from both circuits, each circuit's pressure being applied to one end of the piston. When the pressures are in balance, the piston remains stationary. When one circuit has a leak, however, the greater pressure in that circuit during application of the brakes will push the piston to one side, closing the distributor switch and activating the brake warning light.

In disc brake systems, this valve body also contains a metering valve and, in some cases, a proportioning valve. The metering valve keeps pressure from traveling to the disc brakes on the front wheels until the brake shoes on the rear wheels have contacted the drums, ensuring that the front brakes will never be used alone. The proportioning valve throttles the pressure to the rear brakes so as to avoid rear wheel lock-up during very hard braking.

These valves may be tested by removing the lines to the front and rear brake systems and installing special brake pressure testing gauges. Front and rear system pressures are then compared as the pedal is gradually depressed. Specifications vary with the manufacturer and design of the brake system.

Brake system warning lights may be tested by depressing the brake pedal and holding it while opening one of the wheel cylinder bleeder screws. If this does not cause the light to go on, substitute a new lamp, make continuity checks, and, finally, replace the switch as necessary.

The hydraulic system may be checked for leaks by applying pressure to the pedal gradually and steadily. If the pedal sinks very slowly to the floor, the system has a leak. This is not to be confused with a springy or spongy feel due to the compression of air within the lines. If the system leaks, there will be a gradual change in the position of the pedal with a constant pressure.

Check for leaks along all lines and at wheel cylinders. If no external leaks are apparent, the problem is inside the master cylinder.

Disc Brakes

Instead of the traditional expanding brakes that press outward against a circular drum, disc brake systems utilize a cast iron disc with brake pads positioned on either side of it. Braking effect is achieved in a manner similar to the way you would squeeze a spinning phonograph record between your fingers. The disc (rotor) is a one-piece casting with cooling fins between the two braking surfaces. This enables air to circulate between the braking surfaces making them less sensitive to heat buildup and more resistant to fade. Dirt and water do not affect braking action since contaminants are thrown off by the centrifugal action of the rotor or scraped off by the pads. Also, the equal clamping action of the two brake pads tends to ensure uniform, straightline stops. All disc brakes are inherently self-adjusting.

Drum Brakes

Drum brakes employ two brake shoes mounted on a stationary backing plate. These shoes are positioned inside a circular cast iron drum which rotates with the wheel assembly. The shoes are held in place by springs; this allows them to slide toward the drums (when they are applied) while keeping the linings and drums in alignment. The shoes are actuated by a wheel cylinder which is mounted at the top of the backing plate. When the brakes are applied, hydraulic pressure forces the wheel cylinder's two actuating links outward. Since these links bear directly against the top of the brake shoes, the tops of the shoes are then forced outward against the inner side of the drum. This action forces the bottoms of the two shoes to contact the brake drum by rotating the entire assembly slightly (known as servo action). When pressure within the wheel cylinder is relaxed, return springs pull the shoes back away from the drum.

The drum brakes are designed to self-adjust during application when the car is moving in reverse. This motion causes both shoes to rotate very slightly with the drum, rocking an adjusting lever, thereby causing rotation of the adjusting screw by means of an actuating lever.

Power Brake Boosters

Power brakes operate just as standard brake systems except in the actuation of the master cylinder pistons. A vacuum diaphragm is located on the front of the master cylinder and assists the driver in applying the brakes, reducing both the effort and travel he must put into moving the brake pedal.

The vacuum diaphragm housing is connected to the intake manifold by a vacuum hose. A check valve is placed at the point where the hose enters the diaphragm housing, so that during periods of low manifold vacuum brake assist vacuum will not be lost.

Depressing the brake pedal closes off the vacuum source and allows atmospheric pressure to enter on one side of the diaphragm. This causes the master cylinder pistons to move and apply the brakes. When the brake pedal is released, vacuum is applied to both sides of the diaphragm, and return springs return the diaphragm and master cylinder pistons to the released position. If the vacuum fails, the brake pedal rod will butt against the end of the master cylinder actuating rod, and direct mechanical application will occur as the pedal is depressed.

The hydraulic and mechanical problems that apply to conventional brake systems also apply to power brakes, and should be checked for if the following tests do not reveal the problem.

Test for a system vacuum leak as described below:

1. Operate the engine at idle with the transaxle in Neutral without touching the brake pedal for at least one minute.

2. Turn off the engine, and wait one minute.

3. Test for the presence of assist vacuum by depressing the brake pedal and releasing it several times. Light application will produce less and less pedal travel, if vacuum was present. If there is no vacuum, air is leaking into the system somewhere.

Test for system operation as follows:

1. Pump the brake pedal (with engine off) until the supply vacuum is entirely gone.

2. Put a light, steady pressure on the pedal.

3. Start the engine, and operate it at idle with the transaxle in Neutral. If the system is operating, the brake pedal should fall toward the floor if constant pressure is maintained on the pedal.

Power brake systems may be tested for hydraulic leaks just as ordinary systems are tested, except that the engine should be idling with the transaxle in Neutral throughout the test.

BRAKE SYSTEM

The X-Body cars have a diagonally-split hydraulic system. This differs from conventional practice in that the left front and right rear brakes are on one hydraulic circuit, and the right front and left rear are on the other.

A diagonally-split system necessitates the use of a special master cylinder design. The X-Body master cylinder incorporates the functions of a standard tandem master cylinder, plus a warning light switch and proportioning valves. Additionally, the master cylinder is designed with a quick take-up feature which provides a large volume of fluid to the brakes at low pressure when the brakes are initially applied. The low pressure fluid acts to quickly fill the large displacement requirements of the system.

The front disc brakes are single piston sliding caliper units. Fluid pressure acts equally against the piston and the bottom of the piston bore in the caliper. This forces the piston outward until the pad contacts the rotor. The force on the caliper bore forces the caliper to slide over, carrying the other pad into contact with the other side of the rotor. The disc brakes are self-adjusting.

Rear drum brakes are conventional duo-servo units. A dual piston wheel cylinder, mounted to the top of the backing plate, actuates both brake shoes. Wheel cylinder force to the shoes is supplemented by the tendency of the shoes to wrap into the drum (servo action). An actuating link, pivot and lever serve to automatically engage the adjuster as the brakes are applied when the car is moving in reverse. Provisions for manual adjustment are also provided. The rear brakes also serve as the parking brakes; linkage is mechanical.

Vacuum boost is an option. The booster is a conventional tandem vacuum unit.

Troubleshooting Basic Brake Problems

The Problem	Is Caused By	What to Do
The brake pedal goes to the floor	• Leak somewhere in the system	• Check/correct fluid level; check system
	• Brakes out of adjustment	• Check automatic brake adjusters
Spongy brake pedal	• Air in brake system	• Bleed brake system
	• Brake fluid contaminated	• Drain, refill and bleed system
The brake pedal is hard	• Improperly adjusted brakes	• Adjust brakes (drums only)
	• Worn pads or linings	• Check lining/pad wear
	• Kinked brake lines	• Replace faulty lines
	• Defective power brake booster	• Check booster
	• Low engine vacuum (power brakes)	• Check engine vacuum
The brake pedal "fades" under pressure (repeated hard stops will cause brake fade; brakes will return to normal when they cool down)	• Air in system	• Bleed brake system
	• Incorrect brake fluid	• Check fluid
	• Leaking master cylinder or wheel cylinders	• Check master cylinder and wheel cylinders for leaks
	• Leaking hoses/lines	• Check lines for leaks
The car pulls to one side or brakes grab	• Incorrect tire pressure	• Check/correct tire pressure
	• Contaminated brake linings or pads	• Check linings for grease; if greasy, replace
	• Worn brake linings	• Replace linings
	• Loose or misaligned calipers	• Check caliper mountings
	• Defective proportioning valve	• Have proportioning valve checked
	• Front end out of alignment	• Have wheel alignment checked
Brakes chatter or shudder	• Worn linings	• Check lining thickness
	• Drums out-of-round	• Have drums and linings ground
	• Wobbly rotor	• Have rotor checked for excessive wobble
	• Heat checked drums	• Check drums for heat checking; if necessary, replace drums

Troubleshooting Basic Brake Problems (cont.)

The Problem	Is Caused By	What to Do
Brakes produce noise (squealing, scraping, clicking)	• Worn linings • Loose calipers • Caliper anti-rattle springs missing • Scored or glazed drums or rotors	• Check pad and lining wear • Check caliper mountings • Check calipers for missing parts • Check for glazing (light glazing can be removed with sandpaper)
Brakes drag (will not release)	• Incorrect brake adjustment • Parking brake stuck or adjusted too tight • Caliper pistons seized • Defective metering valve or master cylinder • Broken brake return springs	• Adjust brakes (drums only) • Check cable where it enters the brake backing plate. In winter, water frequently freezes here • Check calipers; rebuild or replace • Check hydraulic circuit • Check brake return springs, replace if necessary
Brake system warning light stays lit	• One part of dual circuit inoperative, defective warning light switch, differential pressure valve not centered	• Check hydraulic circuit

Adjustment
DISC BRAKES

The front disc brakes are inherently self-adjusting. No adjustments are either necessary or possible.

DRUM BRAKES

The drum brakes are designed to self-adjust when applied with the car moving in reverse. However, they can also be adjusted manually. This manual adjustment should also be performed whenever the linings are replaced.

1. Use a punch to knock out the stamped area on the brake drum. If this is done with the drum installed on the car, the drum must then be removed to clean out all metal pieces. After adjustments are complete, obtain a hole cover from your dealer (Part no. 4874119 or the equivalent) to prevent entry of dirt and water into the brakes.

2. Use an awl, a screwdriver, or an adjusting tool especially made for the purpose to turn the brake adjusting screw star wheel. Expand the shoes until the drum can just barely be turned by hand.

3. Back off the adjusting screw 30 notches. If the shoes still are dragging lightly, back off the adjusting screw one or two additional notches. If the brakes still drag, the parking brake adjustment is incorrect or the parking brake is applied. Fix and start over.

4. Install the hole cover into the drum.

5. Check the parking brake adjustment.

On some models, no marked area or stamped area is present on the drum. In this case, a hole must be drilled in the backing plate:

1. All backing plates have two round flat areas in the lower half through which the parking brake cable is installed. Drill a ½ in. hole into the round flat area on the backing plate opposite the parking brake cable. This will allow access to the star wheel.

2. After drilling the hole, remove the drum and remove all metal particles. Install a hole plug (Part no. 4874119 or the equivalent) to prevent the entry of water or dirt.

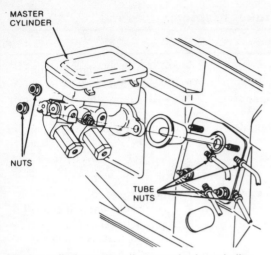

MASTER
CYLINDER

NUTS

TUBE
NUTS

Master cylinder removal; power brakes similar

HYDRAULIC SYSTEM

Master Cylinder
REMOVAL AND INSTALLATION

1. If your car does not have power brakes, disconnect the master cylinder pushrod at the brake pedal inside the car. The pushrod is retained to the brake pedal by a clip; there is a washer under the clip, and a spring washer on the other side of the pushrod.

2. Unplug the electrical connector from the master cylinder.

3. Place a number of cloths or a container under the master cylinder to catch the brake fluid. Disconnect the brake tubes from the master cylinder; use a flare nut wrench if one is available. Tape over and open ends of the tubes.

NOTE: *Brake fluid eats paint. Wipe up any spilled fluid immediately, then flush the area with clear water.*

4. Remove the two nuts attaching the master cylinder to the booster or firewall.

5. Remove the master cylinder.

6. To install, attach the master cylinder to the firewall or booster with the nuts. Torque to 22–30 ft lbs (30–45 Nm.).

7. Reconnect the pushrod to the brake pedal with non-power brakes.

8. Remove the tape from the lines and connect to the master cylinder. Torque to 120–180 in. lbs (13–20 Nm.). Connect the electrical lead.

9. Bleed the brakes.

OVERHAUL

This is a tedious, time-consuming job. You can save yourself a lot of trouble by buying a rebuilt master cylinder from your dealer or parts supply house. The small difference in price between a rebuilding kit and a rebuilt part usually makes it more economical, in terms of time and work, to buy the rebuilt part.

1. Remove the master cylinder.

2. Remove the reservoir cover and drain the fluid.

3. Remove the pushrod and rubber boot on non-power models.

4. Unbolt the proportioners and failure warning switch from the side of the master cylinder body. Discard the O-rings found under the proportioners. Use new ones on installation. There may or may not be an O-ring under the original equipment failure warning switch. If there is, discard it. In either case, use an O-ring upon assembly.

5. Clamp the master cylinder body in a vise, taking care not to crush it. Depress the primary piston with a wooden dowel and remove the lock ring with a pair of snap-ring pliers.

6. The primary and secondary pistons can be removed by applying compressed air into one of the outlets at the end of the cylinder and plugging the other three outlets. The primary piston must be replaced as an assembly if the seals are bad. The secondary piston seals are replaceable. Install these new seals with the lips facing outwards.

7. Inspect the bore for corrosion. If any corrosion is evident, the master cylinder body must be replaced. Do not attempt to polish the bore with crocus cloth, sandpaper, or anything else. The body is aluminum; polishing the bore won't work.

8. To remove the failure warning switch piston assembly, remove the allen head plug from the end of the bore and withdraw the assembly with a pair of needlenose pliers. The switch piston assembly seals are replaceable.

9. The reservoir can be removed from the master cylinder body if necessary. Clamp the body in a vise by its mounting flange. Use a pry bar to remove the reservoir. If the reservoir is removed, remove the reservoir grommets and discard them. The quick take-up valves under the grommets are accessible after the retaining snap-rings are removed. Use snap-ring pliers; no other tool will work.

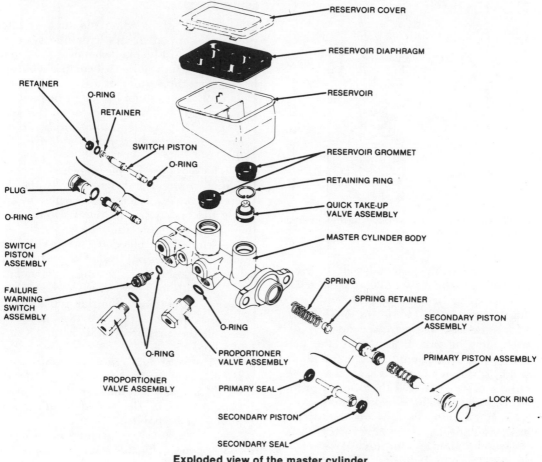

RESERVOIR COVER

RESERVOIR DIAPHRAGM

RESERVOIR

RETAINER

O-RING

RETAINER

SWITCH PISTON

O-RING

RESERVOIR GROMMET

RETAINING RING

QUICK TAKE-UP VALVE ASSEMBLY

PLUG

O-RING

SWITCH PISTON ASSEMBLY

FAILURE WARNING SWITCH ASSEMBLY

MASTER CYLINDER BODY

SPRING

SPRING RETAINER

SECONDARY PISTON ASSEMBLY

PRIMARY PISTON ASSEMBLY

O-RING

O-RING

PROPORTIONER VALVE ASSEMBLY

PROPORTIONER VALVE ASSEMBLY

PRIMARY SEAL

SECONDARY PISTON

SECONDARY SEAL

LOCK RING

Exploded view of the master cylinder

10. Clean all parts in denatured alcohol and allow to air dry. Do not use anything else to clean, and do not wipe dry with a rag, which will leave bits of lint behind. Inspect all parts for corrosion or wear. Generally, it is best to replace *all* rubber parts whenever the master cylinder is disassembled, and replace any metal part which shows any sign whatsoever of wear or corrosion.

11. Lubricate all parts with clean brake fluid before assembly.

12. Install the quick take-up valves into the master cylinder body and secure with the snap-rings. Make sure the snap-rings are properly seated in their grooves. Lubricate the new reservoir grommets with clean brake fluid and press them into the master cylinder.

13. Install the reservoir into the grommets by placing the reservoir on its lid and pressing the master cylinder body down onto it with a rocking motion.

14. Lubricate the switch piston assembly

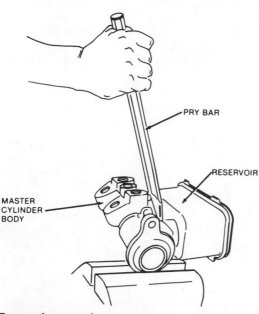

PRY BAR

RESERVOIR

MASTER CYLINDER BODY

Reservoir removal

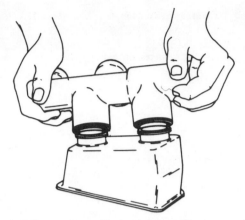

Install the master cylinder body to the reservoir with a rocking motion

with clean brake fluid. Install new O-rings and retainers on the piston. Install the piston assembly into the master cylinder and secure with the plug, using a new O-ring on the plug. Torque is 40–140 in. lbs (5–16 Nm.).

15. Assemble the new secondary piston seals onto the piston. Lubricate the parts with clean brake fluid, then install the spring, spring retainer and secondary piston into the cylinder. Install the primary piston, depress, and install the lock ring.

16. Install new O-rings on the proportioners and the failure warning switch. Install the proportioners and torque to 18–30 ft lbs (25–40 Nm.). Install the failure warning switch and torque to 15–50 in. lbs (2–6 Nm.).

17. Clamp the master cylinder body upright into a vise by one of the mounting flanges. Fill the reservoir with fresh brake fluid. Pump the piston with a dowel until fluid squirts from the outlet ports. Continue pumping until the expelled fluid is free of air bubbles.

18. Install the master cylinder, and bleed the brakes. Check the brake system for proper operation. Do not move the car until a "hard" brake pedal is obtained and the brake system has been thoroughly checked for soundness.

Proportioning Valves and Failure Warning Switch

These parts are installed in the master cylinder body. No separate proportioning or metering valve is used. Replacement of these parts requires disassembly of the master cylinder. See the preceding master cylinder overhaul for replacement instructions.

Bleeding

The purpose of bleeding the brakes is to expel air trapped in the hydraulic system. The system must be bled whenever the pedal feels spongy, indicating that compressible air has entered the system. It must also be bled whenever the system has been opened or repaired. You will need a helper for this job.

CAUTION: *Never reuse brake fluid which has been bled from the brake system.*

1. The sequence for bleeding is right rear, left front, left rear and right front. If the car has power brakes, remove the vacuum by applying the brakes several times. Do not run the engine while bleeding the brakes.

2. Clean all the bleeder screws. You may want to give each one a shot of penetrating solvent to loosen it up; seizure is a common problem with bleeder screws, which then break off, sometimes requiring replacement of the part to which they are attached.

3. Fill the master cylinder with DOT 3 brake fluid.

NOTE: *Brake fluid absorbs moisture from the air. Don't leave the master cylinder or the fluid container uncovered any longer than necessary. Be careful handling the fluid—it eats paint.*

Check the level of the fluid often when bleeding, and refill the reservoirs as necessary. Don't let them run dry, or you will have to repeat the process.

4. Attach a length of clear vinyl tubing to the bleeder screw on the wheel cylinder. Insert the other end of the tube into a clear, clean jar half filled with brake fluid.

5. Have your assistant slowly depress the brake pedal. As this is done, open the

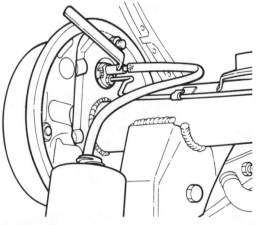

Bleeding the brakes

bleeder screw ⅓–½ of a turn, and allow the fluid to run through the tube. Then close the bleeder screw before the pedal reaches the end of its travel. Have your assistant slowly release the pedal. Repeat this process until no air bubbles appear in the expelled fluid.

6. Repeat the procedure on the other three brakes, checking the level of fluid in the master cylinder reservoir often.

After you're done, there should be no sponginess in the brake pedal feel. If there is, either there is still air in the line, in which case the process should be repeated, or there is a leak somewhere, which of course must be corrected before the car is moved.

FRONT DISC BRAKES

Pads

INSPECTION

The pad thickness should be inspected every time that the tires are removed for rotation. The outer pad can be checked by looking in at each end, which is the point at which the highest rate of wear occurs. The inner pad can be checked by looking down through the inspection hole in the top of the caliper. If the thickness of the pad is worn to within 0.030 in. (0.76 mm) of the rivet at either end of the pad, all the pads should be replaced. This is the factory-recommended measurement; your state's automobile inspection laws may not agree with this.

NOTE: *Always replace all pads on both front wheels at the same time. Failure to do so will result in uneven braking action and premature wear.*

REMOVAL AND INSTALLATION

1. Siphon ⅔ of the brake fluid from the master cylinder reservoir. Loosen the wheel lug nuts and raise the car. Remove the wheel.

2. Position a C-clamp across the caliper so that it presses on the pads and tighten it until the caliper piston bottoms in its bore.

NOTE: *If you haven't removed some brake fluid from the master cylinder, it will overflow when the piston is retracted.*

3. Remove the C-clamp.

4. Remove the allen head caliper mounting bolts. Inspect the bolts for corrosion, and replace as necessary.

5. Remove the caliper from the steering knuckle and suspend it from the body of the

car with a length of wire. Do not allow the caliper to hang by its hose.

6. Remove the pad retaining springs and remove the pads from the caliper.

7. Remove the plastic sleeves and the rubber bushings from the mounting bolt holes.

8. Install new sleeves and bushings. Lubricate the sleeves with a light coating of silicone grease before installation. These parts must always be replaced when the pads are replaced. The parts are usually included in the pad replacement kits.

9. Install the outboard pad into the caliper.

10. Install the retainer spring on the in-

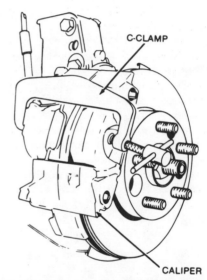

Install a C-clamp to retract the disc brake pads

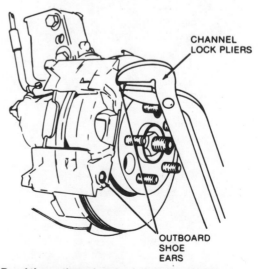

Bend the outboard pad ears into place with a large pair of slip joint pliers

board pad. A new spring should be included in the pad replacement kit.

11. Install the new inboard pad into the caliper. The retention lugs fit into the piston.

12. Use a large pair of slip joint pliers to bend the outer pad ears down over the caliper.

13. Install the caliper onto the steering knuckle. Tighten the mounting bolts to 21–35 ft lbs (28–47 Nm.). Install the wheel and lower the car. Fill the master cylinder to its proper level with fresh brake fluid meeting DOT 3 specifications. Since the brake hose wasn't disconnected, it isn't really necessary to bleed the brakes, although most mechanics do this as a matter of course.

Caliper

REMOVAL AND INSTALLATION

1. Follow Steps 1, 2 and 3 of the pad replacement procedure.

2. Before removing the caliper mounting bolts, remove the bolt holding the brake hose to the caliper.

3. Remove the allen head caliper mounting bolts. Inspect them for corrosion and replace them if necessary.

4. Installation is the reverse. Mounting bolt torque is 21–35 ft lbs (28–47 Nm.) for the caliper. The brake hose fitting should be tightened to 18–30 ft lbs (24–40 Nm.).

OVERHAUL

1. Remove the caliper.

2. Remove the pads.

3. Place some cloths or a slat of wood in front of the piston. Remove the piston by applying compressed air to the fluid inlet fitting. Use just enough air pressure to ease the piston from the bore.

CAUTION: *Do not try to catch the piston with your fingers, which can result in serious injury.*

4. Remove the piston boot with a screwdriver, working carefully so that the piston bore is not scratched.

5. Remove the bleeder screw.

6. Inspect the piston for scoring, nicks, corrosion, wear, etc., and damaged or worn chrome plating. Replace the piston if any defects are found.

7. Remove the piston seal from the caliper bore groove using a piece of pointed wood or plastic. Do not use a screwdriver, which will damage the bore. Inspect the caliper bore for nicks, corrosion, and so on. Very light wear can be cleaned up with crocus cloth. Use finger pressure to rub the crocus cloth around the circumference of the bore—

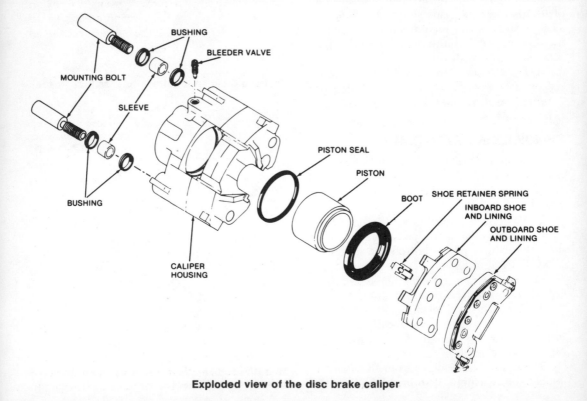

Exploded view of the disc brake caliper

do not slide it in and out. More extensive wear or corrosion warrants replacement of the part.

8. Clean any parts which are to be reused in denatured alcohol. Dry them with compressed air or allow to air dry. Don't wipe the parts dry with a cloth, which will leave behind bits of lint.

9. Lubricate the new seal, provided in the repair kit, with clean brake fluid. Install the seal in its groove, making sure it is fully seated and not twisted.

10. Install the new dust boot on the piston. Lubricate the bore of the caliper with clean brake fluid and insert the piston into its bore. Position the boot in the caliper housing and seat with a seal driver of the appropriate size, or G.M. tool no. J-29077.

11. Install the bleeder screw, tightening to 80–140 in. lbs (9–16 Nm.). Do not overtighten.

12. Install the pads, install the caliper, and bleed the brakes.

Disc (Rotor)

REMOVAL AND INSTALLATION

1. Remove the caliper.
2. Remove the rotor.
3. Installation is the reverse.

INSPECTION

1. Check the rotor surface for wear or scoring. Deep scoring, grooves or rust pitting can be removed by refacing, a job to be referred to your local machine shop or garage. Minimum thickness is stamped on the rotor

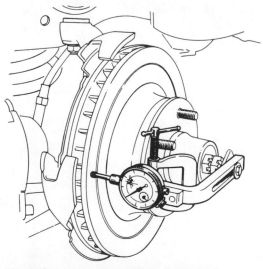

Check the rotor runout with a dial indicator

(0.965 in., or 24.47 mm). If the rotor will be thinner than this after refinishing, it must be replaced.

2. Check the rotor parallelism; it must vary less than 0.0005 in. (0.013 mm) measured at four or more points around the circumference. Make all measurements at the same distance in from the edge of the rotor. Refinish the rotor if it fails to meet this specification.

3. Measure the disc runout with a dial indicator. If runout exceeds 0.005 in. (0.127 mm), and the wheel bearings are OK (if runout is being measured with the disc on the car), the rotor must be refaced or replaced as necessary.

REAR DRUM BRAKES

Brake Drums

REMOVAL AND INSTALLATION

1. Loosen the wheel lug nuts. Raise and support the car. Mark the relationship of the wheel to the axle and remove the wheel.

2. Mark the relationship of the drum to the axle and remove the drum. If it cannot be slipped off easily, check to see that the parking brake is fully released. If so, the brake shoes are probably locked against the drum. See the "Adjustment" section earlier in this chapter for details on how to back off the adjuster.

3. Installation is the reverse. Be sure to align the matchmarks made during removal. Lug nut torque is 102 ft lbs (140 Nm.).

INSPECTION

1. After removing the brake drum, wipe out the accumulated dust with a damp cloth.
WARNING: *Do not blow the brake dust out of the drums with compressed air or lungpower. Brake linings contain asbestos, a known cancer causing substance. Dispose of the cloth used to clean the parts after use.*

2. Inspect the drums for cracks, deep grooves, roughness, scoring, or out-of-roundness. Replace any drum which is cracked; do not try to weld it up.

3. Smooth any slight scores by polishing the friction surface with fine emery cloth. Heavy or extensive scoring will cause excessive lining wear and should be removed from the drum through resurfacing, a job to be referred to your local machine shop or garage.

The maximum finished diameter of the drums is 7.894 in. (200.64mm). The drum must be replaced if the diameter is 7.924 in. (201.40 mm) or greater.

Brake Shoes

INSPECTION

After removing the brake drum, inspect the brake shoes. If the lining is worn down to within $1/32$ in. (0.76 mm) of a rivet, the shoes must be replaced.

NOTE: *This figure may disagree with your state's automobile inspection laws.*

If the brake lining is soaked with brake fluid or grease, it must be replaced. If this is the case, the brake drum should be sanded with crocus cloth to remove all traces of brake fluid, and the wheel cylinders should be rebuilt. Clean all grit from the friction surface of the drum before replacing it.

If the lining is chipped, cracked, or other-wise damaged, it must be replaced with a new lining.

NOTE: *Always replace the brake linings in sets of two on both ends of the axle. Never replace just one shoe, or both shoes on one side.*

Check the condition of the shoes, retracting springs, and hold-down springs for signs of overheating. If the shoes or springs have a slight blue color, this indicates overheating and replacement of the shoes and springs is recommended. The wheel cylinders should be rebuilt as a precaution against future problems.

REMOVAL AND INSTALLATION

1. Loosen the lug nuts on the wheel to be serviced, raise and support the car, and re-move the wheel and brake drum.

NOTE: *It is not really necessary to remove the hub and wheel bearing assembly from the axle, but it does make the job easier. If*

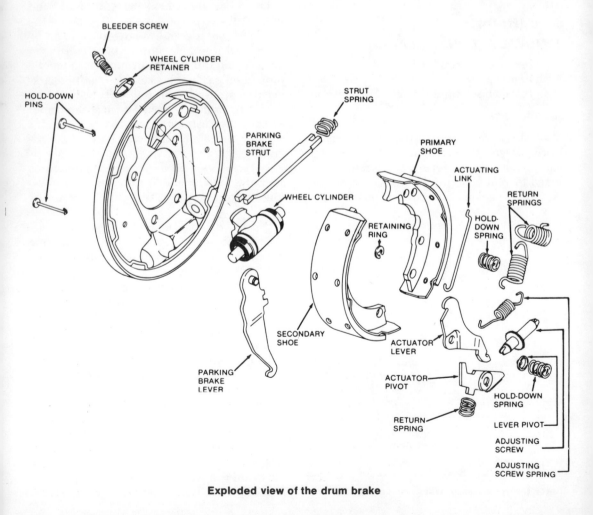

Exploded view of the drum brake

you can work with the hub and bearing assembly in place, skip down to Step 3.

2. Remove the four hub and bearing assembly retaining bolts and remove the assembly from the axle.

3. Remove the return springs from the shoes with a pair of needle nose pliers. There are also special brake spring pliers for this job.

4. Remove the hold down springs by gripping them with a pair of pliers, then pressing down and turning 90°. There are special tools to grab and turn these parts, but pliers work fairly well.

5. Remove the shoe hold-down pins from behind the brake backing plate. They will simply slide out once the hold-down spring tension is relieved.

6. Lift up the actuator lever for the self-adjusting mechanism and remove the actuating link. Remove the actuator lever, pivot, and the pivot return spring.

7. Spread the shoes apart to clear the wheel cylinder pistons and remove the parking brake strut and spring.

8. If the hub and bearing assembly is still in place, spread the shoes far enough apart to clear it.

9. Disconnect the parking brake cable from the lever. Remove the shoes, still connected by their adjusting screw spring, from the car.

10. With the shoes removed, note the position of the adjusting spring and remove the spring and adjusting screw.

11. Remove the C-clip from the parking brake lever and remove the lever from the secondary shoe.

12. Use a damp cloth to remove all dirt and dust from the backing plate and brake parts. See the warning about brake dust in the drum removal procedure.

13. Check the wheel cylinders by carefully pulling the lower edges of the wheel cylinder boots away from the cylinders. If there is excessive leakage, the inside of the cylinder will be moist with fluid. If leakage exists, a wheel cylinder overhaul is in order. Do not delay, because brake failure could result.

NOTE: *A small amount of fluid will be present to act as a lubricant for the wheel cylinder pistons. Fluid spilling from the boot center hole, after the piston is removed, indicates cup leakage and the necessity for cylinder overhaul.*

14. Check the backing plate attaching bolts to make sure that they are tight. Use

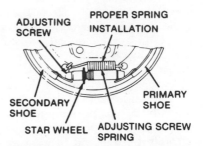

Proper spring installation is with the coils over the adjuster, not the star wheel

fine emery cloth to clean all rust and dirt from the shoe contact surfaces on the plate.

15. Lubricate the fulcrum end of the parking brake lever with brake grease specially made for the purpose. Install the lever on the secondary shoe and secure with the C-clip.

16. Install the adjusting screw and spring on the shoes, connecting them together. The coils of the spring must *not* be over the star wheel on the adjuster. The left and right hand springs are *not* interchangeable. Do not mix them up.

17. Lubricate the shoe contact surfaces on the backing plate with the brake grease. Be certain when you are using this stuff that none of it actually gets on the linings or drums. Apply the same grease to the point where the parking brake cable contacts the plate. Use the grease sparingly.

18. Spread the shoe assemblies apart and connect the parking brake cable. Install the shoes on the backing plate, engaging the shoes at the top temporarily with the wheel cylinder pistons. Make sure that the star wheel on the adjuster is lined up with the adjusting hole in the backing plate, if the hole is back there.

19. Spread the shoes apart slightly and install the parking brake strut and spring. Make sure that the end of the strut without the spring engages the parking brake lever. The end with the spring engages the primary shoe (the one with the shorter lining).

20. Install the actuator pivot, lever and return spring. Install the actuating link in the shoe retainer. Lift up the actuator lever and hook the link into the lever.

21. Install the hold-down pins through the back of the plate, install the lever pivots and hold-down springs. Install the shoe return springs with a pair of pliers. Be very careful not to stretch or otherwise distort these springs.

22. Take a look at everything. Make sure

the linings are in the right place, the self-adjusting mechanism is correctly installed, and the parking brake parts are all hooked up. If in doubt, remove the other wheel and take a look at that one for comparison.

23. Measure the width of the linings, then measure the inside width of the drum. Adjust the linings by means of the adjuster so that the drum will fit onto the linings.

24. Install the hub and bearing assembly onto the axle if removed. Tighten the retaining bolts to 35 ft lbs (55 Nm.).

25. Install the drum and wheel. Adjust the brakes using the procedure given earlier in this chapter. Be sure to install a rubber hole cover in the knock-out hole after the adjustment is complete. Adjust the parking brake.

26. Lower the car and check the pedal for any sponginess or lack of a "hard" feel. Check the braking action and the parking brake. The brakes must not be applied severely immediately after installation. They should be used moderately for the first 200 miles of city driving or 1000 miles of highway driving, to allow the linings to conform to the shape of the drum.

Wheel Cylinders

REMOVAL AND INSTALLATION

1. Loosen the wheel lug nuts, raise and support the car, and remove the wheel. Remove the drum and brake shoes. Leave the hub and wheel bearing assembly in place.

2. Remove any dirt from around the brake line fitting. Disconnect the brake line.

3. Remove the wheel cylinder retainer by using two awls or punches with a tip diameter of ⅛ in. or less. Insert the awls or

punches into the access slots between the wheel cylinder pilot and retainer locking tabs. Bend both tabs away simultaneously. Remove the wheel cylinder from the backing plate.

4. To install, position the wheel cylinder against the backing plate and hold it in place with a wooden block between the wheel cylinder and the hub and bearing assembly.

5. Install a new retainer over the wheel cylinder abutment on the rear of the backing plate by pressing it into place with a 1⅛ in. 12-point socket and an extension.

6. Install a new bleeder screw into the wheel cylinder. Install the brake line and tighten to 120–180 in. lbs (13–20 Nm.).

7. The rest of installation is the reverse of removal. After the drum is installed, bleed the brakes using the procedure outlined earlier in this chapter.

OVERHAUL

As is the case with master cylinders, overhaul kits are available for the wheel cylinders. And, as is the case with master cylinders, it is usually more profitable to simply buy new or rebuilt wheel cylinders rather than rebuilding them. When rebuilding wheel cylinders, avoid getting any contaminants in the system. Always install new high-quality brake fluid; the use of improper fluid will swell and deteriorate the rubber parts.

1. Remove the wheel cylinders.

2. Remove the rubber boots from the cylinder ends. Discard the boots.

3. Remove and discard the pistons and cups.

4. Wash the cylinder and metal parts in denatured alcohol.

CAUTION: *Never use mineral-based solvents to clean the brake parts.*

5. Allow the parts to air dry and inspect the cylinder bore for corrosion or wear. Light

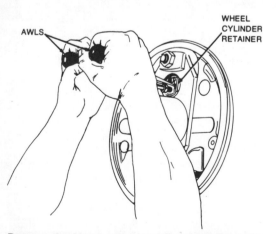

Remove the wheel cylinder retainer from the backing plate with a pair of awls or punches

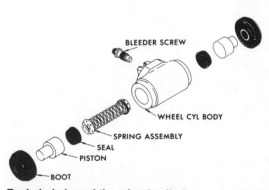

Exploded view of the wheel cylinder

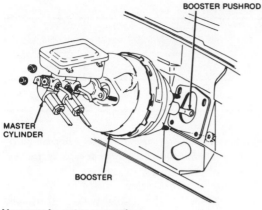

BOOSTER PUSHROD

MASTER
CYLINDER

BOOSTER

Vacuum booster mounting

corrosion can be cleaned up with crocus cloth; use finger pressure and rotate the cloth around the circumference of the bore. Do not move the cloth in and out. Any deep corrosion or pitting or wear warrants replacement of the parts.

6. Rinse the parts and allow to dry. Do not dry with a rag, which will leave bits of lint behind.

7. Lubricate the cylinder bore with clean brake fluid. Insert the spring assembly.

8. Install new cups. Do not lubricate prior to assembly.

9. Install the new pistons.

10. Press the new boots onto the cylinders by hand. Do not lubricate prior to assembly.

11. Install the wheel cylinders. Bleed the brakes after installation of the drum.

VACUUM BOOSTER

REMOVAL AND INSTALLATION

1. Remove the master cylinder from the booster. It is not necessary to disconnect the lines from the master cylinder. Just move the cylinder aside.

2. Disconnect the vacuum booster pushrod from the brake pedal inside the car. It is retained by a bolt. A spring washer lives under the bolt head, and a flat washer goes on the other side of the pushrod eye, next to the pedal arm.

3. Remove the four attaching nuts from inside the car. Remove the booster.

4. Install the booster on the firewall. Tighten the mounting nuts to 22–33 ft lbs (30–45 Nm.).

5. Connect the pushrod to the brake pedal.

6. Install the master cylinder. Mounting torque is 25 ft lbs (40 Nm.).

OVERHAUL

This job is not difficult, but requires a number of special tools which are expensive, especially if they're to be used only once. Generally, it's better to leave this job to your dealer, or buy a rebuilt vacuum booster and install it yourself.

PARKING BRAKE

ADJUSTMENT

1. Raise and support the car with both rear wheels off the ground.

2. Depress the parking brake pedal exactly two ratchet clicks.

3. Loosen the equalizer locknut, then tighten the adjusting nut until the left rear wheel can just be turned backward using two hands, but is locked in forward rotation.

4. Tighten the locknut.

5. Release the parking brake. Rotate the rear wheels—there should be no drag.

6. Lower the car.

Cable

REMOVAL AND INSTALLATION

Front Cable

1. Depress the parking brake pedal.

2. Clamp a pair of locking pliers on the upper cable where it enters the casing.

3. Pull the brake release, and remove the cable from the control assembly.

4. Release the locking tabs on the casing and remove the casing from the control assembly.

5. Push the grommet and the cable through the firewall into the engine compartment.

6. Remove the cable from its guide bracket on the firewall.

7. Remove the cable from the rear cable guide. Unhook the cable from the equalizer lever.

8. Installation is the reverse. Coat all areas in sliding contact with white waterproof grease. Adjust the parking brake after cable installation.

Brake Specifications

Model	Lug Nut Torque (ft/lb)	Master Cylinder Bore	Brake Disc		Brake Drum			Minimum Lining Thickness	
			Minimum Thickness	Maximum Run-Out	Diameter	Max Machine O/S	Max Wear Limit	Front	Rear
All	103	0.874	0.965	0.005	11.00	7.894	7.924	①	①

① Minimum lining thickness is to $\frac{1}{32}$ of rivet

NOTE: *Minimum lining thickness is as recommended by the manufacturer. Because of variations in state inspection regulations, the minimum allowable thickness may be different than recommended by the manufacturer.*

Right Rear Cable

1. Raise and support the car. Remove the wheel and the brake drum.

2. Insert a screwdriver between the brake shoe and the top part of the adjuster bracket. Push the bracket to the front and release the top adjuster bracket rod.

3. Remove the rear hold-down spring and remove the actuator lever and return spring.

4. Remove the adjuster screw spring.

5. Remove the top rear brake shoe return spring.

6. Unhook the parking brake cable from the parking brake lever.

7. Pull the cable casing from the backing plate after the retaining legs have been released.

8. Remove the equalizer retaining bolt. Remove the nut attaching the cable to the pivot. Remove the cable casing from the cable guide bracket behind the equalizer by releasing the retaining legs.

9. Unhook the cable from the connector that attaches to the left cable.

10. Installation is the reverse. Apply white grease to all parts in sliding contact. Adjust the parking brake after installation.

Left Rear Cable

1. Perform Steps 1–7 of the right rear cable procedure.

2. Remove the cable casing from the rear axle.

3. Disconnect the cable at the connector at the center of the axle.

4. Installation is the reverse. Lubricate all parts in sliding contact with white waterproof grease, and adjust the parking brake after installation.

9

Body

The list of tools and equipment you may need to fix minor body damage ranges from very basic hand tools to a wide assortment of specialized body tools. Most minor scratches, dings and rust holes can be fixed using an electric drill, wire wheel or grinder attachment, half-round plastic file, sanding block, various grades of sandpaper (#120, which is coarse through #600, which is fine, in both wet and dry types), auto body plastic, primer, touch-up paint, spreaders, newspaper and masking tape. If you intend to try straightening any dents, you'll probably also need a slide hammer (dent puller).

Most auto body repair kits contain all the materials you need to do the job right in the kit. So, if you have a small rust spot or dent you want to fix, check the contents of the kit before you run out and buy any additional tools.

ALIGNING BODY PANELS

Doors

There are several methods of adjusting doors. Your vehicle will probably use one of those illustrated.

Whenever a door is removed and is to be reinstalled, you should matchmark the posi-

tion of the hinges on the door pillars. The holes of the hinges and/or the hinge attaching points are usually oversize to permit alignment of doors. The striker plate is also moveable, through oversize holes, permitting up-and-down, in-and-out and fore-and-aft movement. Fore-and-aft movement is made by adding or subtracting shims from behind the striker and pillar post. The striker should be adjusted so that the door closes fully and remains closed, yet enters the lock freely.

DOOR HINGES

Don't try to cover up poor door adjustment with a striker plate adjustment. The gap on each side of the door should be equal and uniform and there should be no metal-to-metal contact as the door is opened or closed.

1. Determine which hinge bolts must be loosened to move the door in the desired direction.

2. Loosen the hinge bolt(s) just enough to allow the door to be moved with a padded pry bar.

3. Move the door a small amount and check the fit, after tightening the bolts. Be sure that there is no bind or interference with adjacent panels.

4. Repeat this until the door is properly positioned, and tighten all the bolts securely.

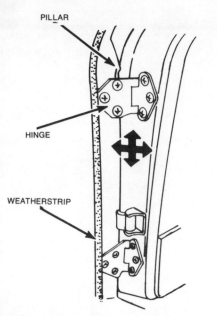

Door hinge adjustment

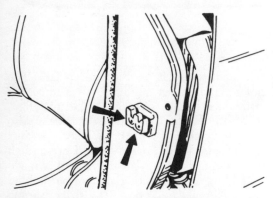

Move the door striker as indicated by arrows

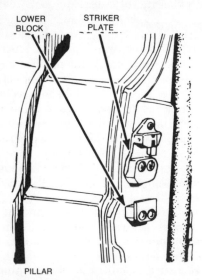

Striker plate and lower block

Hood, Trunk or Tailgate

As with doors, the outline of hinges should be scribed before removal. The hood and trunk can be aligned by loosening the hinge bolts in their slotted mounting holes and moving the hood or trunk lid as necessary. The hood and trunk have adjustable catch locations to regulate lock engagement. Bumpers at the front and/or rear of the hood provide a vertical adjustment and the hood lockpin can be adjusted for proper engagement.

The tailgate on the station wagon can be adjusted by loosening the hinge bolts in their slotted mounting holes and moving the tailgate on its hinges. The latchplate and

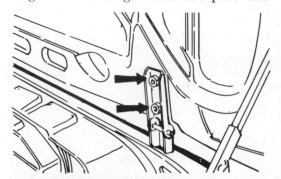

Loosen the hinge boots to permit fore-and-aft and horizontal adjustment

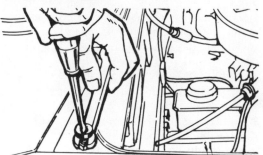

The hood is adjusted vertically by stop-screws at the front and/or rear

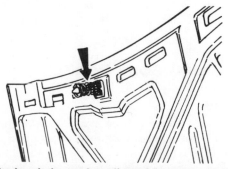

The hood pin can be adjusted for proper lock engagement

latch striker at the bottom of the tailgate opening can be adjusted to stop rattle. An adjustable bumper is located on each side.

RUST, UNDERCOATING, AND RUSTPROOFING

Rust

About the only technical information the average backyard mechanic needs to know about rust is that it is an electro-chemical process that works from **the inside out** on unprotected ferrous metals such as steel and iron. Salt, pollution, humidity—these things and more create and promote the formation of rust. You can't stop rust once it starts. Once rust has started on a fender or a body panel, the only sure way to stop it is to replace the part.

It's a lot easier to prevent rust than to remove it, especially if you have a new car and most late model cars are pretty well rustproofed when the leave the factory. In the early seventies, it seemed like cars were rusting out faster than you could pay them off and Detroit (and the imports) realized that better protection was needed.

Undercoating

Contrary to what most people think, the primary purpose of undercoating is not to prevent rust, but to deaden noise that might otherwise be transmitted to the car's interior. Since cars are pretty quiet these days anyway, dealers are only too willing to promote undercoating as a rust preventative. Undercoating will of course, prevent some rust, but only if applied when the car is brand-new. In any case, undercoating doesn't provide the protection that a good rustproofing does. If you do decide to undercoat your car and it's not brand-new, you have a big clean-up job ahead of you. It's a good idea to have the underside of the car professionally steam-cleaned and save yourself a lot of work. Spraying undercoat on dirty or rusty parts is only going to make things worse, since the undercoat will trap any rust causing agents.

Rustproofing

The best thing you can do for a new or nearly new car is to have it properly rust-proofed. There are two ways you can go about this. You can do it yourself, or you can have one of the big rustproofing companies do it for you. Naturally, it's going to cost you a lot more to have a big company do it, but it's worth it if your car is new or nearly new. If you own an older car that you plan to hang onto for a while, then doing it yourself might be the best idea. Professional rust-proofing isn't cheap ($100–$250), but it's definitely worth it if your car is new. The rustproofing companies won't guarantee their jobs on cars that are over three months old or have more than about 3000 miles on them because they feel the corrosion process may have already begun.

If you have an older car that hasn't started to rust yet, the best idea might be to purchase one of the do-it-yourself rustproofing kits that are available, and do the job yourself.

Drain Holes

Rusty rocker panels are a common problem on nearly every car, but they can be prevented by simply drilling some holes in your rocker panels to let the water out, or keeping the ones that are already there clean and unclogged. Most cars these days have a series of holes in the rocker panels to prevent moisture collection there, but they frequently become clogged up. Just use a small screwdriver or penknife to keep them clean. If your car doesn't have drain holes, it's a simple matter to drill a couple of holes in each panel.

Repairing Minor Body Damage

Unless your car just rolled off the showroom floor, chances are it has a few minor scratches or dings in it somewhere, or a small rust spot you've been meaning to fix. You just haven't been able to decide whether or not you can really do the job. Well, if the damage is anything like that presented here, there are a number of auto body repair kits that contain everything you need to repair minor scratches, dents, and rust spots. Even rust holes can be repaired if you use the correct kit. If you're unsure of your ability, start out with a small scratch. Once you've mastered small scratches and dings, you can work your way up to the more complicated repairs. When doing rust repairs, remember that unless all the rust is removed, it's going to come back in a year or less. Just sanding the rust down and applying some paint won't work.

Repairing Minor Surface Rust and Scratches

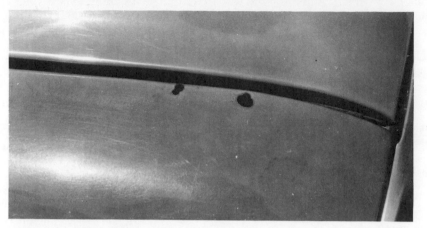

1. Just about everybody has a minor rust spot or scratches on their car. Spots such as these can be easily repaired in an hour or two. You'll need some sandpaper, masking tape, primer, and a can of touch-up paint.

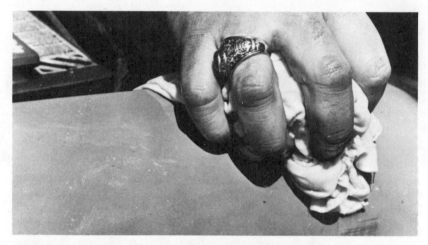

2. The first step is to wash the area down to remove all traces of dirt and road grime. If the car has been frequently waxed, you should wipe it with thinner or some other wax remover so that the paint will stick.

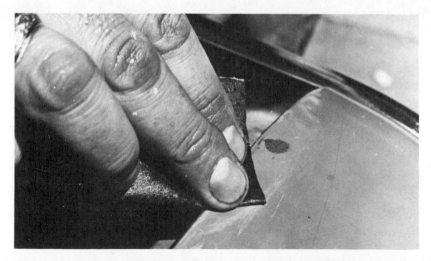

3. Small rust spots and scratches like these will only require light hand sanding. For a job like this, you can start with about grade 320 sandpaper and then use a 400 grit for the final sanding.

4. Once you've sanded the area with 320 paper, wet a piece of 400 paper and sand it lightly. Wet sanding will feather the edges of the surrounding paint into the area to be painted. For large areas, you could use a sanding block, but it's not really necessary for a small job like this.

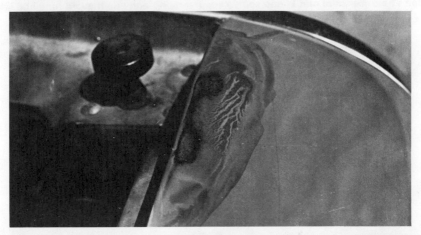

5. The area should look like this once you're finished sanding. Wipe off any water and run the palm of your hand over the sanded area with your eyes closed. You shouldn't be able to feel any bumps or ridges anywhere. Make sure you have sanded a couple of inches back in each direction so you'll get good paint adhesion.

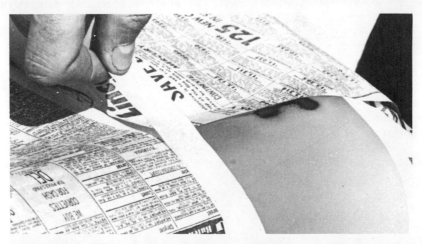

6. Once you have the area sanded to your satisfaction, mask the surrounding area with masking tape and newspaper. Be sure to cover any chrome or trim that might get sprayed. You'll have to mask far enough back from the damaged area to allow for overspray. If you mask right around the sanded spots, you'll end up with a series of lines marking the painted area.

7. You can avoid a lot of excess overspray by cutting a hole in a piece of cardboard that approximately matches the area you are going to paint. Hold the cardboard steady over the area as you spray the primer on. If you haven't painted before, it's a good idea to practice on something before you try painting your car. Don't hold the paint can in one spot. Keep it moving and you'll avoid runs and sags.

8. The primered area should look like this when you have finished. It's better to spray several light coats than one heavy coat. Let the primer dry for several minutes between coats. Make sure you've covered all the bare metal.

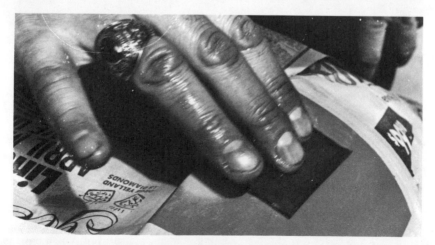

9. After the primer has dried, sand the area with wet 400 paper, wash it off and let it dry. Your final coat goes on next, so make sure the area is clean and dry.

10. Spray the touch-up paint on using the cardboard again. Make the first coat a very light coat (known as a fog coat). Remember to keep the paint can moving smoothly at about 8–12 inches from the surface.

11. Once you've finished painting, let the paint dry for about 15 minutes before you remove the masking tape and newspaper.

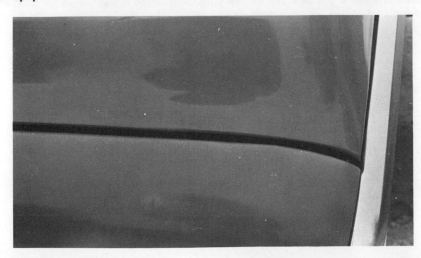

12. Let the paint dry for several days before you rub it out lightly with rubbing compound, and the finished job should be indistinguishable from the rest of the car. Don't rub hard or you'll cut through the paint.

Repairing Rust Holes With Fiberglass

1. The job we've picked here isn't an easy one mainly because of the location. The compound curves make the work trickier than if the surface were flat.

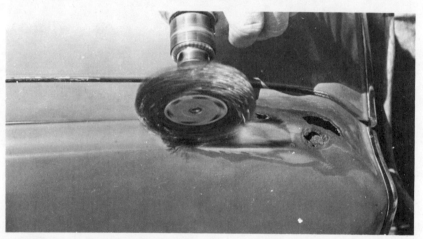

2. You'll need a drill and a wire brush for the first step, which is the removal of all the paint and rust from the rusted-out area.

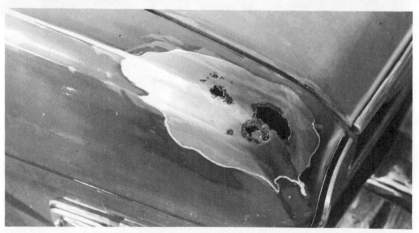

3. When you've finished grinding, the area to be repaired should look like this. Grind the paint back several inches in each direction to ensure that the patch will adhere to the metal. Remove all the damaged metal or the rust will return.

4. Tap the edges of the holes inward with a ballpeen hammer to allow for the thickness of the fiberglass material. Tap lightly so that you don't destroy any contours.

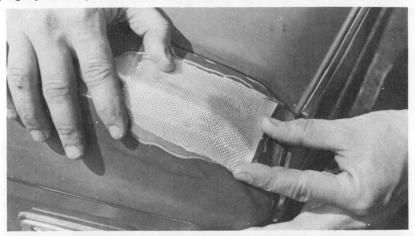

5. Follow the directions of the kit you purchase carefully. With fiberglass repair kits, the first step is generally to cut one or two pieces of fiberglass to cover the hole. Quite often, the procedure is to cut one patch the size of the prepared area and one patch the size of the hole.

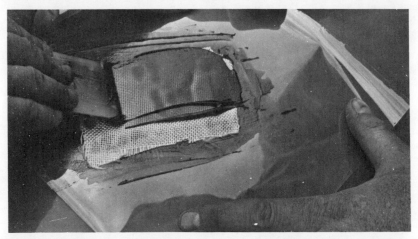

6. Mix the fiberglass material and the patching compound together following the directions supplied with the kit. With this particular kit, a layer type process is used, with the entire mixture being prepared on a piece of plastic film known as a release sheet. Keep in mind that not all kits work this way. Be careful when you mix the catalyst with the resin, as too much catalyst will harden the mixture before you can apply it.

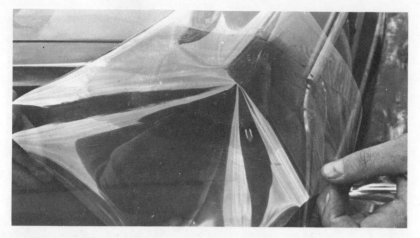

7. Spread the material on the damaged area using the release sheet. This process is essentially meant for smooth flat areas, and as a result, the release sheet would not adhere to the surface properly on our test car. If this happens to you, you'll probably have to remove the release sheet and spread the fiberglass compound out with your fingers or a small spreader.

8. This is what the fiberglass mixture looked like on our car after it had hardened. Because of the contours, we found it nearly impossible to smooth the mixture with a spreader, so we used our fingers. Unfortunately, it makes for a messy job that requires a lot of sanding. If you're working on a flat surface, you won't have this problem.

9. After the patch has hardened, sand it down to a smooth surface. You'll probably have to start with about grade 100 sandpaper and work your way up to 400 wet paper. If you have a particularly rough surface, you could start with a half-round plastic file.

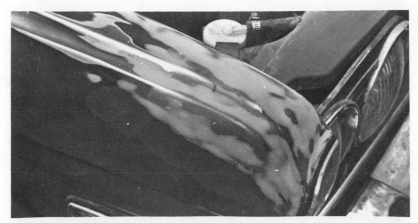

10. This is what the finished product should look like before you apply paint. Many of the kits come with glazing compound to fill in small imperfections left after the initial sanding. You'll probably need some. We did. The entire sanding operation took about an hour. Feather the edges of the repaired area into the surrounding paint carefully. As in any other body job, your hand is the best indicator of what's smooth and what isn't. It doesn't matter if it looks smooth. It's got to feel smooth. Take your time with this step and it will come out right.

11. Once you've smoothed out the repair, mask the entire area carefully, and spray the repair with primer. Keep the spray can moving in steady even strokes, overlap every stroke, and keep the spray can about 8–12 inches from the surface. Apply several coats of primer, letting the primer dry between coats.

12. The finished product (in primer) looks like this. If you were going to just spot paint this area, the next step would be to spray the correct color on the repaired area. This particular car is waiting for a complete paint job.

Appendix

General Conversion Table

Multiply by	To convert	To	
2.54	Inches	Centimeters	.3937
30.48	Feet	Centimeters	.0328
.914	Yards	Meters	1.094
1.609	Miles	Kilometers	.621
.645	Square inches	Square cm.	.155
.836	Square yards	Square meters	1.196
16.39	Cubic inches	Cubic cm.	.061
28.3	Cubic feet	Liters	.0353
.4536	Pounds	Kilograms	2.2045
4.226	Gallons	Liters	.264
.068	Lbs./sq. in. (psi)	Atmospheres	14.7
.138	Foot pounds	Kg. m.	7.23
1.014	H.P. (DIN)	H.P. (SAE)	.9861
—	To obtain	From	Multiply by

Note: 1 cm. equals 10 mm.; 1 mm. equals .0394″.

Conversion—Common Fractions to Decimals and Millimeters

Common Fractions	Decimal Fractions	Millimeters (approx.)	Common Fractions	Decimal Fractions	Millimeters (approx.)	Common Fractions	Decimal Fractions	Millimeters (approx.)
1/128	.008	0.20	11/32	.344	8.73	43/64	.672	17.07
1/64	.016	0.40	23/64	.359	9.13	11/16	.688	17.46
1/32	.031	0.79	3/8	.375	9.53	45/64	.703	17.86
3/64	.047	1.19	25/64	.391	9.92	23/32	.719	18.26
1/16	.063	1.59	13/32	.406	10.32	47/64	.734	18.65
5/64	.078	1.98	27/64	.422	10.72	3/4	.750	19.05
3/32	.094	2.38	7/16	.438	11.11	49/64	.766	19.45
7/64	.109	2.78	29/64	.453	11.51	25/32	.781	19.84
1/8	.125	3.18	15/32	.469	11.91	51/64	.797	20.24
9/64	.141	3.57	31/64	.484	12.30	13/16	.813	20.64
5/32	.156	3.97	1/2	.500	12.70	53/64	.828	21.03
11/64	.172	4.37	33/64	.516	13.10	27/32	.844	21.43
3/16	.188	4.76	17/32	.531	13.49	55/64	.859	21.83
13/64	.203	5.16	35/64	.547	13.89	7/8	.875	22.23
7/32	.219	5.56	9/16	.563	14.29	57/64	.891	22.62
15/64	.234	5.95	37/64	.578	14.68	29/32	.906	23.02
1/4	.250	6.35	19/32	.594	15.08	59/64	.922	23.42
17/64	.266	6.75	39/64	.609	15.48	15/16	.938	23.81
9/32	.281	7.14	5/8	.625	15.88	61/64	.953	24.21
19/64	.297	7.54	41/64	.641	16.27	31/32	.969	24.61
5/16	.313	7.94	21/32	.656	16.67	63/64	.984	25.00
21/64	.328	8.33						

Conversion—Millimeters to Decimal Inches

mm	inches	mm	inches	mm	inches	mm	inches	mm	inches
1	.039 370	31	1.220 470	61	2.401 570	91	3.582 670	210	8.267 700
2	.078 740	32	1.259 840	62	2.440 940	92	3.622 040	220	8.661 400
3	.118 110	33	1.299 210	63	2.480 310	93	3.661 410	230	9.055 100
4	.157 480	34	1.338 580	64	2.519 680	94	3.700 780	240	9.448 800
5	.196 850	35	1.377 949	65	2.559 050	95	3.740 150	250	9.842 500
6	.236 220	36	1.417 319	66	2.598 420	96	3.779 520	260	10.236 200
7	.275 590	37	1.456 689	67	2.637 790	97	3.818 890	270	10.629 900
8	.314 960	38	1.496 050	68	2.677 160	98	3.858 260	280	11.032 600
9	.354 330	39	1.535 430	69	2.716 530	99	3.897 630	290	11.417 300
10	.393 700	40	1.574 800	70	2.755 900	100	3.937 000	300	11.811 000
11	.433 070	41	1.614 170	71	2.795 270	105	4.133 848	310	12.204 700
12	.472 440	42	1.653 540	72	2.834 640	110	4.330 700	320	12.598 400
13	.511 810	43	1.692 910	73	2.874 010	115	4.527 550	330	12.992 100
14	.551 180	44	1.732 280	74	2.913 380	120	4.724 400	340	13.385 800
15	.590 550	45	1.771 650	75	2.952 750	125	4.921 250	350	13.779 500
16	.629 920	46	1.811 020	76	2.992 120	130	5.118 100	360	14.173 200
17	.669 290	47	1.850 390	77	3.031 490	135	5.314 950	370	14.566 900
18	.708 660	48	1.889 760	78	3.070 860	140	5.511 800	380	14.960 600
19	.748 030	49	1.929 130	79	3.110 230	145	5.708 650	390	15.354 300
20	.787 400	50	1.968 500	80	3.149 600	150	5.905 500	400	15.748 000
21	.826 770	51	2.007 870	81	3.188 970	155	6.102 350	500	19.685 000
22	.866 140	52	2.047 240	82	3.228 340	160	6.299 200	600	23.622 000
23	.905 510	53	2.086 610	83	3.267 710	165	6.496 050	700	27.559 000
24	.944 880	54	2.125 980	84	3.307 080	170	6.692 900	800	31.496 000
25	.984 250	55	2.165 350	85	3.346 450	175	6.889 750	900	35.433 000
26	1.023 620	56	2.204 720	86	3.385 820	180	7.086 600	1000	39.370 000
27	1.062 990	57	2.244 090	87	3.425 190	185	7.283 450	2000	78.740 000
28	1.102 360	58	2.283 460	88	3.464 560	190	7.480 300	3000	118.110 000
29	1.141 730	59	2.322 830	89	3.503 903	195	7.677 150	4000	157.480 000
30	1.181 100	60	2.362 200	90	3.543 300	200	7.874 000	5000	196.850 000

To change decimal millimeters to decimal inches, position the decimal point where desired on either side of the millimeter measurement shown and reset the inches decimal by the same number of digits in the same direction. For example, to convert 0.001 mm to decimal inches, reset the decimal behind the 1 mm (shown on the chart) to 0.001; change the decimal inch equivalent (0.039″ shown) to 0.000039″.

Tap Drill Sizes

Screw & Tap Size	*National Fine or S.A.E. Threads Per Inch*	*Use Drill Number*
No. 5	44	37
No. 6	40	33
No. 8	36	29
No. 10	32	21
No. 12	28	15
1/4	28	3
5/16	24	1
3/8	24	Q
7/16	20	W
1/2	20	29/64
9/16	18	33/64
5/8	18	37/64
3/4	16	11/16
7/8	14	13/16
1 1/8	12	1 3/64
1 1/4	12	1 11/64
1 1/2	12	1 27/64

Tap Drill Sizes

Screw & Tap Size	*National Coarse or U.S.S. Threads Per Inch*	*Use Drill Number*
No. 5	40	39
No. 6	32	36
No. 8	32	29
No. 10	24	25
No. 12	24	17
1/4	20	8
5/16	18	F
3/8	16	5/16
7/16	14	U
1/2	13	27/64
9/16	12	31/64
5/8	11	17/32
3/4	10	21/32
7/8	9	49/64
1	8	7/8
1 1/8	7	63/64
1 1/4	7	1 7/64
1 1/2	6	1 11/32

Decimal Equivalent Size of the Number Drills

Drill No.	Decimal Equivalent	Drill No.	Decimal Equivalent	Drill No.	Decimal Equivalent
80	.0135	53	.0595	26	.1470
79	.0145	52	.0635	25	.1495
78	.0160	51	.0670	24	.1520
77	.0180	50	.0700	23	.1540
76	.0200	49	.0730	22	.1570
75	.0210	48	.0760	21	.1590
74	.0225	47	.0785	20	.1610
73	.0240	46	.0810	19	.1660
72	.0250	45	.0820	18	.1695
71	.0260	44	.0860	17	.1730
70	.0280	43	.0890	16	.1770
69	.0292	42	.0935	15	.1800
68	.0310	41	.0960	14	.1820
67	.0320	40	.0980	13	.1850
66	.0330	39	.0995	12	.1890
65	.0350	38	.1015	11	.1910
64	.0360	37	.1040	10	.1935
63	.0370	36	.1065	9	.1960
62	.0380	35	.1100	8	.1990
61	.0390	34	.1110	7	.2010
60	.0400	33	.1130	6	.2040
59	.0410	32	.1160	5	.2055
58	.0420	31	.1200	4	.2090
57	.0430	30	.1285	3	.2130
56	.0465	29	.1360	2	.2210
55	.0520	28	.1405	1	.2280
54	.0550	27	.1440		

Decimal Equivalent Size of the Letter Drills

Letter Drill	Decimal Equivalent	Letter Drill	Decimal Equivalent	Letter Drill	Decimal Equivalent
A	.234	J	.277	S	.348
B	.238	K	.281	T	.358
C	.242	L	.290	U	.368
D	.246	M	.295	V	.377
E	.250	N	.302	W	.386
F	.257	O	.316	X	.397
G	.261	P	.323	Y	.404
H	.266	Q	.332	Z	.413
I	.272	R	.339		

Anti-Freeze Chart

Temperatures Shown in Degrees Fahrenheit +32 is Freezing

Cooling System Capacity Quarts	Quarts of ETHYLENE GLYCOL Needed for Protection to Temperatures Shown Below													
	1	2	3	4	5	6	7	8	9	10	11	12	13	14
10	+24°	+16°	+ 4°	−12°	−34°	−62°								
11	+25	+18	+ 8	− 6	−23	−47		For capacities over 30 quarts divide true capacity by 3. Find quarts Anti-Freeze for the ⅓ and multiply by 3 for quarts to add.						
12	+26	+19	+10	0	−15	−34	−57°							
13	+27	+21	+13	+ 3	− 9	−25	−45							
14			+15	+ 6	− 5	−18	−34							
15			+16	+ 8	0	−12	−26							
16			+17	+10	+ 2	− 8	−19	−34	−52°					
17			+18	+12	+ 5	− 4	−14	−27	−42					
18			+19	+14	+ 7	0	−10	−21	−34	−50°				
19			+20	+15	+ 9	+ 2	− 7	−16	−28	−42				
20				+16	+10	+ 4	− 3	−12	−22	−34	−48°			
21				+17	+12	+ 6	0	− 9	−17	−28	−41			
22				+18	+13	+ 8	+ 2	− 6	−14	−23	−34	−47°		
23				+19	+14	+ 9	+ 4	− 3	−10	−19	−29	−40		
24				+19	+15	+10	+ 5	0	− 8	−15	−23	−34	−46°	
25				+20	+16	+12	+ 7	+ 1	− 5	−12	−20	−29	−40	−50°
26					+17	+13	+ 8	+ 3	− 3	− 9	−16	−25	−34	−44
27					+18	+14	+ 9	+ 5	− 1	− 7	−13	−21	−29	−39
28					+18	+15	+10	+ 6	+ 1	− 5	−11	−18	−25	−34
29					+19	+16	+12	+ 7	+ 2	− 3	− 8	−15	−22	−29
30					+20	+17	+13	+ 8	+ 4	− 1	− 6	−12	−18	−25

For capacities under 10 quarts multiply true capacity by 3. Find quarts Anti-Freeze for the tripled volume and divide by 3 for quarts to add.

To Increase the Freezing Protection of Anti-Freeze Solutions Already Installed

Cooling System Capacity Quarts	Number of Quarts of ETHYLENE GLYCOL Anti-Freeze Required to Increase Protection													
	From +20° F. to					From +10° F. to					From 0° F. to			
	0°	−10°	−20°	−30°	−40°	0°	−10°	−20°	−30°	−40°	−10°	−20°	−30°	−40°
10	1¾	2¼	3	3½	3¾	¾	1½	2¼	2¾	3¼	¾	1½	2	2½
12	2	2¾	3½	4	4½	1	1¾	2½	3¼	3¾	1	1¾	2½	3¼
14	2¼	3¼	4	4¾	5½	1¼	2	3	3¾	4½	1	2	3	3½
16	2½	3½	4½	5¼	6	1¼	2½	3½	4¼	5¼	1¼	2¼	3¼	4
18	3	4	5	6	7	1½	2¾	4	5	5¾	1½	2½	3¾	4¾
20	3¼	4½	5¾	6¾	7½	1¾	3	4¼	5½	6½	1½	2¾	4¼	5¼
22	3½	5	6¼	7¼	8¼	1¾	3¼	4¾	6	7¼	1¾	3¼	4½	5½
24	4	5½	7	8	9	2	3½	5	6½	7½	1¾	3½	5	6
26	4¼	6	7½	8¾	10	2	4	5½	7	8¼	2	3¾	5½	6¾
28	4½	6¼	8	9½	10½	2¼	4¼	6	7½	9	2	4	5¾	7¼
30	5	6¾	8½	10	11½	2½	4½	6½	8	9½	2¼	4¼	6¼	7¾

Test radiator solution with proper hydrometer. Determine from the table the number of quarts of solution to be drawn off from a full cooling system and replace with undiluted anti-freeze, to give the desired increased protection. For example, to increase protection of a 22-quart cooling system containing Ethylene Glycol (permanent type) anti-freeze, from +20° F. to −20° F. will require the replacement of 6¼ quarts of solution with undiluted anti-freeze.

Index

25 Ways

TO BETTER GAS MILEAGE

The Federal government's goal is to cut gasoline consumption 10% by 1985. In addition to intelligent purchase of a new vehicle and efficient driving habits, there are other ways to increase gas mileage with your present car or truck.

Tests have shown that almost ¾ of all vehicles on the road need maintenance in areas that directly affect fuel economy. Using this book for regular maintenance and tune-ups can increase fuel economy as much as 10%, depending on your vehicle.

1. **Replace spark plugs regularly.** New plugs alone can increase fuel economy by 3%.

2. **Be sure the plugs are the correct type and properly gapped.**

3. **Set the ignition timing to specifications.**

4. If your vehicle does not have electronic ignition, **check the points, rotor and cap as specified.**

5. **Replace the air filter regularly.** A dirty air filter richens the air/fuel mixture and can increase fuel consumption as much as 10%. Tests show ⅓ of all vehicles have air filters in need of replacement.

6. **Replace the fuel filter** at least as often as recommended.

7. **Be sure the idle speed and carburetor fuel mixture are set to specifications.**

8. **Check the automatic choke.** A sticking or malfunctioning choke wastes gas.

9. **Change the oil and filter as recommended.** Dirty oil is thick and causes extra friction between the moving parts, cutting efficiency and increasing wear.

10. **Replace the PCV valve** at regular intervals.

11. **Service the cooling system** at regular recommended intervals.

12. **Be sure the thermostat is operating properly.** A thermostat that is stuck open delays engine warm-up, and a cold engine uses twice as much fuel as a warm engine.

13. **Be sure the tires are properly inflated.** Under-inflated tires can cost as much as 1 mpg. Better mileage can be achieved by over-inflating the tires (never exceed the maximum inflation pressure on the side of the tire), but the tires will wear faster.

14. **Be sure the drive belts (especially the fan belt) are in good condition** and properly adjusted.

15. **Be sure the battery is fully charged for fast starts.**

16. **Use the recommended viscosity motor oil to reduce friction.**

17. **Use the recommended viscosity fluids in the rear axle and transmission.**

18. **Be sure the wheels are properly balanced.**

19. **Be sure the front end is correctly aligned.** A misaligned front end actually has wheels going in different directions, creating additional drag.

20. **Correctly adjust the wheel bearing.** Wheel bearings adjusted too tight increase rolling resistance.

21. **Be sure the brakes are properly adjusted and not dragging.**

22. **If possible, install radial tires.** Radial tires deliver as much as ½ mpg more than bias belted tires.

23. **Install a flex-type fan** if you don't have a clutch fan. Flex fans push more air at low speeds when more cooling is needed. At high speeds the blades flatten out for less resistance.

24. **Check the radiator cap for a cracked or worn gasket.** If the cap doesn't seal properly, the cooling system will not function properly.

25. **Check the spark plug wires for bad cracks, burned or broken insulation.** Cracked wires decrease fuel efficiency by failing to deliver full voltage to the spark plugs.